THE REFERENCE SHELF   VOLUME 39 NUMBER 4

NEW LIGHT ON
JUVENILE DELINQUENCY

EDITED BY
RONALD STEEL

THE H. W. WILSON COMPANY
NEW YORK   1967

THE REFERENCE SHELF

The books in this series contain reprints of articles, excerpts from books, and addresses on current issues and social trends in the United States and other countries. There are six separately bound numbers in each volume, all of which are generally published in the same calendar year. One number is a collection of recent speeches; each of the others is devoted to a single subject and gives background information and discussion from various points of view, concluding with a comprehensive bibliography.

Subscribers to the current volume receive the books as issued. The subscription rate is $12 ($15 foreign) for a volume of six numbers. Single numbers are $3 each.

PREFACE

Juvenile delinquency is both an old and a new problem in America. As long as there have been young people, there have been youthful offenders against the law. It is a problem that was as common to the ancient world as it is to ours—a problem that today exists not only in the United States, but in Argentina, Italy, Japan, and Soviet Russia. Wherever young people come into conflict with the law, there is a problem of juvenile delinquency.

Yet although the phenomenon is ancient, it also has a new element that has dramatically magnified its dimensions. For the first time, young people form a class totally apart from their elders. They are not merely young adults learning to do adults' work. Rather, they are adolescents, somewhere between childhood and adult status. Often they are capable of performing adult tasks. But society, for various reasons, keeps them in a state of dependency. They form an in-between class. They are teen-agers—a group with a culture and an identity of its own. Teen-agers look at the adult world with mixed feelings. They want to be accepted as adults and to have the freedom of adults. Yet they often resent much of the adult world and its values. Some rebel in minor ways. Others express their tensions by criminal acts that come into direct conflict with the law. This is what adults call juvenile delinquency.

Delinquent behavior is criminal behavior—at least as society defines criminality. Adults deplore juvenile delinquency and express bewilderment over the misbehavior of the young. They find it particularly hard to understand why delinquency is just as great a problem among privileged children from wealthy families as it is among the poor. They blame the laxity of the law, or the loosening of moral standards, and they call for harsher punishment. Yet society itself is not without fault. As the psychiatrist Robert Coles has written in one of the selections in this compilation: "If we are at present appalled at a soaring, reckless criminality in our middle-class children, it is likely we are really appalled at what has happened to ourselves, because much of what horrifies us is our own

3

assumptions and actions come to expression and perpetuation by those who know us best and are our most eager followers."

The selections in this volume are an attempt, as the title indicates, to throw new light on the familiar, but often misunderstood, problem of juvenile delinquency. The first section deals with some of the causes and manifestations of delinquency in the modern world. The following section describes the delinquent's world of gangs, truants, and drug addicts. In the third section the phenomenon of a separate "youth culture" is examined, and the ways in which the disaffection of youth leads to violence. The fourth section deals with the conflict between youth and a society which has often failed to provide an adequate outlet for youthful energies and talents. The final section describes various means of preventing delinquency, and of dealing with it once it has occurred. It is the hope of the editor that this volume may help, in some small way, to bridge the gap between the world of misunderstood youth and the world of baffled, often indignant, adults.

The editor would like to thank the various authors, publishers, and organizations that have granted permission for the use of materials included in this book. He would also like to thank Lavinia Dobler, Lucy Evankow, and Catha Maslow for their kind assistance.

RONALD STEEL

July 1967

CONTENTS

I. WHAT MAKES A DELINQUENT?

EDITOR'S INTRODUCTION

Although the delinquent has become a part of our culture, and although the term "juvenile delinquency" has entered the everyday vocabulary, we still have much to learn about the causes of delinquent behavior. Who is a delinquent? By what standards can delinquency be measured? What is the line between delinquent and "acceptable" behavior? Is there a clear connection between delinquency and poverty? Why is society so intent on repressing those it labels as delinquents?

There has been a great deal of investigation and research into the causes of juvenile delinquency. Yet the more we learn about this widespread phenomenon, the more perplexing it becomes. Where it was once regarded simply as aberrant behavior on the part of an individual, it is now viewed in a larger social context. Delinquency, we are told by psychiatrists, sociologists, and criminologists, is a youthful reaction against certain aspects of society. It must, therefore, be viewed within the larger framework of the society itself—its values, its goals, its rewards, its opportunities.

The articles in this introductory section were chosen to place the problem of delinquency in perspective. The opening piece is taken from a report by a Senate subcommittee investigating juvenile delinquency and the kind of legislation which may help to correct it. This is followed by an article by Julius Horwitz, author and former welfare worker, which translates the cold statistics of delinquency into graphic examples of human tragedy. The third article is taken from an interview with Professor Sheldon Glueck and his wife, Eleanor T. Glueck, renowned criminologists on the staff of the Harvard Law School. The final article in this section, dealing with delinquency as a worldwide phenomenon, is by William C. Kvaraceus, a professor at Tufts University and a leading figure in the study of youth problems.

DELINQUENCY AND ITS CAUSES [1]

It is sometimes said even by those who should have expert knowledge regarding the scope of youth crime in this nation that only 2 per cent or less of our young people appear before the courts as juvenile delinquents.

Unfortunately there is little comfort in this figure because those who use it as a measure of delinquency fail to realize that it is an annual figure; that each year approximately 70 per cent of this 2 per cent represents different children. When the juvenile population in the 8 years between 10 through 17 is considered, the chances are that about 11 per cent of these children, including boys and girls, have been referred to the juvenile court for delinquent behavior (excluding traffic). And when boys alone are considered, it is estimated that over 16 per cent or about 1 in 6 have faced the court at one time or another. This group has been referred to as the "delinquency generation." Stated quantitatively, at any given point in time there are almost 2 million young males who are either currently or recently delinquent and who have experienced single or multiple appearances before a juvenile court. And when females are included, the figure surpasses the 2.5 million mark.

But even these statistics are a conservative indication of the amount of delinquency in the nation because we know that only about half of the young offenders who come in contact with the police are referred to the juvenile court and it is further estimated that in some cities only a third of the young people involved in delinquency known to the police is reflected in any statistical record.

Furthermore, our figures do not include the unknown and undeterminable number of so-called hidden delinquents whose offenses are never reported to any agency and which are beyond official recognition and review. If we take into account these other factors, the total number of young people in the "delinquency generation" is even higher than the 2.5 million known delinquents.

The Juvenile Delinquency Subcommittee is not primarily a statistics gathering agency. We have relied heavily upon the com-

[1] From *Juvenile Delinquency;* a report of the Committee on the Judiciary, United States Senate, made by its Subcommittee to Investigate Juvenile Delinquency, pursuant to S. Res. 52 (S. Rep. no 1664) 89th Congress, 1st session. Supt. of Docs. Washington, D.C. 20402. '66. p 2-8.

petent work performed in this area both by the United States Children's Bureau and the Federal Bureau of Investigation. But as part of our inquiry into the causes of youth crime and the necessary control measures, we are faced with the need to accurately estimate the size of the problem. For developing delinquency prevention projects such as those created under the Juvenile Delinquency and Youth Offenses Control Act and the antipoverty programs, it is most important to know how many young people are in need of preventive or rehabilitative treatment.

Such broad preventive effort, it should be emphasized, must take into account not only the repeaters and new delinquents who are reported in the court statistics in a particular year, but also the children who have appeared one or more times before a juvenile court in previous years, who may still be engaging in antisocial behavior but who simply do not appear in the current annual statistics.

The number of children that must be considered according to such an approach is not 591,000 but possibly between 3 and 4 million.

From a legislative perspective we must deal not in terms of short-range statistics, but rather in terms of the total delinquent population concept. This deals with that segment of the population in the 10 through 17 age range which manifest problems associated with delinquency over and above the specifically unlawful behavior reflected in court and police records.

Aside from the segments of the delinquent population mentioned above, there are in addition the so-called agency delinquents, handled either by private or public social agencies without judicial intervention. Many deviant or disturbed middle- or upper-class young people are handled in this manner. A large number of female delinquents would also fit into this category because of the tendency to protect females from the criminogenic process.

In addition, we must consider those children showing signs of emotional disturbance in the general school population. These children are actually considered to be worthy of treatment, so deep is their pathology. Based on studies and surveys conducted by the various behavioral sciences, it is estimated that 10 per cent of our total school population falls into this category. And this is an admittedly conservative estimate. Even though most of these children are probably not officially delinquent, the majority are highly vulnerable to this disorder. Furthermore, we must consider the school dropouts, about 30 per cent of our high school students, who because of their inadequate preparation for employment are in a high delinquency risk category. Both the employed and unemployed members of this group are subject to drastic limitations on their opportunities for economic and social advancement and, as a result, to pressures conducive to delinquency. . . .

Every year the growing delinquent population in the nation places increasing pressures on the experts in human behavior to develop plausible explanations for this phenomenon. Indeed, better understanding in this field is vital if we are to be successful in establishing effective delinquency prevention and control measures.

Today there are still serious gaps in our knowledge. We understand many of the causes of delinquency, but since the society grows increasingly more complex new causes come to the surface every year, apparently faster than we are able to evaluate them.

Recently a popular explanation has been that the majority of delinquency is caused by the lack of opportunity for legitimate occupational and economic advancement among the so-called lower-class youths. These young people, often because of their minority group backgrounds, have been educationally deprived. Their rural heritage which has been passed on from generation to generation has not equipped them to function in a mechanized society where heavy emphasis is placed on trade training and formal education.

Perhaps an even more significant explanation of an increasing youth crime rate must include a consideration of the general relationship between delinquency and poverty.

When the existence of this relationship is proposed by social scientists, it is a common mistake on the part of the general public to seek a direct relationship between crime and economic deprivation. And when none is readily apparent it is easy to criticize the Government and its current antipoverty programs as misconceived and ineffective for controlling this problem.

Such criticism is unfortunate because the connection here although hard to pinpoint is overwhelming. The very complexity of our society and the tremendous prosperity that we have come to enjoy militate against the victim of crime and delinquency.

As the society relies more on automation and mechanization and less on unskilled manpower in farming or other manual occupations heavy pressures are brought to bear on each individual to conform to certain educational and occupational specifications. In previous decades an unskilled, untrained person could find employment in various manual occupations or he could retain independence and provide for his family as a small farmer or farm laborer. His skills could be general, his competence acquired from practice rather than from formal training.

Today this era has largely passed and each individual is required to fit into a niche in the economy even though his background has not enabled him to make this kind of adjustment. And the economy even while setting up these requirements is failing to establish sufficient means for meeting them.

There are several reasons why many people cannot adjust to specific requirements established by the social and economic structure. Cultural background and discrimination are some of them. Keener competition in view of population growth and the changing shape of the labor market from predominantly unskilled to predominantly skilled jobs are still others.

All of these factors, of course, must be taken together.

And from all of them we can draw the conclusion that it is more difficult for marginal individuals to exist in our urban society.

The point is that poverty today is more difficult to live with than in times past. Except for social welfare and unemployment programs, when employment is lost, incomes stop, rental payments stop, and food supplies stop. There are fewer ways to obtain part-time jobs, or makeshift jobs, it is less common for neighbors or even relatives to help out one another, and communities are less able to organize themselves to overcome a crisis affecting some of its members.

We have seen in this century a growth of governmental programs designed to promote the health and welfare of our citizens.

We have seen even more recently gross modification of our social and cultural structure by legislative enactments as exemplified by the school integration decision and by subsequent civil rights legislation. Equal opportunity for every type of achievement has been the hallmark of the middle decades of the twentieth century. These advances along with the progress of our technology and economic life has been lauded by the press and the mass media to such an extent that our entire society is virtually obsessed with material success and achievement. This is the theme of our profile to the world. This is the theme of our advertising content dealing with products from detergents to automobiles and this is the theme of our apparent value system acquired by children in the home, in the school and not the least from television.

But while our nation's progress has been swift and spectacular there are serious distortions in its portrayal to the public.

The publicity given to every civil rights achievement, every anti-poverty law and every new employment program is mounted without giving recognition to the fact that there are segments of our population whose way of life, whose education, and whose economic achievement have remained far below average as compared to our over-all growth. Indeed, progress has distorted the lives of whole segments of our population by urban renewal, by geographic relocation, by new welfare and relief programs, and by unrealistic requirements for legitimate adjustment.

Thus we have segments of our people who feel betrayed and by-passed by the glitter of progress all around them. They are promised a share of this progress by new laws and administrative measures enunciated by the Government, yet they cannot see the results of all this. They do not see the tangible concrete changes that they are led to expect in their lives and the consequence is often little more than confusion and disillusionment.

These are conditions that have given rise to militant groups particularly among young Negroes. These are conditions that are largely at the base of the Watts riots and other urban disturbances we have experienced in recent years, and these are undoubtedly conditions that contribute to every other type of deviant and destructive behavior throughout the nation.

Even though we may have today a level of prosperity unequaled at any time in the history of this country and even though the percentage of the poor in our midst is smaller than ever before, it appears that where poverty does exist it is more absolute, more tragic, and more disorganizing.

The level of disorganization and demoralization is certainly expressed in crime and delinquency, which are outgrowths of individual and group insecurity, frustration, and inadequacy.

It is not that people steal because they are hungry, which would be a direct relationship between poverty and crime. It is, rather, that individuals choose criminal behavior because they feel that they have no chance of success in the legitimate world. They commit crimes both against property and persons out of anxiety, fear, and confusion rather than because of legitimate and immediate material needs.

There is another set of conditions which accentuates the relationship between poverty and criminality.

This is the inadequacy of prevention and control programs and facilities to handle either the youth or the adult crime problems.

When families were close knit, when towns were small and most people knew one another and the economy was less complicated, many delinquents and marginal delinquents—the "black sheep"— were still sheltered by their families and friends and neighbors by being given jobs and other means of existence. In those days many criminals and delinquents were handled informally and effectively without burdening formal control facilities. Only the poorest, most rejected and disorganized criminal offenders were dependent on the state and perhaps because we have never had excellent facilities for handling the poor, our correctional and penal facilities developed as largely inadequate institutions where the most dejected members of society were kept out of its collective hair. Throughout history with little exception, it has been the poor and disadvantaged who have gone to prison, while those with means have managed to make some sort of adjustment even when involved in criminal litigation of one type or another.

Certainly this has been true regarding children or juvenile delinquents, with very few offspring of wealthy parents ever going to training schools or even detention homes or other temporary shelters.

Thus the prisons, the reformatories, and the training schools, not to speak of houses of correction, have always been places of refuge for the indigent and it appears that the development of correctional practice has been strongly colored by this association with poverty. Until very recently the poor have been taken for granted as an unsolvable problem in society and all facilities, institutions, and services for them have been of an inferior caliber.

Today with other advances in our society, with greater complexity and regimentation in all institutions, private adjustments of criminality and delinquency are no longer possible. Thus increasingly the Government must extend its programs of crime control and treatment even as it has found it necessary to move against poverty itself, an effort largely unthinkable less than half a century ago.

As the war on poverty lifts the social and economic base of the lower classes, as more people are convinced that participation in this effort can give tangible results and as more of them absorb the middle-class values and success goals, the line of demarcation between those individuals who succeed and those who fail will grow sharper. And as this happens, the correctional field will be faced with a more complex task of rehabilitating the criminal or delinquent to a higher level of performance than was required in past decades.

This conclusion is in line with the proposition set forth above that in a complex society marginal adjustment as measured by old standards will not be sufficient.

When a large portion of our population lived in comparative poverty, when many people were unskilled, and when manual jobs of various kinds made up the largest part of the occupational structure, the criminal released from a penal institution could blend back into society without feeling that his lot in life was grossly different from the experiences of those around him.

Today, on the other hand, when most good jobs require systematic training and experience, when hiring presupposes detailed listing of qualifications, background investigations, character witnesses, and in many cases bonding of employees, any deviation from the norm is a serious handicap. Today a man who falls short of the standards or whose progress has been stunted because of delinquency and institutional commitment may never catch up without professional assistance.

Thus the regimentation of our modern social and economic structure may encourage crime and delinquency by rejecting those handicapped by inadequacies of one type or another. It also places a great strain on our preventive and correctional machinery to transform the delinquent or marginal delinquent into a highly trained, stable, and respectable citizen.

The summary of factors contributing to delinquency and crime presented in this section of the report represents some of the most recent interpretations of the causes of these problems developed by social scientists. *IN SUMMARY*

It must be emphasized that lack of opportunity or poverty in today's society are not the only causes of delinquent behavior. There are still more basic causes ranging from individual conditions such as inadequacies in the personality makeup, character disorders, and mental diseases to social conditions such as family discord, faulty socialization of children by parents, crime-ridden neighborhoods, delinquent companions, and others. It should be stressed, however, that the nature and structure of the social institutions which place severe limits on the opportunities for social, educational, and economic advancement in the more deprived levels of our society reinforce these basic causal factors of crime and delinquency and thus contribute to a disproportionate increase of these problems.

THE ARITHMETIC OF DELINQUENCY [2]

There are 69 million children in the United States under the age of eighteen. Of the 69 million, 12 million live in absolute poverty, which means just enough milk, bread, meat, clothing and shelter to keep from starving to death or freezing to death. The intellectual and moral starvation is catastrophic. A vast number of children in America cannot read. And the reason they cannot read

[2] From article by Julius Horwitz, author of several books on social problems. New York *Times Magazine.* p 12+. Ja. 31, '65. © 1965 by The New York Times Company. Reprinted by permission of William Morris Agency, Inc.

is that they do not believe there is a good reason for them to read. A vast number of American children commit crime. And the reason they commit crime is that they are trying to tell America just how sick they are.

How many children commit crimes? The FBI report for 1963 states that 706,252 children were taken into custody. Nobody knows how many children commit crimes who are not apprehended. But every authority knows that the sharpest increase has been in serious crimes—murder, rape, assault, larceny, theft. Children, kids age ten to fourteen, who should be playing cops and robbers, are taking part in the final charade of a mental disorder: their fantasy playing has become real. They will do anything to cry out their pain, their loneliness, their separation from the human race.

In 1963, the New York City police arrested forty thousand children. The New York State Training Schools operate at full capacity. A brand new youth detention center is already overcrowded. The probation officers carry a caseload of 85 and more cases when they should be handling a maximum of 40 cases involving children. Since 1945, there has been a 500 per cent increase in the crime rate for children in New York City and most crime and delinquency do not result in an arrest.

What do these insane figures mean? Why should children rob, assault, murder, rape? What makes a sixteen-year-old boy in Brooklyn kick an eighty-seven-year-old woman to death? What makes 10 per cent of the eighth-grade boys in a New York neighborhood consider sticking heroin into their systems?

Who is responsible? Children are not born murderers, rapists, thieves (though now the New York City hospitals are experiencing the birth of children who are addicted to drugs at birth because their mothers are drug addicts).

The scientific investigation of delinquency and crime is almost as ancient as the investigation of cancer. And the two follow the same path: the identification often comes when it is too late. Some cancer patients survive their illness. Some delinquents never become adult criminals. But the rate of recidivism in children charged with crime overwhelms the institutional authorities. In 1934, Sheldon and Eleanor Glueck, the criminologists from Harvard University, revealed in a study that 88 per cent of 1,000 delinquent boys who appeared in a Boston juvenile court between 1917 and 1922 continued their delinquencies. I don't think any authority would seriously contest these figures for today's population of children committed to institutions for delinquency.

In 1952, the New York City Youth Board decided to test the Social Prediction Table developed by the Gluecks, who made an exhaustive study of 500 delinquent and 500 nondelinquent boys in the Boston area. Their findings were published in 1950 in their book *Unraveling Juvenile Delinquency*. The Glueck study stated that it would be possible to determine at the age of five or six if a child would become delinquent or nondelinquent, by considering five factors in the environment of the child. The factors were: discipline of the boy by the father, supervision of the boy by the mother, affection of the father for the boy, affection of the mother for the boy, the cohesion of the home. The Gluecks had worked from the records of boys who were already delinquent. It was apparent that it would be necessary to follow the lives of a substantial number of boys for at least ten years in order to determine the accuracy of the Social Prediction Table. In New York State, a delinquent is a person at least seven years old and less than sixteen years of age who does an act which, if committed by an adult, would be a crime.

Last December [1964] the Youth Board issued a report based on a ten-year study of the Glueck table. The Board followed the lives of 301 boys for a period of ten years and reported the following results: of 33 boys predicted as delinquent, 28 became delinquent, an 84.8 per cent accuracy in predicting delinquency. Of the 243 cases predicted as nondelinquents, 236 or 97.1 per cent were nondelinquent. Of the 25 boys who were predicted as having an almost even chance of becoming delinquent or remaining nondelinquent, 9 were delinquent and 16 remained nondelinquent. The findings were published in a booklet, *A Manual of Procedures for Application of the Glueck Prediction Table*. The price of the manual is one dollar and the Youth Board said that the demand was so great that it is the first publication in the Board's history that will show a profit.

The Youth Board study was prepared under the direction of Mrs. Maude Craig, director of research of the Youth Board. Mrs. Craig was assisted by Dr. Selma Glick, who had made a retrospective study of the Glueck table at the Hawthorne-Cedar Knolls School. The Youth Board selected a "high delinquency neighborhood"—a slum. A slum is a neighborhood where people infect one another with the virus of failure, and where children are infected long before the virus is detected.

The Bronx is a borough of 1,425,000 people and the South Bronx is one of its ugliest stretches. It was in this neighborhood that the Youth Board, with the cooperation of the Board of Education, selected for study all of the boys entering first grade in two public schools. The total number of boys was 303—130 of them white, 131 Negro, 42 Puerto Rican. The Youth Board sent skilled case workers into the homes of all the boys to gather social data for rating the boys on the Glueck table.

The case workers gained entry into all 303 homes and prepared case records for each family. Over 50 per cent of the families were receiving public assistance and 89 per cent of the families eventually became known to the Department of Welfare.

The completed case records were rated according to the five factors isolated by the Gluecks. Each factor was given a numerical weight. The weights were added together and a score was entered for each child, representing his probable chance of becoming delinquent before his sixteenth birthday.

This is how the table worked for Dennis James, aged six. (The name, as with other case histories reported here, is fictitious.) Dennis was given no chance for surviving the social factors that molded the first six years of his life.

His first year of school started with a prophetic boom, for nothing in his existence had prepared him to accept school, to feel that school was important. This is his teacher's observation in the first grade: Dennis's behavior is impossible. He is a terrible fighter. He does not work. He can't sit with the rest of the class. He can't be put in line with another child. He seems to resent being told what to do. He just looks at his teacher with a blank stare.

Why should a six-year-old boy look at his teacher with a blank stare in the wonder world of polished desks, books, a green-tinted blackboard, chalk, crayons, a record player, the scrubbed faces of other children?

This is what the case workers reported: Dennis never saw his father. He vanished before he was born. Dennis never asked about his father. He doesn't know what a father is. The mother works. Dennis is supervised by a sixty-seven-year-old woman in the South Bronx. The mother works in a bakery. Dennis is more affectionate toward his mother than she is to him. What is the cohesion in the home? There appears to be no yelling or screaming. What marks did Dennis get on the Social Prediction Table? Supervision by mother, 57.5, discipline by mother 82.9, cohesion of the family 61.3, total 201.7 or an 89.2 probability of becoming delinquent.

Why is there no rating for the father? After preparing its original ratings based on the five-factor table the Youth Board realized it had penetrated into a world where there is no father. The welfare world of New York is a fatherless world. The father is an impregnator. He vanishes after he has planted his seed. He is frightened of the bloom. He will not buy his child a Golden Book, a pair of roller skates, a kite, a Good Humor ice cream, take him to a movie, or for a walk in the park. How can you rate a father if he doesn't exist? The Youth Board dropped its ratings for the affection shown by the father, the discipline shown by the father to his son, in deference to reality.

What did the teacher say in the second grade? Dennis won't listen. He won't behave without constant supervision. He can't count above three. He can't read. He can't write his name. He recognizes the number 1, and is delighted when he is called upon to identify the number 1 for the class. He brought a knife to school. He claims he needs it for protection.

Class CRMD 2. Dennis is identified as mentally retarded and is assigned to a class with this designation, which stands for Children with Retarded Mental Development. He is already a victim. A victim of the impact of a disadvantaged environment on learning, resulting in nonorganic mental retardation. Dennis has no organic pathology. His retardation is man-made and he is not alone. The President's Panel on Mental Retardation reports that out of 5.5 million retarded persons in the United States, 4.5 million of the retarded have no organic pathology and are retarded because of exposure to an environment that destroys the learning capacity of an otherwise normal child.

What happens later, in CRMD 7? Dennis's behavior is bad. He knocks down chairs. He does not appear to be vicious but he does hit other children. He is now reading on a first-grade level. On a Bronx subway Dennis tries to steal a package. His first contact is made with the police.

In junior high school Dennis is still reading first-grade primer books. He talks in class about traveling in the subway late at night, going long distances underground. He speaks with no emotion, no sense that he is doing anything wrong. A psychiatrist is asked for an evaluation: Boy could be helped with a sympathetic, understanding adult, but the adult must be constantly with him to channel his energies. It is questionable if he can get through life on his own. The diagnosis: moderate mental retardation with sociopathic features.

What happened to Dennis before his sixteenth birthday? How did his prediction come through? Dennis knocked down an old lady on a Bronx street and kept kicking her in the face until he was grabbed by a police officer.

Here is Charles Burns with a 50-50 chance of delinquency. At six years of age he entered the first grade. His mother is on welfare. His father deserted before he was born, and never supported the family. Three of his brothers and sisters were born out of wedlock. His mother has been hospitalized twice at Central Islip State Hospital. Each time the mother is released from the hospital the father appears from out of the street, impregnates her and vanishes before he can see the face of his child.

One night the mother is found naked on a Brooklyn street, carrying her infant baby, sobbing for help. The mother is sent to Rockland State Hospital and comes out again to have another child. Charles is looked after by his grandmother. The grandmother runs the family. She reads the Bible to the children and hopes that God will listen.

What happens in 1-4, the first grade? Charles tells his teacher that his father beat up his mother, that his father is in jail. The teacher isn't sure that this is true and thinks it may be a fantasy.

In 2-1, the teacher reports: Charles has no idea of what he is doing.

In 3-1, the teacher reports that Charles is a "creep." But the teacher is aware that Charles comes up to her after class, that he tells her little things, little stories; he wants her to listen to him and she is candid enough to report that she doesn't like to listen to him.

In 5-6, the teacher reports: Charles just exists. Doesn't extend himself. Nothing seems to reach him.

In 6-2, Charles is reading on a second-grade level. Charles is bitten by a rat. His mother is in Bellevue. A welfare investigator reports that the children are dirty, the house dirty, the children piled up in one filthy room, sleeping four in a bed. The mother comes out of Bellevue, has a new man in her bed and is pregnant again. The children are placed with the grandmother.

And the grandmother saved Charles—at least at the point the study was concluded. He did not come into contact with the police, the courts, he did not commit serious and persistent acts, which if committed by an adult would be a crime.

The Youth Board followed the lives of 301 boys for a period of ten years, a remarkable achievement in the history of social research. Only one boy was lost to the researchers and one boy could not be rated. Out of the 301 boys, 44 became delinquent and 257 did not become delinquent. The board had 100 per cent accuracy in predicting nondelinquency in the white group, 97 per cent accuracy for the Puerto Ricans and 93.8 per cent accuracy for the Negroes.

In 54 of the families the boys lived only with their mothers, and no fathers or males were present; 32 of these families were Negro. In 68.5 per cent of the families, the homes were broken before the rated child was six years old. The study revealed a total of 124 broken homes. A "broken home" means there is no father, either in presence or in substance.

Illegitimacy was found in 80 per cent of the families of the boys who become delinquent and in 25 per cent of the families of nondelinquent boys. The white families had a 14.6 per cent rate of illegitimacy, the Puerto Rican families 22 per cent and the Negro families 47.7. The average number of people in a household was 4.5. In the delinquent families, 84.1 per cent received welfare and altogether 51.8 per cent of the total families were known to a bewildering array of social agencies. The 44 delinquents had 238 social-agency contacts.

Of the 301 families, 96 had one or more members who had a criminal record or a court record and 75 per cent of the 44 delinquent families had one or more members who were also delinquent.

Of the 44 delinquent boys, 18.2 per cent were mentally retarded and not one was rated by his teachers as possessing above average or superior intelligence. Of the 301 boys, 159 were behavior problems to their teachers, and 145 of the 159 were behavior problems in the first to third grades.

The police had contact with 108 of the boys and the 44 delinquents had 169 contacts with the police. Fourteen of the 44 delinquents were serious and persistent delinquents before the age of ten, and 10 of the boys became delinquent between the ages of eleven and twelve. Only five of the delinquent boys were known to be members of organized street gangs.

Most shocking, 39 of the 44 delinquents were classified as recidivists, which means the courts, the psychologists, the teachers, the guidance counselors, the training schools, couldn't put Humpty Dumpty together again.

What does this sickening array of statistics tell us? Are they news? Did you skip over them? Go back again. Each unit of the statistic is a human being, a child entering the first grade, in the richest city in the world, with the most elaborate network of social organizations in modern history.

The critics of the Youth Board study told me that the prediction tables, if used in the schools or by large government organizations, will stigmatize and label children and will repeat the disastrous impact of the IQ tests on slum children, which resulted in the teachers creating an expectancy of failure in the children because their IQ's already doomed them to failure. The Youth Board states that the Social Prediction Table is a reasonable diagnostic tool for the early identification of boys who are likely to be a problem. The Board does not say the table can prevent delinquency; the table can only point to the need for intervention, for prevention.

What is to be done?

I asked Pedro Ramos. Pedro is twenty-six. He grew up in East Harlem. He was a member of a street gang until he moved to Oregon at the age of fourteen. He has just returned to New York with his own family. He remembers East Harlem from the 1950's, when it was impossible to walk down a street without protection and when the gangs ruled the sidewalk.

"It was bad, then, bad. The Dragons were killers. The Viceroys just liked to beat you up. . . . It was like war. But there was no dope then. I think I got out just in time. . . . One of my brothers got shot by the police. Guys were killed that you never read about in the newspapers. I've been thinking about those days. Why didn't I wind up in Otisville or Elmira? I think it was my mother. She saw to it that I always had a job, that I was always busy with school. I used to sweep out the market on East 116th Street when I was eight years old. I always had a job. But most of the guys didn't. They were just like nothing. They had nothing to say. Nothing to do. I'm going to see that my kids make it. . . ."

"Do you remember the old gang members?"

"Sure."

"Can you remember thinking about them, in the house, with your brothers, talking about which ones would make it, the ones that would wind up in jail?"

"We used to do that. Predicting."

"Let's go down the list. Do you remember any names?"

"Emanuel. I said he would wind up dead. He didn't. He killed a guy on East 114th Street and he's doing twenty years."

"Who else?"

"Ralph had a mother and father who were drunks. I thought he wouldn't make it. But he wound up a priest. There was Eddie. He once pointed a shotgun at a kid's head but the gun didn't go off. He didn't make it. He's a bum now. He's on drugs. . . ."

"What about your kids? You're living now in East Harlem. Everything around you is supposed to be bad for the kids. How do you feel about it, I mean raising the kids?" Pedro has three children. The oldest boy is four.

"I keep my kids in, off the streets. If you want to see the kids who won't make it look at their mothers. You don't have too many fathers around. There's a woman here on the top floor. There's no father. She has nine kids. They run around naked even in the winter. She doesn't give a damn about them. They hit the street in the morning and stay there. They don't think this is a house they live in. They throw garbage, . . . they scream, fight, they're wild. Kids like somebody to tell them what to do. They need authority. You can't frighten kids. How in the hell does a kid of five, six, seven, know what to do?"

What is to be done? Obviously, as Pedro Ramos told me after I explained the Social Prediction Table to him, somebody has to interfere, quick, with know-how.

We need to undo what we are now doing. We need to redeploy the existing social welfare world to meet the needs of children in trouble. The emphasis must begin before the child is in trouble. The social agencies cannot wait for the child in trouble to come to them, nor can the government agencies wait. If the Youth Board study, despite the intense criticism surrounding it, does anything, it will help create the need for a social body to take the responsibility for meeting the needs of children before they become delinquent, before they are unreachable.

The professional social world needs to listen to itself. Not one of the professions through its own efforts can meet the problem of working with delinquent children. Each profession has a contribution to make. Today there is no one to direct the individual professions toward the goal of preventing delinquency. As fantastic as it sounds, there is no project director. Imagine trying to send up a space capsule without a project director.

A Youth Department is required to take the responsibility of directing the professional social welfare world in services to children and their families, simply because no such responsibility now exists either in the social welfare world, or more profoundly, in the homes of tens of thousands of children, who have their link to the South Bronx.

We need to penetrate into the home, as though a plague were raging, all the adults dead and the children moaning in their cribs for help. The "unavailable mother"—unwed, indigent or surviving on welfare payments, socially deprived, economically deprived, intellectually deprived, often friendless, depressed, mentally disturbed, lonely, frightened, unable to supply the needs of a newborn child, already burdened with children she has rejected—the unavailable mother produces the unreachable child. This is the woman who needs the attention of the social welfare world.

I would recommend, as the first step in a preventive delinquency program, the establishment of a Mother's Aid Agency, to meet the needs of the unavailable mother. It would be a bold step in the prevention of delinquency and dependency problems, if every indigent woman, either wed or unwed, who leaves a hospital with a child, would be visited by a Mother's Aid, a woman trained to overcome the gap between the lonely destructive world of a slum-based environment and the natural endowment of a bawling healthy infant. . . .

What is practical is obvious. Somebody has to take the responsibility. We have to learn to identify the children who are most likely to become delinquent if left unhelped. We have to learn to recognize the symptoms that affect children long before their pain is expressed in words or action. The accident of birth can be remedied. Children removed from troubled homes and placed with foster families have shown a 20-30 point increase in the IQ's.

Today children are removed from the home only at the point of emergency. Children in trouble are only recognized at the point of emergency. We rush them into courts, we rush them into detention centers. Obviously, in a democratic society, we are not going to start removing children from their homes just because they are born poor, or born to an unwed mother, or born to a family dependent on government payments for survival.

But we now know that in given census tracts of a large city, a sizable proportion of the infants are predestined for a stunted existence if no intervention takes place. We know that the damage to the infant takes place long before he sees the dirt, the drunks, the drug addicts, the spilled garbage of the slum; the damage takes place when the unavailable mother brings her child home from the hospital and realizes she hates him for being alive.

Today we subsidize millions of these children with direct government money payments. Another kind of subsidy is required:

recognition, love, attention, talk, affection, play, dedication, intelligence, dreams, authority. It seems clear that this can be provided only in an institution. And we had better start thinking of what form the institution will take. For the form it takes will mask our own face.

Is more proof required? Imagine your own child if you never spoke to him all day, if you never read him a book, never took him for a walk, to visit friends, to see a dinosaur in the museum, if you never made him believe that another human being cared for him.

I visited one of the two schools where the boys in the Youth Board study entered the first grade. The corridors are broad, clean. The children looked scrubbed, neat, well dressed. Slum children are always neat, scrubbed, well dressed in elementary school. I watched the children in the lunch room, in the corridors, the gym, the playground. Some fought. Some played. Some laughed. The school was new a decade ago when the Youth Board made the decision to follow the lives of 303 boys. I watched the children through the eyes of the Youth Board study. The statistics leapt to life. The children leapt to their doom.

WHY YOUNG PEOPLE "GO BAD" [3]

Q. Professor and Mrs. Glueck, is poverty at the root of juvenile crime in America today?

A. In some cases, yes. Poverty is involved, for instance, in the case of the mother who has to work outside the home in order to support her family.

But poverty, by itself, doesn't make a delinquent. There are working mothers who somehow manage to give their children a good upbringing.

We do not mean to say that the "war on poverty" is not desirable. What we are saying is that, by itself, it will not bring a substantial decrease in delinquency. You cannot make good parents out of bad ones simply by raising their income or moving them into a new house.

[3] From interview with Professor and Mrs. Sheldon Glueck (Eleanor T. Glueck), eminent criminologists of the Harvard Law School. *U.S. News & World Report.* 58:56-60+. Ap. 26, '65. Reprinted from *U.S. News & World Report.* Copyright 1965 U.S. News & World Report, Inc.

You know, some of the most important individuals in America today came out of the slums. In the old days, we often spoke of "the respectable poor."

In Boston, our research investigators could often tell just as soon as a tenement door opened up whether they were entering the home of a delinquent or of a nondelinquent. All the families in the neighborhood would be poor, but there would be enormous variation in the under-the-roof atmosphere from one household to the next.

On the other hand, it is probable that, in a suburban neighborhood of middle income, you could find similar variations.

Q. Even in affluent families?

A. Oh, yes. You can find low standards of behavior and neglected children in well-to-do families. In fact, delinquency seems to be rising in suburban areas, and the causes for it, we think, are basically the same that you find in the slum areas.

There are mothers of ample income who neglect their children just as much as tenement mothers do, and there are fathers who might as well not be there, for all the time they spend with their children. You see, the things that count the most in raising children do not depend so much on dollars and cents as they do on the parents' affection. Parental love is not purchasable. And you don't express this love through overindulgence, or by bribing a child with presents to make up for the lack of that parental love and concern day by day.

Q. Could affluence actually cause delinquency?

A. Sometimes it could, where it builds up a never-ending thirst for material things, such as high-powered cars.

One problem of our affluent society is that it has not yet defined a meaningful role for adolescents. Once there were chores around the house to make a child feel important and useful. Adventuresome youngsters could join a sailing ship or head west. There were many outlets for energy and adventure.

Today, the tendency is to hand everything on a platter to the adolescent. Very little effort is required on his part, so he has really become bored with life, in a sense.

Back of all this, however, is the problem of the inadequate parents. Their children, like those in the slums, grow up with a sense of neglect and insecurity—and this is what lays the foundation for delinquency.

Q. At what age does this tendency become evident in the child?

A. That would vary a great deal. Our basic research shows that about 50 per cent of the delinquents we studied began to show clear signs of maladjusted behavior at the age of eight or under. Virtually 90 per cent showed these signs at the age of ten or under.

Now we have found it possible to arrive at some idea of the child's delinquency potential even before those years by identifying certain pathologic aspects of his family life. The studies we have carried out show that this can be done at the school-entering age—between five-and-one-half years and six-and-one-half. At the present time we are working at and, we hope, succeeding in studies to identify predelinquents at an even earlier age, by combining parental factors and certain childhood traits.

Q. Will parents be able to recognize these traits in their preschool youngsters?

A. Perhaps. But a trained observer is needed. A pediatrician, for example, would recognize them if he had some briefing in the relationship of these traits to later delinquency.

Q. What are some of the traits that point to delinquency?

A. Stubbornness, emotional instability, destructiveness, defiance, for example.

Q. Couldn't some of these be found in healthy youngsters?

A. Indeed, they could. However, it is a question of how these characteristics combine in an unfavorable home atmosphere. If a child has only one or two and there is parental affection and understanding, you wouldn't worry. But suppose he has a combination of them together with neglectful and hostile or unconcerned parents. Then you would have a piling up which might lead to aggressive behavior in the years ahead.

Q. Is there a constitutional factor in juvenile misbehavior?

A. In terms of general health, no. Our studies indicate no significant differences in the bodily health of delinquents and nondelinquents.

Nor, we might add, do there seem to be significant differences in basic intelligence, except that delinquents appear to have less capacity in dealing with abstractions and symbols and more "manipulative" capacity—in doing things with their hands—for instance.

The troubles that delinquents often have in their school work stem more from emotional causes than from a lack of intelligence.

What we do find in our studies of delinquents and nondelinquents is some indirect relationship between a child's body structure and predelinquent behavior.

You see, William Sheldon and other authorities in physical anthropology have noted that people can be classified into roughly four types of body structure:

One is the mesomorph. He is the compact, adventurous, energetic type. Shakespeare's shrew-tamer, Petruchio, might be an illustration.

Then there is the ectomorph, who is linear, fragile and rather inclined to be sensitive and reflective. Hamlet might be considered an example of this type.

The third type is the endomorph, who is inclined to be soft and fat and easygoing, like Sir John Falstaff.

Finally, you have a fourth type who combines, in about equal measure, the qualities of the other three.

Now we have found, in comparing 500 persistent delinquents with 500 true nondelinquents, that almost two thirds of the delinquents were mesomorphic, while less than one third of the control sample of nondelinquents had this kind of build.

We might add that the youngsters we studied were first matched in terms of age, intelligence, ethnic or racial derivation, and residence in the extreme slums of the Greater Boston area.

Q. Why are there more mesomorphs than other types among troublemakers? Do delinquents tend to be athletic?

A. The mesomorph is energetic. He is more assertive and less submissive to authority. He is less sensitive than other types. He isn't nearly as inclined as the ectomorph or endomorph to internalize his emotions. Rather, he is uninhibited in his responses.

The mesomorph tends to have fewer emotional conflicts than the other types do.

Q. Would you call such youngsters inherently bad?

A. No, not at all. A large proportion of law-abiding people in the general population are mesomorphs.

What our studies do point to is this: Mesomorphic predelinquents are more energetic than others and, unless this drive is diverted into acceptable channels by parents and teachers, such children are going to seek outlets elsewhere. Rather than accept strictly supervised recreation, they're likely to seek their adventures in railway yards, wharves and junk yards. In classrooms, they are going to rebel if held too tightly in line for long periods of time. They can't sit through an hour without a change.

Actually, however, body structure is only one signpost in the direction of identifying a child's traits that could lead to trouble.

And his likelihood of getting into trouble or staying out of it rests finally with the parents. It is when we look at them that we get our real look at a child's destination.

Q. In what way?

A. When we set out to see if there was a way to predict the likelihood of delinquency in a child or not, we evolved a table based on five factors, as follows:

Affection of the mother for the child

Affection of the father for the child

Supervision of the child by the mother

Discipline by the father

Cohesiveness of the family

By evaluating the performance of the parents in each of these aspects, we could arrive at a total score which would indicate whether or not the youngster was headed for delinquency.

Now, we had to change this table a little more than ten years ago for a study that the New York City Youth Board wanted to make of a selected group of boys, aged five and a half to six and a half. The reason was that the study involved so many families in which the father was absent.

After some experimenting, we found that we could get just as good predictive results by eliminating the factors of the father's affection and discipline. You know, of course, that this does not mean that the father is not important in child rearing.

Well, this study went on for ten years, and just a few months ago it was announced that 84.6 per cent of the youngsters considered, under our predictive table, likely to become delinquent actually did so. And 97 per cent of those thought unlikely to become delinquents did not.

There was a small group of boys whose chances of delinquency were considered about 50-50. In that group, nine actually did become delinquent.

Q. Are you saying, "This child is sure to become delinquent," or "'That child will not become delinquent"?

A. Indeed not. We predict the likelihood of delinquency on the assumption that conditions in the home will remain relatively unchanged. Over the years, our position has always been that we are not predicting a child's destiny, but his destination—and his destination can be changed by effective action.

Q. What seems to be causing delinquency to grow so fast nowadays?

A. There are many causes for this. For the most part, however, what we are seeing now is a process that has been going on since the second World War.

First, you have had more and more mothers going to work. Many have left their children more or less unattended, at home or in the streets. This has deprived children of the constant guidance and sense of security they need from their mothers in their early years.

Along with that change, parental attitudes toward disciplining their young have changed quite rapidly. In the home and outside, the trend has been steadily toward more permissiveness—that is, placing fewer restraints and limits on behavior.

Q. Is this permissive trend new?

A. It's not a new trend, really. Today's parents themselves are the products of somewhat permissive parents of the time before the second World War. There was much support for the philosophy of child rearing which said that, since a child is "creative," it should be permitted to experiment more or less at will, and so on.

Well, just how much that philosophy had to do with permissive parenthood can be argued, but many people feel that it started the whole trend toward permissiveness.

Q. How has that philosophy worked out in practice?

A. Not very well, it seems. Life requires a certain amount of discipline. You need it in the classroom, you need it in the home, you need it in society at large. After all, the Ten Commandments impose a discipline. Unless general restraints are built into the character of children, you can arrive eventually at social chaos.

Q. Are you saying that moral values are crumbling?

A. This is part of the picture. Not only parents but others are uncertain in many cases as to what is morally right or wrong, and that makes discipline harder to enforce.

For instance, children today are being exposed to all kinds of motion pictures and books. It is difficult to decide what motion pictures and books should be censored.

In a broad sense, actually, you might feel that censorship in general is undesirable. Yet you also know that restraint must be imposed at some point—especially where children are involved. But in trying to decide at what point restraint should be imposed, it very often turns out that no restraint at all results. And it is this lack of restraint in the home and on the outside that is back of so much of our delinquency.

Q. Is it bad parents, then, who make bad children?

A. In large measure. It is the affection and discipline the child gets in the home that shape his attitudes and ideals as child and adult.

Q. Does that mean that more discipline is needed?

A. Discipline is always needed. Fifty years ago, much more than now, there was discipline. Children knew the limits on their behavior. They lived in smaller neighborhoods where they were under the eye of parents and neighbors—and what the neighbors thought was important. Religion, too, seemed to have a greater influence on personal behavior.

Also, the home setting itself encouraged parental control. Children were taught by example that each had his or her work to do without question: The father worked out in the field, the mother cleaned the house and cooked the family's food, and the children carried in the wood and helped out.

Today, in our urban centers, the situation is totally different. There are all kinds of distractions for children. Mothers are either working outside the home or preoccupied with all the problems of day-to-day running of the home. Fathers, too, spend more time away from home.

There is less work for children to do around the house, and the parents can't think of other ways to fill up the void, so they leave it to the child himself to work out the problem. In that situation, parental authority is not likely to be strong.

Q. With what result?

A. With the result that the child considers it his right to do as he pleases and to ignore parental wishes. . . .

Q. Is a spanking, or some other form of corporal punishment, an answer to the problem?

A. We do not rule out corporal punishment, provided it is clearly related in the child's mind to the misdeed he has committed. But more use should be made of deprivation of privileges—sending a child to bed earlier if he misbehaves, or not letting him see his favorite television program—as a means of discipline. What is really required is great firmness administered with love.

You see, love is the essential element. We think that it is even possible for a parent to be overstrict at times or too lenient at other times, yet be an effective parent if he really loves the child—because the child then will accept these variations. But if a parent is overstrict or vacillating or lax, and doesn't really love the child, the child very quickly senses this and either takes advantage or rebels.

Now, the earlier in the child's life he senses parental love and guidance, the sooner he will acquire self-discipline—and the less of a disciplinary problem he's going to be as he grows up.

Q. Why do Chinese-Americans, for instance, seem to have few youngsters in trouble, while some other ethnic groups seem to have a high ratio of delinquency?

A. In any group, the incidence of delinquency derives from the strength of the family life. Years ago, we thought of doing a study of Chinese-American delinquents. But we found in our preliminary survey that there were simply not enough Chinese delinquent boys in New York or San Francisco to give us an adequate sample.

Why was this? We think it is because of the strong sense of family, the respect for parents and elders, that exists among the Chinese.

On the other hand, in the ethnic groups where the delinquency rate is high, you tend to find a great deal of desertion by fathers, and much illegitimacy. Even when a mother does show affection for her children, often her efforts to administer discipline are not supported by a strong sense that family reputation is at stake.

Q. What kind of action is needed? Is social work the answer?

A. Actually, we have not seen that the treatment usually given to predelinquent or delinquent children does a great deal of good.

We know of two studies—one in Washington, D.C., and another in the Cambridge-Somerville area of Massachusetts—where treatment was given one group of delinquent children and not to another. In both of these studies, the children had the benefit of some clinical treatment, friendly supervision, recreational activities, neighborhood meetings, health examinations, counseling, and so on. But unfortunately the kind of aid that was given seemed to make little difference in their delinquency rate compared with those children who didn't get treatment.

Q. How would you explain that?

A. As we see it, too much attention or therapy is being directed at the children, and not at the family condition that made them delinquent. This is the sort of social work that delinquent children so often get. In other words, it is the parents who need reeducation more than the child.

Q. How can that be accomplished?

A. By teaching the parents the importance of affection and discipline in their relationship to the child.

Many parents also have emotional problems of their own which need to be worked out if they're going to become effective parents. Clinics for the reeducation of ineffective parents are a major need in preventing delinquency.

Actually, we see training for parenthood as a process beginning in childhood—and certainly young couples about to marry should know what is going to be expected of them in the successful raising of a family.

Now, the earlier this understanding and training can be given in the predelinquency period—before the first signs of trouble are developing in a child—the better chance there will be that corrective measures will succeed.

Q. Can all parents be helped through training?

A. Not all—and, in extreme cases, children should be removed from an environment that is likely to lead them into delinquency. Many could benefit from placement in foster homes, which seem to us much preferable to institutional care, at least of the kind now given to neglected children.

But it is our feeling that many more parents could be helped than is generally realized. So much of the emotional damage to children is the result of downright ignorance on the part of parents.

In that connection, we are much interested to learn that a rehabilitation center in a troublesome area of Louisville, Kentucky, will try not only to rehabilitate delinquent boys but also to provide weekly counseling and other services to parents to try to improve their relationship to the boys.

Q. Can police and courts help reduce juvenile crime?

A. By the time a child walks into juvenile court, much of the damage to his character has been done, and it is much harder to correct damage than to prevent it.

Q. Do juvenile courts tend to be too soft on youngsters?

A. Sometimes, yes, but more often there is inconsistency because judges have wide discretion, and they may rely on intuition or hunches rather than use of predictive data which their staff could gather for them on each case.

Q. Then is stern punishment a deterrent to further crime?

A. Certainty of punishment is definitely a deterrent. After all, fear is a primary emotion in man. It plays an important part in his training. We have gone rather far in the other direction, in letting the child feel that he isn't going to be punished for misdeeds.

Of course, it is wrong to rely exclusively on fear of punishment to restrain the child. But it is equally wrong to do away with this deterrent.

Q. Can schools help in keeping children from developing into troublemakers?

A. They certainly can. As we have said, there are children whose energies are not suited to long periods of sitting still and whose adventuresomeness has to be satisfied in some acceptable way.

We also think that one of the basic needs of schools, along with other elements of society, is a general recognition that rules must be observed—that, without rules, you drift into chaos and into tyranny and into taking the law into your own hands. You see it not only among delinquents but among young college students, in their demand for more and more freedom from restraints and from higher authority.

Q. What else is needed to keep delinquency from growing?

A. It seems to us that business and industry can help a great deal by providing recreational facilities and nurseries for the very young children of working mothers. This would not be aimed at providing mothers with a free baby-sitting service and nothing more. Rather, it would enable the mother to see her child or children occasionally during the day and maintain warm contact with them.

We have seen something like this system in the Israeli *kibbutzim*, or communal settlements, and we are told that some factories in Europe are beginning to provide this sort of service.

Finally, our administration of criminal justice needs a complete revision. We need to get better men and women into this field. There has to be a better training on the part of judges, prosecutors, defense lawyers, probation officers and others in law, psychology, sociology, biology and other disciplines in attacking the increasingly complex problems that are arising in our modern society. As a start in that direction, we have proposed—and Senator Edward M. Kennedy, of Massachusetts, is sponsoring—legislation to create a national academy of criminal justice which might be considered analogous to West Point in this field.

Q. Do you look for crime and delinquency to continue to grow?

A. Probably. Our own feeling is that, unless much is done to check the vicious cycles involved, we are in for a period of violence beyond anything we have yet seen.

All you have to do is to read about the murders and assaults taking place in New York subways. Only a few years ago nobody thought of public conveyances as being unsafe.

We foresee no letup in this trend. A delinquent child often grows up to produce delinquent children—not as a matter of heredity, but of his own unresolved conflicts which make him an ineffective parent.

In our principal study, we found that 45 per cent of the mothers of the delinquents we interviewed had a history of criminality themselves, compared with 15 per cent of the mothers of nondelinquents. Sixty-six per cent of the fathers had a similar history, contrasted with 32 per cent of the fathers of nondelinquents.

Our trouble is that everyone is so busy managing the children who are already delinquents that they don't have time to think of how to break the vicious cycle that is building up delinquency. We are not doing the main thing that must be done to prevent the predelinquent from becoming a full-fledged delinquent by correcting conditions in the home.

That has been one of our purposes in working for so many years on tracing the roots and the development of delinquency—to provide our authorities with the information they need to act at the earliest possible period in a child's life when trouble signs appear.

DELINQUENCY IN THE MODERN WORLD [4]

What Is a Juvenile Delinquent?

Almost every language in the world now yields a phrase labeling those youngsters of many nations whose behavior or tastes are different enough to incite suspicion if not alarm. They are the *teddy boys* in England, the *nozem* in the Netherlands, the *raggare* in Sweden, the *blousons noirs* in France, the *tsotsis* in South Africa, the *bodgies* in Australia, the *halbstarken* in Austria and Germany, the *taipau* in Taiwan, the *mambo boys* or *taiyozuku* in Japan, the

[4] Article entitled "Juvenile Delinquency: A Problem for the Modern World," by William C. Kvaraceus, professor of education and director of youth studies, Lincoln Filene Center for Citizenship and Public Affairs, Tufts University. *Federal Probation*. 28:12-18. S. '64. (This article presents in condensed form excerpts from Dr. Kvaraceus' Unesco book of the same title. © Unesco 1964.) Reprinted by permission

tapkaroschi in Yugoslavia, the *vitelloni* in Italy, the *hooligans* in Poland, and the *stiliagyi* in the U.S.S.R.

But it is not our right to assume that every *teddy boy* or every *blouson noir* is actively engaged in delinquency. These names often mislead people. It is unjust to assume automatically that a youngster who likes rock 'n' roll music or bizarre clothing is on his way to becoming a delinquent if he is not one already. Too often, the adult world has used the word "delinquent" to express anger or bewilderment at adolescent tastes.

Nor should every minor who breaks a rule or behaves offensively be considered a delinquent. The behavior of young people rarely consistently conforms with the standards and expectations that adults have for them.

What are the offenses and what are the penalties? The differences from country to country only indicate how divided the world is on who is a delinquent, who is not, and what should be done about it.

A widespread form of delinquency in Cairo is the collection of cigarette butts from the street. A recent survey in India, conducted in Lucknow and Kampur, indicated that the second most common juvenile offense was vagrancy. A few years ago in Hong Kong, juveniles brought before the magistrate's court reached the startling figure of more than 55,000 and yet over 90 per cent of them had committed only technical breaches of the law such as hawking without a license. Information from Lagos, Nigeria, shows that a delinquent there is primarily an offender against the unwritten laws of the home: disrespect and disobedience are regarded as serious offenses.

So we see that the numbers of children cited for delinquent acts can sometimes be misleading unless we are to know the nature of the offenses and what particular law they violate.

Yet even when we take the most cautious attitude towards statistics on delinquency from all corners of the world, the evidence mounts. The offenses are varied. They range from stealing, vandalism and property offenses, petty extortion and gambling to violent behavior, rowdiness, truancy, immoral or indecent conduct, drinking, and drug addiction.

In almost every city in the world where delinquency exists, so does the juvenile gang which looms up as a modern social institution. These gangs, innocent or evil, are an important element in the over-all pattern of juvenile delinquency. Looking at delinquency in a worldwide context, one does not often see individual youngsters becoming delinquent each in his own fashion, but rather as a number of boys participating in joint activities that derive their meaning and pleasure from a set of common sentiments, loyalties, and rules.

The majority of these gangs often engage in acts which do not always bring financial gains and to the rest of the world seem almost purposeless in their malice.

In Poland, teen-age gangs have damaged railroad trains and molested passengers for no apparent reason. In Saskatchewan, Canada, groups of boys have entered private homes and mutilated expensive furnishings without attempting to steal a single object. In Chiengmai, Thailand, a band of male minors, with a symbol of a white eagle tattooed on their arms, found their greatest diversion in terrorizing or injuring outsiders. In Argentina, gangs of boys have gathered in cafés or bars to insult or humiliate customers.

Some juvenile delinquents, however, have clearer goals in mind. Racketeering or petty extortion are good examples. A gang in Detroit, Michigan, which was composed of fifteen boys from thirteen to sixteen years of age, organized a racket in which all the smaller children of the neighborhood were forced to pay five cents for the insurance of not being molested on the way to and from the local cinema. A report from India indicates that gangs of young boys and girls have learned to be highly successful smugglers of illicit liquor and drugs.

In the past, tabulations on the backgrounds of a cross section of the juvenile delinquents always seemed to indicate that these children were reared in poor living conditions. A recent United Nations report, however, points to a strong change in this tendency. There are numerous and increasing indications that children from the higher-income brackets are becoming delinquents. In France, the expression *blousons dorés* (jackets of gold) is a somewhat sarcastic reference to delinquents from richer families than those of the *blousons noirs.*

In the United States, a recent survey revealed that a relatively large number of teen-age boys admitted that they had committed serious acts of delinquency which had never become a matter of court record. These were sons of middle- and upper-income families.

One of the richest collections of twentieth century myths surrounds the subject of delinquency. Usually, they are oversimplified versions of what causes delinquency. But generalizations are useless. Such explanations as slum living, "broken" homes, films, and deprivation fail to provide us with universal and realistic reasons. Sometimes, each of these may be one among many factors that shape a child's life but no factor can be accepted as the single over-all reason for the thousands and thousands of delinquent cases.

To begin to understand the problem, we must realize that delinquents often do the same thing for vastly different reasons and to achieve vastly different results.

Three Case Histories

To illustrate these differences—as far as reasons and results go—here are examples of boys each of whom might be considered a juvenile delinquent.

A fifteen-year-old American, John G., from Los Angeles, California, is one of twelve members of a street gang called the "Sharks." The gang has an inflexible code of values, standards, and morals. All the members have sworn allegiance to this peculiar code, and for John G. it is the most serious and important emotional commitment of his life. Last summer, he and four other gang boys stole a car that was parked in the neighborhood. They abandoned the car, a mile and a half away, the next morning around 4 A.M. When John G. was questioned by a juvenile court he did not feel anxious to explain why he had done it and there was not the slightest attempt to show he was sorry. He had previously been in trouble for breaking windows and slashing the roofs of convertible cars with a razor.

His background showed that both parents worked and their combined incomes were meager. Their apartment was too small for the five members of the family. John G.'s record in school was dismal and his teachers resented his pose of boredom and contempt. His attitude, in school and outside, was spiteful and malicious, yet a psychiatric examination revealed no pronounced emotional disturbances and a normal intelligence.

By conventional standards, John G. might be considered a disgrace to his law-abiding parents, a failure by his school, and a threat by his community. And yet there is a telling logic in what he does. All of this delinquent's most offensive acts won the approval and respect of the people he most admires: gang members of the "Sharks." His conduct is right by the standards of his own street-corner subculture, although it happens to be wrong to the outside world.

A thirteen-year-old English boy, Basil P., comes from a prosperous family in London. Basil does not do well in school, much to the distress of his father who also studied there and achieved a reputation as a student. Basil's most conspicuous difficulty is poor reading; in any subject requiring much effort in reading he is apt to become distracted or lazy. He might have remained an anonymous or inadequate student, but for the fact that several of his teachers and many of his classmates know that Basil has a habit of taking things.

The child makes no attempt to deny it. For a long period of time he has been pilfering objects from other boys, stealing both valuable and trifling things. Basil does not hoard them but often gives them away to classmates, consciously increasing the risk that the original owner will see his possession and claim it. Once, in London on a holiday, Basil stole three gramophone records from a music store. He says he is "sorry" he steals, he does not know why he does it, and he wishes he could stop. A psychiatric examination revealed that on a deep symbolical level the objects Basil stole stand for or substitute for something unconsciously desired but somehow forbidden or unattainable. It was recommended, and agreed, that he would receive psychiatric help and treatment.

A seventeen-year-old African, Pierre N., traveled from his home village on the Ivory Coast to try to find a job in the nearest city. He hoped to be employed in a hotel. Pierre N. could read and write, speak two languages, and was a bright youngster. In the city he was caught by a clerk when trying to steal a shirt from a store. To the judge of a court Pierre explained that his own clothes were shabby, he had no money, and he hoped a new shirt would make a better impression when he looked for a job.

The considerable differences between these three case histories give only some indication of the hazards of lumping all adolescent transgressions under the label of juvenile delinquency.

Why Delinquency Exists

Delinquent behavior, which stems from so many combinations of factors, cannot be treated or controlled until several scientifically evolved theories about the individual offender have been checked. The boy must be considered apart from his conspirators. His life at home, his problems at school, his relationships with his parents, his own self-image, and his personality must all be carefully revealed and evaluated.

One theory says that delinquency results from severe frustrations suffered by a growing child. Another, that it is an expression of rebellion. Yet another theory suggests that juvenile delinquency is perhaps the failure of a young male to be able to identify himself with what is professionally referred to as a "male authority figure." This naturally means the child's father, the dominating and consistent male influence in his life. If there is no father, if he is rarely at home, or even if he is a dim or withdrawn figure in the child's life, a small boy may come to feel a very deep insecurity about his own image of himself as a man.

In some families the child does not lack a "male authority figure"—there is a father and an assertive one. But what happens when the mother derides the father and constantly reminds the child of his faults? The child comes to understand that to be loved and accepted he must somehow be different from the man who is his father—the one man it is most natural for him to idealize. It is more than possible that a youngster in this situation will have the same fears about himself as the child who lacks a father.

In the broadest sense, any adolescent who is unsure of himself can appease his worries—or will try to—by being aggressive. Here is where one of the rare positive statements about all delinquent behavior can be made: it is remarkably aggressive. Aggression may be verbal, it may consist of destructive acts, it may be sexual. Aggression may be directed towards one's self, towards the world, or both.

A very simple illustration of how some boys dispel their doubts about their own masculinity by extremely aggressive behavior—stealing of cars—is contained in a report from Sweden: "A phrase often heard is: 'If you've got a car, you'll get a girl.' At the same time one is struck by the extreme inadequacy of this category of car thieves in their dealings with girls. A great many of them cannot dance, even though they are of the 'dancing age.' This means they lack not only the skill to dance, but also have no way with girls and are completely without confidence in their own manliness."

A deep questioning in the child's mind about his own value as a human being can cripple him so that he is almost unable to make any honest or lasting attachment with other people. For if his parents have not loved and accepted him and admitted him, how can a child believe that someone else will? Children who feel they are not loved or wanted can be very severely damaged by such deprivation—real or imaginary. Maladjusted adolescents are usually those youngsters who have suffered from these feelings.

Sometimes even genuine love is not enough. In the case of a family where the mother is the head of the house, the provider, and the voice of authority, a rebellion may occur. Young boys wishing to become young men must break from this world of feminine rule, even if it means defying the mother, and assert themselves as males. When there is no man around the house on a permanent basis this becomes difficult. The boy is under a peculiar sort of stress. It is possible that because of this stress he will try to take on attributes which will symbolize to him, and to the world, an unassailable masculinity. There are a number of activities and even possessions which symbolize clear-cut and irreproachable masculinity. For example, there is ability in combat, ownership of a car or motorcycle, techniques in violence or sadism, or even a vocabulary. There are forms of dress. One has only to think of the much-publicized American juvenile delinquent who owns a motorcycle and wears a black leather jacket and blue jeans.

In most societies it is accepted and understood that adolescence is the period when a youngster forms his own identity, usually by a meaningful conflict with his parents or the older generation. Nothing in this world causes as much concern to the adolescent as this question of his own identity: how he sees himself and how he feels the rest of the world sees him. Even a negative identity—and more than one habitual delinquent child has described himself as "plain mean"—can be satisfying.

Young people usually want and need parental models either to imitate or reject. Few children might actively complain about the increasing tolerance and permissiveness of their parents, but their behavior often reflects their own inner confusion. Where there are no clear boundaries in a child's life, when the "rules" are never defined, when neither his father nor his mother represents certain values and certain commitments to life, it becomes harder for the child to discover a true image of himself and to set limits of behavior.

So much for the interior forces that may shape the child so crucially at the beginning of his life. There is also the outside world which begins to intrude upon his thoughts and feelings when he is very young.

For example, a young person who grows up in a deprived area learns certain kinds of behavior as naturally and normally as the middle-class boy learns exactly the opposite. A middle-class child might be taught to fear poor marks in school, fighting, cursing, and being rude to his teacher. But the slum child, conversely, might fear doing well in school and being friendly with his teacher, for this would set him apart from the other children and possibly evoke their anger or ridicule. All too often he learns that the best way to express his aggressions is with his fists.

It cannot be assumed that all deprived areas are jungles of violence. What is clearly shown in many scientific research projects is that while they are never the one and only cause for delinquency, they can provide a different set of traditions which are unfamiliar to outsiders. Many children who are exposed to values which almost encourage delinquency do not automatically become delinquents. Others prove more vulnerable.

The child who lives in an underprivileged neighborhood may often resent the limits that he feels society has imposed. This may be illustrated through hundreds of case histories. One example could be the boy who knows he will never make enough money to buy the car he wants. Another is the child who knows that it is impossible for him to attend college. These are frustrations that society creates and they can often be as disturbing as the frustrations that are emotionally aroused by a lack of inner security.

Industrialization and Changing Society

Many complex problems in human behavior have been traced to intense industrialization. Sociologists have remarked very often about the type of work that absorbs years of men's lives when their entire working day consists only of pressing buttons and pulling levers or switches. The assembly line hardly offers a man a sense of joy or fulfillment in his work. He has no commitment, no sense of achievement, no pride in craftsmanship, and no sense of social purpose. For a young boy who can look forward only to many years of this sort of monotony, delinquency can often serve as the best and most exciting sort of protest against a dreary and unacceptable future.

Added to this, there is a frightening freedom for people who live in big cities, divorced from the traditional values and familiar standards that shaped their lives. Very often, they are anonymous and alone, cut off from the smaller society from which they came.

When normal values and traditions break down, and cannot be so easily replaced, it is often the adolescents who feel the most stress. It has been said that the social problem of one generation is a psychological problem for the next. In the case of societies undergoing modernization, it is often the rate—the degree of acceleration—of these changes much more than the changes themselves that must be considered.

There are many conclusions to be drawn from understanding and appreciating the viewpoints of the specialists on the subject of juvenile delinquency. One conclusion must always be remembered. There is not one cause for delinquency but rather a sequence of interlocking factors in the child's life that can result in delinquency. Different factors sometimes can result in the same type of delinquent behavior; on the other hand, different kinds of delinquent behavior are often caused by the same factors.

Juvenile Delinquency: What a Community Can Do

What emerges clearly from many studies and reports and surveys is that delinquent behavior must be the concern of the entire community, not just dismissed as a problem to be handled by local schools, police courts, or professional agencies. Professionals will always be needed but the impetus must come from the community itself.

One of the most crucial forces, if we consider only the number of years during which it exerts an influence over the child, is the school. Together with the home it provides the basic learning experience for all children. The teacher, who is a trained observer, can detect evidence or incipient signs of personal or social problems that are affecting the child and perhaps offer the pupils some form of help and relief. He can do much to make the child aware of his own basic values and teach him how to develop them.

Ideally, specialized professional personnel are needed to reinforce and augment the assistance a teacher can give to a pupil. Through timely and skillful use of auxiliary services, the school can often help a child from becoming a failure. The visiting teacher who can establish a close contact with a child's parents, the school social worker, or the psychiatric worker are all trained to evaluate and relieve the pressures that often contribute to a child's defeat in the classroom.

Many educators have expressed the opinion that far too many schools adhere too rigidly to a curriculum that has no significance or value to every pupil. If we agree that the child who might become a good mechanic is not to be considered a human being inferior to the child with an interest in medicine, then we must also acknowledge that a single school should accommodate and benefit both of them. Pouring all students into a single academic mold causes many children who might be vulnerable to delinquency to come a good deal closer to it. What can and should be considered by the authorities and the community is the establishment of different types of school experiences for children who cannot benefit by a standard academic education or those children who, for any number of reasons, cannot hold their own in the regular classroom.

Some large cities have attempted to diminish their delinquency problems among other objectives by establishing separate vocational or technical high schools, and through work-study programs. The programs of these schools are realistically connected both to the employment situation and to the requirements of the apprentice system in various trades.

Every community will not be able to establish a vocational high school. But there are other possibilities. Some schools have adopted the system of an optional period during the week: there is a class in vocational training for those who elect it, other pupils can study foreign languages. In other places, schools and local industries have developed cooperative work-study programs for selected youngsters.

Delinquents, for a variety of reasons, frequently do not have an accepting or reassuring relationship with their parents. Any education program or any counseling that the community makes available to parents, provided it is wisely presented, can often be a turning point.

Many things can be meant by parent education. It is not always helpful to tell a mother outright to be a better mother, but, sometimes, by relieving her of economic or health worries she is freer to love and consider her children.

In many instances, the very parents of the children most exposed to delinquency have very little concept of what it means to be a member of a community and belong to an organization. They may react suspiciously or resent the visit of an outsider wishing to advise them on their family problems. Very often, hostility can be overcome if the parents are contacted, not with a reproachful or condescending attitude by others, but with an invitation to contribute something to the life of the community. The larger the number of adults from all backgrounds that one community can interest in belonging to some type of stable and enduring organization, the easier it will be to reach them as parents and possibly direct them.

Some city communities have established neighborhood centers where informal educational activities are conducted. These activities include parent discussion groups. Through these neighborhood centers, people of all backgrounds who have a natural ability for different kinds of leadership can be found and involved in committee or recreational work.

The importance of the police in a community with delinquency can hardly be overrated since they often represent the first official contact between the young offender and the law. The policeman or juvenile officer is the one who must frequently decide whether to let the child off with a reprimand or to refer him to a juvenile court or some other agency set up to deal with such children.

In some countries the evolution of the work of the police has given rise to more definite forms of action of a preventive nature. In Liverpool, since 1949, there has been developed a city police program known as the Juvenile Liaison Scheme. Its object is to deal with youngsters under seventeen years of age who manifest some behavior disorders or who have already committed petty offenses. The police officials try, after an interview with a child, to secure the cooperation of the individual family and school. Then they often contact appropriate services such as youth clubs, probation officers, and family service units in order to provide suitable help.

The liaison officer visits the child and parents often. He tries to advise and assist them in various ways. What is most significant about the Liverpool plan is that it improves the relations between the police and the public in general. It is claimed that this special operation was a contributory factor to diminishing the figures of juvenile delinquency in Liverpool, a city with the unhappy distinction of once having the highest delinquency rate in England.

Very often a separate division or bureau in the police department, specially for juvenile aid, can accomplish much. A juvenile aid bureau generally handles all the cases of youngsters who are picked up either by the regular police force or by a juvenile squad. The staff also may carry on research concerning any local youth problems; they can assume a good share of the responsibility for enforcing child labor laws, supervising children in street trades and checking on those local danger spots which often foster delinquent behavior.

If there are a number of boys who have left school in one particular neighborhood with a high incidence of delinquency most people would hope that they would find jobs instead of loitering on street corners. But it is not enough to find them jobs—any job—just to keep them out of trouble. What has to be done is to make youngsters who are vulnerable to delinquent behavior *more* employable in addition to creating new employment opportunities for them.

One possible remedy, especially in poorer neighborhoods, is a community-organized youth jobs center, the function of which would be to help the young person enter the world of work. Such a center could offer guidance and counseling, placement service, and help redirect the youngster to a training program. The aim should be to make the boy more employable by improving his social, academic, and job skills.

New Outlooks: Involving the Delinquent

In the long run, only the delinquent can solve the delinquency problem. In the past, many agencies working with the delinquent encouraged him to be passive. The professional workers tended to moralize over him, scold him, threaten him, study him, relocate him, and treat him. Today, hopefully, the emphasis in many parts of the world is to encourage the delinquent to play a much more active and decisive role in the solution of his own problems.

This must be done with considerable skill and patience. Very often, he will refuse to cooperate and refuse to help himself. Involving the delinquent can mean a multitude of things. Here is a very simple example of how one community approached it. At the suggestion of a team of professionals, a group of thirty-four delinquents who had previously been gang members were divided into three squads, according to age. They were encouraged to suggest or consider certain projects for their particular group with an adult adviser. A feeling of mild competition between the three squads was encouraged.

During a two-month period, each squad carried out a certain program. One squad was busy cleaning up an empty lot to use as a recreational area. Another squad operated a darts booth and a lemonade stand at a neighborhood fund-raising carnival in order to make enough money for a summer camping trip. The third squad was engaged in repainting a wing of a local hospital; what money they made went into a fund. In each squad, there was a strong *esprit de corps*; individual and group performance was encouraged; special citations were awarded by community groups—such as a chamber of commerce—for programs that genuinely benefited the community as a whole. The leader of each squad had the responsibility of seeing that each project was carried out within a time limit.

The ideal result of such a project is not to convert every delinquent into a civic-minded prude. It is to show the young delinquents that conformity need not be stifling, and that they themselves are capable of choosing and reaching socially acceptable goals.

In trying to involve the delinquent in his own reeducation, one thing must be remembered. He already knows failure to an exceptional degree. Therefore, caution must be taken not to involve him in an adult plan or set up such difficult expectations that he would face still another failure. Neither should he be so protected and supervised that he is not permitted to make mistakes in judgment.

II.   TRUANTS, GANGS, AND ADDICTS

EDITOR'S INTRODUCTION

The world of the juvenile delinquent is a complicated one that adults cannot penetrate—one they rarely understand. It has its own rules, its own set of values, and even its own code of honor. The forms that delinquency takes are influenced by the demands placed upon youth and by the opportunities that are open to young people to fit into the larger society. They are also determined by the values of the society—whether its standards and its rewards seem worthwhile to young people. Delinquency, thus, is not simply a result of poverty or deprivation. It can be found in the most "respectable" families of wealthy communities, just as in the neglected slums of the great cities. The delinquent is a law-breaker. But to him the law often seems outdated, repressive, or irrelevant. To escape from the confines of a society which does not seem to respond to his needs, the youthful delinquent turns to crime, to gang warfare, to drugs, and to a search for "kicks." This places him outside the law. But it also forces society to recognize the part it has played in creating the causes of delinquency.

The selections in this section deal with various forms of delinquency. The first selection, condensed from a series of articles by staff writers in the Washington *Post*, examines the causes of delinquency among neglected young people. This is followed by an article by Joseph Lelyveld, staff reporter of the New York *Times*, on the strange—but increasingly familiar—phenomenon of delinquency among privileged children from wealthy families. The next selection, taken from a study by Professor Gilbert Geis of Los Angeles State College, deals with the origins of juvenile gangs and why young people find satisfaction and security in them. In the last two selections free-lance writer Jack Harrison Pollack on assignment for the *NEA Journal* and staff writer Martin Arnold of the New York *Times* examine the relatively recent problems of alcoholism and addiction among the young.

THE DELINQUENT'S WORLD [1]

Down on the street in Northeast Washington, the fight—the dirty fight—somehow helps make life bearable.

This is a street where men and women stand on corners and lean from windows and sit on rowhouse stoops for hours, waiting for the single flash of excitement—a neighbor's new dress or a sudden, shouted argument—that can make a whole day memorable.

This is a street where many children live in homes poisoned with contempt or barely warmed by parents' love. So these youngsters go out on the streets for attention or affection or just plain something to do.

Eighty per cent of the youngsters who live on these streets seek and find their love and their status in their homes and schools and jobs. The 80 per cent concentrate on the bigger battle to escape the streets, or at least to endure them.

But the 20 per cent who make the headlines have never had wise counsel at home. They have never known the counsel that can be had at school. And they fear authority so deeply that they will attack its representative—the policeman, the teacher—before their counsel can find voice.

So in the absence of any wise counsel, this 20 per cent will go out on the street.

Like proud Solo, who struts in $40 shoes, basking in the street's knowledge that he stole to get the money for them.

Or like the eleven-year-old boy who wore nine pairs of socks to school to stand as tall as his classmates, then yoked [mugged] a ten-year-old newsboy in the afternoon for a pittance to celebrate his newfound stature.

Or the fourteen-year-old girl who spends long afternoons at home with two other young dropouts, poring over newspaper advertisements, carefully selecting a wardrobe which one of the three will just as carefully shoplift the next day. She wants to be well dressed when she streetwalks on weekend nights and sells herself to find the attention she never gets at home.

[1] From "20% of Slum Children Find Status in Thievery" and "How Experts Explain Making of a Criminal," two articles by staff writer John J. Carmody in a series of twelve entitled "Children and Society: Partners in Crime?" Washington *Post.* My. 8, 12, '65. Reprinted by permission.

Or the seventeen-year-old youth who has fathered a child by a seventeen-year-old girl and faithfully maintains an apartment for them as she lies expecting another baby. He walks the downtown streets on Thursday nights looking for yoke victims because Friday morning is grocery-shopping day for his little family. . . .

Otto, who earned $28 a week for two nights' work as a car hop to make restitution on a housebreaking—until his restaurant employer asked Otto to bring him a police clearance, saw the youth's record, and fired him on the spot.

Or the fourteen-year-old girl whose need for affection led her to a gang of boys whose prerequisite for membership was that every new member's girl must be made pregnant. Desperate to belong there—anywhere—the girl entered into a gentle conspiracy with one of the boys and began adding a T-shirt a month to her girth to convince the other club members that he and she had met the test.

And the sixteen-year-old shoplifter and pickpocket whose pious grandmother takes in his loot and tells him encouragingly that "the good Lord provides even though the Devil brings it home." . . .

Out in the playgrounds the old drunks stagger by and the young dropouts stand ready with a hundred sorry blandishments for the pupils.

The wonder down in the ghetto is not that 20 per cent of the youngsters turn out so bad but that 80 per cent turn out so well.

This is a neighborhood where the only aspirations many children ever have are from television programs—those myopic visions of rich apartments and big cars and bountiful hair and heroes who kill when necessary. . . .

And yet 80 per cent of those youngsters turn out well. They do not rob for attention or sell their bodies.

They do not resent school or the teacher who may be the first man ever to enforce his adult will on them. They do not fight a policeman just to gain a place in a shadowy pantheon of pseudo-heroes.

They do not attack the elderly for purse money or steal a $5,000 car and pretend it is theirs.

This 80 per cent are children who find life bearable down in the slums.

These children walk these streets and see them as a place to escape, at least to endure. In the fight to make life bearable in those streets, they have won.

But Solo has not. He wanders, despite the efforts of many persons to give his life meaning.

The Making of a Criminal

"I was young at the time and I wanted to get a rep. That's actually why I did it, to get a rep."

The speaker: Solo, a young criminal. . . .

"You know why I got into trouble?" asks Leroy, another youth in the ghetto. "All my friends used to go steal and wouldn't let me go with them. They were the only friends I had then. . . . So they let me go once and I got busted [arrested]. . . ."

These boys' own explanations of their beginnings into crime might be heard all through their ghetto.

You ask a psychiatrist who specializes in adolescents' problems and he might point out how Solo and Leroy need attention from their friends, how they strive for it, from buying $40 shoes to bashing someone over the head to get the money for those shoes.

Down where Leroy and Solo live, status is a big thing. After all, there aren't big cars for them to own or much money to go around. Nor are there many jobs or much education.

And so how does a youth, say fifteen or sixteen years of age and a Negro who has dropped out of school, get attention?

Some of them get it by flights into crime.

In their world, say the psychiatrists, violence may even be the norm. When a Leroy or a Solo steps out into the street and when one of them smashes the face of a passerby, the behavior isn't all that abnormal. Some sociologists even say it's quite normal behavior, under the circumstances.

"It's a warm night and nothing else to do. There's never nothing else to do. You're just walking down the street and you see a car with the keys in it. So you take it."

The speaker now is Tommy, the suburban counterpart of Solo and Leroy. . . . His milieu is different, certainly.

He, too, seeks status and attention, says the psychiatrist. But Tommy can't copy the college-bound boys at his suburban high school, so he tries to stand out by abnormal behavior.

A United States Children's Bureau report on youth crime points out that, indeed, some delinquency is "normal." It's a logical identification youngsters make with their group or neighborhood.

In the case of Leroy and Solo and Tommy, the people who think about social problems and children might also point up the similarities of their weak home lives.

One settlement house worker . . . , for instance, points out that most children in trouble seem to have an unsatisfactory home life.

Says . . . [an] employee who specializes in youth:

I've been impressed by the similarity of the city and the suburban delinquent. I don't believe the only kind of deprivation is economic or material.

For example, you find the successful father who is away sixteen hours a day. You have the same situation in the city with the absent alcoholic father.

With wealthy parents who have a governess and maids, often the children are in fact abandoned by those parents. By the same token, however, the attentive mother on welfare in the slums may well do a good job.

A judge emphasizes, however, that the size and solutions to the problems in the city and suburbs are widely disparate.

The suburbs possess the machinery to win back the relatively rare wandering youth, while the cities' crime-fighting apparatus is clogged to saturation.

This, he contends, is why an antipoverty problem is so urgently needed, to nudge the cities back from their points of crisis.

And a juvenile judge points out: "No child is born a delinquent. The earlier you can provide a decent environment at home, the better. The last place some of these kids want to go at one in the morning is back to a home that is unhappy."

And in the suburbs, the Children's Bureau points out, "The family is weakened as a means of social control by the freedom of adolescents, their mobility and the preoccupation of parents in their own social and job success."

One lingering tragedy of weak home life is the emotional deprivation that ensues. Says another psychiatrist:

"This can result in a low-grade rage that can last a lifetime. Mother is too busy or dad is too drunk and the primary result of this deprivation is a mistrust of everybody."

A psychiatrist at Laurel Youth Center points out that the Tommys and Leroys "want to do something valuable but there is seldom the old-fashioned business of working on projects as a family for these troubled children."

And a consultant at Johns Hopkins University goes even farther and laments:

"The family is working least well of all of today's institutions. In the last twenty years the role of the family in respect to the child has been diminishing. Adults as well as children are now associating by age group rather than by family . . . the family has abdicated responsibility."

Psychiatrists also note there is an important gap between childhood and adulthood.

The Children's Bureau report paints this picture:

Youngsters don't adjust gradually from childhood to adulthood. It's a sharp break, for which they get no preparation, though many hunger for it. For some of them, delinquency fills the gap by introducing them to the adult world where they have to be responsible for their actions. This is true when they get caught. It may be the first time they've ever had to be responsible.

This drive to accept responsibility is often evident in the Juvenile Court. One judge reports that youths on probation to the court sometimes violate their parole just before their probationary time is over.

"He uses his probation officer as a prop," says the judge.

But another judge adds another factor here: "The probation officer may be the only one who'll speak kindly to these youngsters."

In both unhappy slum homes and unhappy suburban homes, the television set often sits in for the parent.

It may serve to remind a Leroy, the Children's Bureau points out, that his family, even if loving, is a disadvantaged family. He sees the programs with all their slick hearthsides and he can't help finding flaws in those around him and in their values.

As the director of a college criminology department points out, the TV set gives Leroy aspirations that he can't possibly realize and at the same time heightens his frustration and resentments and feelings of rejections.

The settlement house worker, seeing the unhappiness at home, says the youngster "needs somebody to latch onto that he can't find in his family. He finds he has to go outside into the strange environment of the streets and find it primarily among his own peers."

Out in the streets, the youngsters find their gangs.

"In the suburbs as well as the city," says a legal psychiatrist . . . "there are groups of youngsters who hang around together and there is a group culture with members under pressure to conform to behavior."

This is where the fight for teen-age status turns into a group movement, whether it's in the suburbs with Tommy and the Colonels, or down in the slums with Leroy and his friends.

"In these group activities," says a psychiatrist, "the vast majority join only to save their own necks. They actually feel they would get hurt by their own kind if they didn't. Most of these hangers-on are innocent, good kids, basically."

The experts stress that the Leroys and Tommys need a strong, guiding hand, and that the schools should be one place to help lend that hand to build respect.

Instead, as a leading juvenile judge points out, "truancy from school seems to be the first step in the delinquent career."

Out in the suburbs, truancy is rare. For instance, occasionally a child drops out because of imagined or real family pressure to succeed.

Down in the slums, the very ease of the act of truancy helps.

The tragedy, says one of Washington's probation officers, is that "many of the kids drift into trouble in plain view of the 'establishment'—the social workers, police, school teachers. Yet no one intervenes to provide the helping hand at the crucial moment."

An official of the National Council on Crime and Delinquency adds: "All the studies about predictability are saying that children who withdraw in class or cause trouble at home are waving their own red flag. Now we identify kids as heading for trouble, but that's all. Then when they get into serious difficulty we look for a legal way to expel them from school and put them away."

One crime expert says that a weak home life or truancy or poverty are only a few factors amid a myriad of them.

"As long as the police and the city fathers wink at numbers games and bookies," he says, "how are the values of troubled children ever going to change?"

Whatever the theories, and there are hundreds, the problems exist. They most harshly affect the man or woman who is maimed by a wayward youth on a darkened street, and the troubled youths themselves. In time those youths, too, will have children, and these children too, the odds will say, might easily fall into the same distressful condition.

THE AFFLUENT DELINQUENT [2]

Everyone knows, of course, what juvenile delinquency is. Like stoopball, it is a pastime of the poor, the oppressed and the crowded. Its causes are multiple and complex. Its cures are better houses, better schools, broader economic opportunities—"a chance," as it's sometimes put, "to get a piece of the American dream."

But if that is what juvenile delinquency is, what is it when the son of a business executive or a professional man steals a battery from a parked car—or the entire car? Clearly, since he is supposed to be living the American dream full time, it cannot be juvenile delinquency. It must be a prank or a mistake. Then, when many cars are stolen and taken for joy rides by teen-agers in the suburbs, is it a wave of mistakes?

Somewhere deep in the American consciousness is the idea that money and virtue reinforce each other, so we easily assume that any misbehavior by the well to do and comfortable is a kind of sport (if not in the sense that means diversion, at least in the sense that means mutation). But the point comes when the wave is big enough to sweep away such assumptions and command the attention of the whole community.

That, for instance, is what happened with the . . . discovery in Yonkers of an alarming incidence of narcotic addiction among teen-

[2] From "The Paradoxical Case of the Affluent Delinquent," by Joseph Lelyveld, staff reporter. New York *Times Magazine.* p. 13+. O. 4, '64. © 1964 by The New York Times Company. Reprinted by permission.

agers from middle-class homes. It happened, too, in Greenburgh, New York, with a couple of knifings and a threatened gang fight. And it happened . . . in Rye, when the merchants on Purchase Street summoned all the parents' groups in town to a meeting and announced they could no longer afford to ignore systematic shoplifting by high school students, who had become so brazen that they were taking orders for specific items of loot, correct sizes and colors guaranteed. The merchants said they had looked the other way, not wanting to get into any hassles with parents, until their businesses were actually endangered.

This solicitude for the feelings of parents often carries over to the authorities. The reasoning seems to be that there is no point in visiting the sins of the sons on the fathers, so long as the fathers are willing to pay the bills.

But—in one case where the bill couldn't be paid—a judge in fashionable Darien, Conn., decided . . . that this was a backward approach to youthful crime. So he signed warrants for the arrest of parents and other adults who had permitted the serving of hard drinks to teen-agers at house parties. . . . Following the parties, two youngsters were involved in a car crash in which a seventeen-year-old girl was killed. Among the parents arrested was a psychiatrist.

Usually, it is not just the reputations of the parents and their children that are shielded, but the reputations of the towns themselves. Suburban towns place a high value on being known as calm islands at the edge of the stormy urban sea. Nevertheless, when they are assured that their identities will be protected, most officials and merchants will say that delinquency seems to become more commonplace as the suburbs grow in size and prosperity.

The typical range of offenses is not large: from trespassing and vandalism to burglary and auto theft. The youths usually operate in bands of only two or three. Compared with New York City, Police Commissioner Edward F. Carey of New Rochelle declares, any suburban town is still "Peaceful Valley." What shocks suburban communities is not uncontrollable outbreaks of juvenile crime, but outbreaks in precisely those areas where they are least expected. Periodically, in one town after another, they reach epidemic size.

"Three years ago," one police chief remarked, "if you asked me whether I had a delinquency problem, I would have told you—sincerely—that this town was clean. Now if any community in Westchester County says it doesn't have a problem with teen-agers, you know damn well they're lying."

One probation officer, however, dissented from the view that there has recently been a significant rise in crimes by teen-agers with well-to-do backgrounds. More probably, he said, the only real increase has been in the number of reports the police bothered to make.

Social workers in Westchester customarily refer to middle-class delinquency as "hidden delinquency." Their meaning is that much of it, perhaps most of it, never finds its way onto the official records. Often parents manage to keep the matter out of court by promising to send an offending youth to a boarding school—not infrequently a military school—or to a psychiatrist. It is very unusual for a teen-ager from a well-off family to be sent to a state correctional institution. An official at one detention home for suburban youths said he had seen a thousand teen-agers from lower-class families come and go, but only a few from moneyed families.

There are many ways of covering up, including that of the officer on the beat who knows he is likely to be rewarded if he takes a delinquent youngster directly home rather than to the station house. "These things happen," a police chief conceded. "I find out when I'm at a party and someone comes up to thank me for getting his kid off the hook when I never even knew the kid was in trouble."

But the ones who look the other way the most are the parents themselves. . . . There is a standing order at one station house that when teen-agers are picked up on the streets for loitering at three and four in the morning, the parents are to be called and asked to come down and retrieve them. Not infrequently no one is home. Usually if the parents are there, they are indignant. "Why can't you bring them home yourselves?" they demand of the police. Or, "Don't you have anything better to do than harass our kids?"

Even when it is a crime that brings parents to the police station, they often react with indignation. "You're crucifying my son!" a mother shrieked at a detective who had arrested the boy for vandalizing some thirty yachts.

"I'll take my oath on this," one policeman declared. "I've never had a parent come in here when the first question wasn't, 'Will it be in the papers?' If we started printing the names, then you'd see the parents act as if they cared."

Cases of vandalism and property damage can usually be handled by a father with a check. Once the account has been squared, the chances are that the injured party will be reluctant to press charges.

"Of course, there's a code," a school principal remarked "The parents say it would be a tragedy if the boy's future were spoiled by just one mistake. So he gets a second chance and a third chance and a fourth chance. Sometimes the result is a much greater tragedy."

The principal recalled one parent who paid a visit to the school after his son got into—and out of—some serious trouble. "What can I do for him?" the father asked. "If you were in my place, would you promise him a car, or would you promise him a yacht?"

"I know you're a very busy man," the principal replied, "but if I were in your place, I'd get some lumber and some plans for a boat —any kind of boat, a rowboat—and I'd build it with the boy." The father frowned. Later the principal heard that the father had arrived at his own solution. He had bought his son *both* the car and the yacht.

Actually, most teen-agers seem to resent fiercely such attempts to purchase their good behavior and affection. One young man put it this way:

"I always had the feeling that I was an employee of my parents. I was supposed to be something—like their car or their house—that they could point to with pride. But I was never supposed to be an inconvenience. I could have anything they thought of giving me. But I couldn't have any wishes of my own."

Often, say psychiatrists, youths act wildly as a way of demanding the attention, standards and discipline that their parents have failed to provide. And often they seem to want to be caught, and stopped. In one such case, a high school boy went hitchhiking on a main highway carrying a cash register he had just taken from a gas station.

Some observers have put the blame on TV shows for the disturbing patterns of violence in the first television-bred generation. The psychiatrist Fredric Wertham has led a one-man crusade against television, which he calls "a school of violence."

"In this school," he . . . declared, "young people are never, literally never, taught that violence is in itself reprehensible. The lesson they do get is that violence is the great adventure and the sure solution, and he who is best at it wins."

Whatever the causes, a simpler explanation—one that is often overlooked—for the apparent increase in the number of affluent delinquents is the incontrovertible increase in the number of affluent families. Although it is a common assumption that such families produce fewer delinquents than poor families, it is an assumption that cannot possibly be proved because accurate records on affluent delinquency have never existed.

It is the apparent pointlessness of most teen-age delinquency in the suburbs that perplexes parents and the police. The ransacking of vacant homes, for instance. In one case, paintings were slashed with antique sabers; bottles of aged brandy were smashed on the hearth; pieces from a prized ivory collection were splintered. The only theft was incidental: the boys took some precious jewels, but only to give them to their junior high school girl friends.

When the vandals were asked what lay behind their actions they said they didn't know. That, the police find, is the most common answer to the inevitable question: Why? The second most common answer is—"For kicks." And the third, often the most puzzling, is—"To get even." With whom and for what? Usually the response to this is answer No. 1: "I don't know."

But once initial reticence has been peeled away in interviews with probation officers and social workers, the teen-agers search for ways to justify themselves. One interviewer described the change: "When they're all together, they try to talk big. But when they're alone, they talk more like the kids they really are."

From saying "We didn't have anything to do" and "I was just going along with the crowd," they move to discussions of their problems with their families. In most cases they are quick to blame their parents for overindulging them or not indulging them enough, for doting on them or ignoring them altogether. With any encouragement at all from the interviewer, these themes are eagerly pursued.

Rarely do teen-agers in trouble pass moral judgments on what they have done. One boy from an extremely well-off family, caught after twelve housebreakings, was pressed by a social worker to say whether he had done wrong. The most that he would concede was that he had been "unwise."

The son of a broker who vandalized a school was very eager to impress an interviewer with the idea that he was not a vandal. Of course, he had gotten out of line that night, but it should be apparent, he insisted, that he was simply not the sort of person who did what he had done.

Probation officers say that the worst outbreaks of juvenile crime can usually be traced to the influence of one or two very disturbed but highly persuasive youths. In Yonkers, for instance, a former high school baseball star got most of the blame for the introduction of narcotics to a quiet residential neighborhood.

In another community, one boy was said to have been behind some forty to fifty burglaries. In the basement of his home the police found an elaborate workshop where he had turned out homemade housebreaking tools. He had participated in every one of the burglaries. A number of others experimented, going along with him once or twice and then dropping out. The leader, who was universally admired for his "coolness," ended up in a mental institution.

Of course, most suburban teen-agers—by far—never have any trouble with the police. Nevertheless, their lives seem to be affected by the same kind of random wandering and reaching out for thrills that impel those who do get into trouble. After midnight on almost any Main Street, the cars filled with teen-agers drive back and forth between the parking lots of all-night diners. There is ceaseless checking in and out:

"What's up?"

"Nothing here—yet."

"Well, let's take a look down the road."

In some towns, the police call this loitering and tell the youths to keep moving. So they cruise through residential neighborhoods, hunting for parties to crash, or head out to the parkways to race.

Those who stay out of trouble, one school principal observed, "are a pretty wonderful bunch. They're tempted just as much as the others. Sometimes they come very close; they'd be horrified to have their parents know just how close. But they hold on."

The teen-agers turn even police veterans into philosophers. "The youth today," a detective soliloquized, "even those that are active, seem bored. They seem bored with life. I don't know what they expect of it. Nothing seems to give them a kick. It's a sign of the times, I'll tell you that."

Dr. William A. Schonfeld, a White Plains psychiatrist who has dealt extensively with suburban youth problems both in his private practice and in community activities, is in basic agreement with the detective's analysis. Today's teen-age problem, he says, is generally different in kind from that of the past because the adolescent rebellion is not against parental rigidity but the absence of parental concern. Juvenile delinquency, according to the doctor, should be read as a symptom of the disintegration of families.

In his view the family today does not stand for the family in the traditional sense. "And I think that's more true in suburbia than it is in a lot of other places," he observed. "There are the homes broken by divorce. And there are the emotionally broken homes than can be even more catastrophic for youth."

Within their own groups, Dr. Schonfeld continued, the teen-agers caricature the striving for status and possessions of their parents. They seek a sense of identity, and find that this is one thing their parents haven't been able to provide.

"It's a growing problem," he concluded. "And I don't see it stopping. If anything, the kids who get into trouble get younger and younger. The adults themselves don't really accept what they say are the standards—their lives are full of evasions."

It is by now a trite observation that juvenile delinquency, when properly studied, turns out to be parental delinquency. Nevertheless, that was the first response in Yonkers to the revelation of the spread of narcotic addiction among teen-agers in the comfortable northwest corner of that city.

"Where the hell were the parents?" demanded a candy-store owner.

"The parents were behind it," a woman insisted. "You see your kid out at 10:30 and 11 o'clock at night, you break his legs, right?"

The Darien case that led to the arrest of the parents involved can almost be read as a parable and applied to the whole range of teen-age crimes. In defending the serving of hard drinks to their teen-agers, Darien residents said it was better to have them drinking at home than in bars in New York. Should parents, they asked, attempt to enforce social standards that have become generally obsolete? How can they? One obvious answer, of course, is that they certainly can't do it by pouring a dozen Scotch-and-waters into one boy's glass—the amount, according to the medical report, that the youthful survivor of the crash car had consumed.

But if that's too much where is the line to be drawn and who's to draw it?

Some parents seem ready to take all the criticism that can be directed at them. It is a measure of their sense of defeat. They have done everything they can think of, they say, but they are helpless to control their children. When they attempt to set limits, they are invariably met with the protest, "Johnny's parents let *him*. . . ."

One father, trying to explain why this tactic nearly always succeeds, said, "There never was a time, you know, when you could go next door and tell your neighbor how to raise his children."

"The hunger for status," the school principal declared, "makes it impossible for both the kids and the parents to say no. It's blackmail."

Pressed for suggestions, social workers propose that parents and teen-agers try to talk to each other on a community-wide basis. Already youth boards and councils and related study groups are burgeoning throughout the suburbs. According to Marion S. English, the Westchester County Executive's special assistant for youth services, "There are now more communities that have become sensitized to these problems than there are communities that are still trying to sweep them under the rug."

In some towns, parents and teen-agers have sought to draft guides or codes to govern behavior on dates or at parties. None of these documents has proved a remarkable success, but the laborious business of arriving at an agreement is usually taken as something of an achievement in itself.

"The Rye Guide"—four mimeographed pages—represents a combination of two drafts, one by a parents' group and one by teen-agers. Each page is divided into two columns: "Parents' responsibilities" and "Teen-agers' responsibilities." Thus under the heading "When the Party Is Elsewhere," parents are urged to "discuss invitations and plans with your teen-agers and know who the hosts will be, as well as type of party, hours, dress." Teen-agers are urged to "advise your parents of each invitation, and obtain their agreement to the date, place, times, type of party, transportation arrangements and any other plans."

There are many who scoff at such attempts at legislating standards. Parents set standards, they say, by the way they live, not by the codes they draft. This may be. But one of the striking things about "The Rye Guide" is that the teen-agers usually adopted a sterner line than the parents when its provisions were up for debate. One father took particular exception to a proposal requiring parents to be at home when their children returned from parties.

"I'll be damned," he cried, in words that might seem to supply a neat summing up of the teen-age problem, "if I'm going to leave *my* party."

JUVENILE GANGS [3]

Juveniles do not necessarily constitute a separate or separable category of human beings, readily distinguishable from adults and from infants. The fact of adolescence and the particular strains accompanying it have been amply demonstrated to be closely related to the structure of the society in which the adolescent lives. In a classic early study, Margaret Mead vividly showed that in Samoa adolescence constituted a rather placid, barely discernible transition period from dependence to independence, involving the smooth acquisition of adult status and adult skills.

[3] From pamphlet by Gilbert Geis, professor of sociology, Los Angeles State College. President's Committee on Juvenile Delinquency and Youth Crime. Supt. of Docs. Washington, D.C. 20402. '65.

The conclusions of the Mead study and similar inquiries force us to look closely at the social structure in which gangs form and in which they operate in order to obtain an indication of the functions which gangs serve. The conclusions of these studies also lead us to an appreciation of the fact that gangs need not exist—that they are not necessary products of something inherent in the nature of young men. And finally, anthropological research reminds us, lest we be inclined to forget, that the basic ingredients of gang existence probably lie deeply embedded within the fabric of a society, and that products of its social structure and ordering will continue to remain relatively impervious to major alterations so long as dominant social motifs persist.

In the United States, the emphasis on competition and individualism, for instance, which is basic to our way of life, probably could not be altered drastically without social surgery that might be extremely injurious to the general vitality and attractiveness of many aspects of our existence. At the same time, if juvenile delinquency and gang activity are most basically responses to the ethos of the society in which they are found, it is also unlikely that either will be eradicated in any dramatic fashion in the United States in the near future.

Such a conclusion need not be viewed either as a critique of the social structure in the United States or as an indication of its need for drastic overhaul. Delinquency and gang activity may often in a paradoxical manner represent an indication of health, however disconcerting, among dispossessed boys responding with some verve to their conditions. In the same fashion, countries with the least amount of delinquency, such as Italy during the Fascist period may, by the standards of a democracy, be much less admirable than countries with greater amounts of juvenile lawbreaking. These statements must be viewed in proper context, however. That context would indicate that despite the small likelihood that delinquency can be sharply reduced by use of techniques permitted in a democracy, it is of considerable importance that the life chances and general well-being of all individuals in the society be enhanced as much and as quickly as possible. . . .

Throughout recorded history, individuals and groups have always failed to adhere to demands for conformity to the general dictates of their society, and they have resorted to acts which were outlawed or disapproved. It is very difficult to specify with precision those conditions which have particularly encouraged or discouraged illegal aggression or depredations in any society at any time in history. . . . Deprivation alone . . . is hardly adequate to account for phenomena such as crime and gang violence; nor, for that matter, neither is any other single isolated factor sufficient unto itself as an explanation. But it again needs to be emphasized that gang behavior today hardly points to a state of degeneracy and decline in contemporary civilization. . . . It is usually reassuring and always fruitful to try to gain a clearer perspective of current events by looking back into historical annals and archives.

The two most noteworthy parallels to American gang activity in recent European history appear in prewar Germany and in the postrevolutionary Soviet Union. Both seem to indicate a combination of social upheaval and ideological disruption as major ingredients in the emergence of juvenile gangs. . . .

The lesson that might be read from the history of the German and Soviet youth movements is that there are at least two general ways of "reforming" gangs—one is to make them by one means or another conform more closely to the values of the major social system, while the other is to have that system move more closely toward their values. It would seem perhaps to be the better part of social wisdom, granting these choices, to aim for some sort of an intermediate condition: To offer to the gang member some acceptable use and outlet for his talents, feelings, and aspirations by effecting some alterations in the social system or in his ability to cope with it. In response to such widened opportunity, presumably the gang member will come to abandon some of his more unacceptable behavior.

It is extremely important to appreciate the fact, however, that people do not give up things which they have found to provide them with solace or satisfaction unless other things are available which offer greater rewards, deeper pleasure, or superior comfort. It is, of course, never easy to assay the precise quantity of "happiness" involved in a paticular way of life, especially when the possibilities of harm or punishment resulting from it are thrown on to the scale. Some observers, watching gang boys gather night after night, as they stand about and "rank" each other, have commented that their existence appears lamentably joyless and inarticulate. But all pleasures are relative—and those of gang association and activity must be seen in terms of their meaning to the particular individual and must be examined against other alternatives which may be available to him and the particular consequences of such alternatives.

There is another problem involved in convincing any individual to abandon a tested way of behaving in order to pursue one which is said to be superior. First, of course, there is always the lingering doubt regarding the accuracy of the claim of superiority. Is it really better, more fun, to work than to steal, to save than to spend, to channel energy into "constructive" rather than "destructive" paths? Second, even if the avenues opened up by the gang worker are in fact more attractive, there is an element of inertia and of irrationality in all of us. Gang members seem to live in an extremely limited and provincial world and they may not be notably adept at weighing adequately the benefits and demerits of alternative methods of behaving, particularly when the evidence before them is skewed (such as, for example, when they see numerous vivid examples of pleasurable sin and few examples of satisfied conformity). The persistence of heavy smoking in the United States, despite the bombardment of evidence regarding its potentially lethal consequences, is adequate evidence of the irrationality of the human animal in so vital an area as that concerning his very existence.

So, too, with gang members. All the literature that we have regarding working with gangs stresses the great importance of having a worker who can demonstrate by his very attitude, his clothes, his sense of security, his behavior that there is something to be gained by attempting to live as he does. We also have some indication that gang members do appreciate rational considerations, at least to a certain extent, and do respond to them. Fear seems to be a strong underlying motif in gang existence, and procedures will often be accepted by gang members so that they can avoid situations which are laden with threat, if the procedures are such that they do not interfere with other important things—such as the necessity to maintain leadership roles, to save face, to retain a degree of integrity within the gang system.

What else can we learn by examining gang behavior found in American society against a backdrop provided by cross-cultural examples? First, we must be impressed by the extraordinarily widespread nature of ganging among adolescents on the postwar world scene, particularly in the more industrialized and urbanized countries. These gangs may vary in size, in social seriousness, and in other respects in different countries, but their ubiquitous presence should yield some basic information about the general nature of the phenomenon of gangs.

Most countries designate delinquents and gang members by special terms, thus singling them out for the verbal attention we have mentioned earlier. It is only in the United States that a designation as awkward as *juvenile delinquent* has not yielded to a shorter and more colorful term. In England, delinquents are called teddy boys, and a description of some of their behavior sounds quite familiar to an American:

> It is not uncommon for groups of twenty or more city boys, sometimes with girls in tow, to arm themselves with knives, bicycle chains, studded belts, and even cutthroat razors and to sally forth by bus, taxi, private car, and motor bike to dance halls fifty miles away with the express purpose of seeking out the local youth gangs and provoking a fight. On a less dramatic scale, groups of boys on foot come together and wander about the cities looking for mischief and fun, or, in their words, "kicks," wherever such opportunities are to be found.

In Japan, Melvin Belli, a San Francisco lawyer visiting there, found what he called "a modern social malignancy" in the youth gangs, or *shintaro*. Belli reported that gang members affect a wild bushy haircut and the Japanese version of the "zoot suit." In Western Germany and Austria, gangs of provocatively dressed adolescents have been labeled *halbstarke,* or in English, "the half-strong." In Sweden, similar youths are known as the *skinnknutte* or "leather jackets," an appellation that first was applied to youth who were wont to race motorcycles through the streets. France employs the designation *blousons noirs* or "black jackets" for its delinquents. In New Zealand and Australia, we have the "milk bar cowboys" and the "bodgies" (boys) and "widgies" (girls).

Surveying the cross-cultural material, one writer has noted:

> There has probably been no more dramatic discovery in recent years in the field of practical sociology than the fact that the problems of Red Hook, Brooklyn, or Manhattan's East Side cannot only be duplicated in Chicago's South Side but also in London's Notting Hill, Amsterdam's new housing projects, the Lenin Hills area of Moscow, and the crowded factory districts of Tokyo.

A newspaper report from Auckland, New Zealand indicates in further detail some of the overseas attributes of gang behavior, and traces the source of this behavior, probably quite erroneously, to the infiltration of ideas from American motion pictures—such as *The Wild One*—and weapons and styles of dress carried to New Zealand by young British sailors:

> They gather outside milk bars, the equivalent of the American drug stores, play the juke boxes and cause chaos by roaring their motorcycles in large groups through busy city streets. Late at night they ride off to the suburbs to engage in vandalism.
>
> The male wears his hair long, with a fringe hanging down over the collar at the back, or he sweeps it up on the top of his head, with a floppy curl hanging down on the forehead.
>
> His female companion favors vivid make-up, a tight high-necked sweater and tight toreador pants, or even tighter skirt slit up the side.
>
> Several gangs have earned the hostility of the armed forces through a series of attacks on men in uniform found alone on unfrequented streets. Young soldiers, sailors, and airmen have retaliated by moving into the favorite haunts of the gangs and ejecting them into the streets.

Several ugly brawls have started, but large reinforcements of policemen have been able to keep the feud within limits by separating the combatants and arresting the more violent of them.

This news item deserves a closer examination in terms of our understanding of gang behavior. It is particularly instructive as an indication of how the mass media represent and formulate characterizations of gangs. In many ways, of course, the story is extremely superficial. It provides little more than descriptive material on a form of gang behavior. It does not indicate, for instance, how prevalent fighting gangs are in contrast to other kinds of gangs, nor does it provide us with any useful information about the origin and the purposes of gang membership and activity.

The story does, however, particularly when it is combined with numerous similar dispatches from around the world, give us an indication of at least two traits of certain kinds of gangs which seem to appear with some regularity in all settings: First, their distinctive mode of dress; and second, their hostility to authority, as that authority is represented by the police, the military, or adults in general. Dress, of course, serves a basic purpose of putting on view an identity, labeling oneself in clear-cut fashion and indicating how one wants to be treated. . . .

The rebellion against authority that generally marks gang members is equated in psychoanalytical theories with poor experiences in the home, particularly in relation to the father. Other writers are more inclined to see social authority—the power system of the society—as highly restrictive of the aspirations and freedom of gang members and thus truly deserving of their fervid antagonism. . . .

Too often prosaic and tedious jobs are put before the gang boy and the [gang] worker is disappointed when . . . [he] performs erratically on the job and ultimately quits it to return to his former haunts and ways. Many of us labor uninspiredly at tasks which we find dull and unappetizing because we have become dependent upon the monetary rewards of our efforts in order to retain the elements of a good life that we have so far accumulated. But for most gang members there may be little lost by not working. They have long since learned to manage without certain things and to gain greater satisfactions from their fellows in gang undertakings than from the forty-hour week. In addition, it is of course usually possible, granting the risks, to gain considerably greater rewards through illegal than through legal acts. One of the great barriers involved in rehabilitating narcotic addicts, for instance, lies in convincing them to work for relatively small sums when they have been accustomed to spending considerably greater amounts of money merely to support their drug habit. . . .

• A nationwide survey by Saul Bernstein of Boston University suggests that gang fighting is on the decline throughout the United States. From a seven-month study of nine cities, Bernstein concluded that gangs were less obvious than formerly, that their names were no longer splashed on walls, and that they less frequently flaunted dark-colored jackets advertising who they were. In the place of rumbles, Bernstein reported greater indulgence in things such as "snagging" or "japping"—stationing a lookout to observe the daily movements of individuals from rival rangs and then methodically waylaying and beating up such individuals. Bernstein, like many other writers, has called attention to what he defines as a growing emphasis on "coolness" among gang members.

In New York City, Kenneth Clark, a leading civil rights spokesman, has attempted to trace the decline in fighting gangs in Negro neighborhoods to changes in the racial climate of the country:

> Fighting gangs in central Harlem are old-fashioned. The energy of young people today is displaced in two directions: by a civil rights militancy and also by a stagnation, a sort of isolation in marijuana and drugs, and the "cool pattern." What has replaced the gang is probably more destructive to the human spirit, although it does not cause as much overt inconvenience to the larger society.

These changes, of course, challenge social agencies to reformulate their policies and tactics so that they are consonant with the altered nature of the problem with which they are dealing. The changes themselves have been associated wth a number of alterations in the values and social patterns in the neighborhoods giving rise to gangs. One major contribution may have been the work of the Youth Board itself, bringing about new arrangements in those areas where its work has been most effective. . . .

There were said to be more than 500 fighting gangs in the twenty-nine high-hazard areas in New York City less than five years ago. Today, the number is put at about 130, with these showing quite varying characteristics. The Assassins of Manhattan's Park West area may be taken as typical of the transition. In 1959, the Assassins were involved in the worst outbreak of teen-age warfare New York had experienced in years. Several of their leaders were arrested. The police crackdown is said to have contributed to the lessening aggression among the Assassins, and the growing number of gangs in more remote areas brought neighboring gangs, formerly intense rivals, into more relaxed relationship in the face of a defined common enemy. The Assassins gradually shifted to more mild-manner pursuits, even adopting the name Socializers, in line with their new look as a "cool" group. . . .

Today, all of the boys who replaced the former Assassins in the area as they outgrew gang membership smoke marijuana. About 20 per cent are said to use heroin more or less regularly. Use of drugs may, of course, represent even less desirable performances than the former pattern of fighting, which may at least have drained off hatreds and energies which, without outlet now, are turned to escapist stratagems through narcotics. If so, this would be an indication of some of the complex social issues involved in intervention programs and the necessity to ascertain that they are directed to dealing with basic underlying problems rather than only with manifest issues.

TEEN-AGE DRINKING AND DRUG ADDICTION [4]

Although individual cases of teen-age tippling and adolescent addiction to drugs crop up in the news media with alarming frequency, the percentage of high school youth who drink regularly or experiment with drugs is probably quite small. Indeed, youthful drug users doubtless amount to less than 1 per cent of all teen-agers.

Nevertheless, because of growing concern among educators about high school drinking and drug addiction, the *NEA Journal* asked me last fall to make a nationwide survey of these problems and to dis-

[4] Article by Jack Harrison Pollack, free-lance author. *NEA Journal.* 55:8-12. My. '66. Copyright © 1966 by Jack Harrison Pollack. Reprinted by permission.

cover how schools are coping with them. Research for these projects was made possible by travel grants from the Philip M. Stern Family Fund of Washington, D.C., and the Society of Magazine Writers, New York City.

The first thing I learned is that alcoholism and drug addiction cannot be considered the same problem. Many educators and mental health experts are convinced that it is a mistake to teach about alcohol and narcotics in a single unit of instruction. Excessive drinking and drug addiction among high school youth often spring from different motivations and have different consequences (claim the experts), and because of these differences, the problems should be assessed separately.

Boys and girls are growing up today in a nation where an estimated two out of three adults drink, where the use of alcohol is often glamorized. Most children have taken their first drink by their fourteenth year, according to some studies. My own cross-country investigations indicate that many begin to drink at an even earlier age.

"The fact that a teen-ager has had a drink or two doesn't necessarily make him a rider on the skid row toboggan," says Herman E. Krimmel, director of the Cleveland Center on Alcoholism. "Though many teen-agers may drink, most don't drink much. For statistical purposes, a teen-age drinker is often defined as any youngster who has ever had a drink, but many never take more than the first drink except for an occasional sip in the family circle."

Teen-age drinking habits vary sharply in different sections of the country. For example, in a recent study published by the Rutgers Center of Alcohol Studies, involving nearly 2,000 eleventh and twelfth grade public school students in Michigan, only about 1 per cent of the students reported *frequent* drinking, although 92 per cent admitted having tasted alcohol at *some* time, and 23 per cent said they drank *occasionally*.

By contrast, a survey of 2,300 Kansas high school students made several years ago by University of Kansas sociologists E. Jackson Baur and Marston M. McCluggage showed that only half of their sample had used alcoholic beverages at any time.

Even within states, teen-age drinking habits can vary considerably. A recent study of 528 white and Negro high school students in two different Mississippi communities made by Mississippi State University sociologists Gerald Globetti and Gerald O. Windham revealed significant differences in drinking habits. In a flat, fertile Delta community where alcohol is socially acceptable, nearly twice as many youngsters had drunk as in a northern hill community where strong religious objections to drinking prevail.

Why do teen-agers drink? A sixteen-year-old Oregon youth explained: "You go to a party and somebody has a bottle. You don't want to be out of it—so you take a swallow."

"How can you keep from drinking and still have dates?" asked a sixteen-year-old Connecticut girl. Other boys and girls gave these reasons for drinking: "It makes me feel grown up." "Everybody does." "It gives me more self-confidence."

Most youngsters are introduced to alcohol in their own homes under parental supervision, I found. In fact, many adolescents tend to conform to or imitate their parents' drinking habits.

According to studies made over a period of years in five states and the District of Columbia, the high school student least likely to drink is a Protestant girl who lives in a rural area and whose parents do not drink. Studies have shown, however, that in homes where moderate amounts of nondistilled alcoholic beverages are customarily served at the table as a normal, culturally accepted part of the meal—wine, for example, among Italian and Jewish families—boys and girls seldom become problem drinkers.

"Primary responsibility for education about alcohol rests in the home," insists Marvin A. Block, M.D., former chairman of the American Medical Association's Committee on Alcoholism. "Unfortunately, too many parents expect schools to assume the entire responsibility. Parents don't help matters by hurrying their youngsters into adulthood with formal parties for young teen-agers, cocktail parties before proms, and even kiddie cocktails for very young children."

Some children have been so conditioned in their homes that they do not separate drinking from customary hospitality. This is aptly illustrated by the story about the Nativity play put on by elementary school children. The small girl who played the innkeeper, after informing Mary and Joseph that there were no rooms, added graciously, "But won't you come in and have a cocktail?"

Though children usually start drinking under parental auspices, by late adolescence they are, in most instances, doing their drinking away from home, frequently at unchaperoned private parties. "What's a party without booze?" a seventeen-year-old Massachusetts boy asked me.

A major reason offered for the growing teen-age drinking problem is the ease with which youngsters can obtain alcohol. If adolescents can't sneak liquor out of their homes, they usually can readily obtain it elsewhere despite state laws prohibiting the sale of alcohol to minors.

A tall sixteen-year-old New Jersey boy told me, "I buy beer in the grocery store when it's busy." A seventeen-year-old Maryland youth said, "I buy whiskey in the store by borrowing my brother's driving license or draft card."

In Cleveland, two fifteen-year-old boys were haled into juvenile court for bribing a wino to buy them a bottle. In Philadelphia, boys as young as eleven have been known to give skid row bums money to purchase liquor for them.

Other high school youth drink in an effort to ape college students. Just as the idea of starting high school fraternities and sororities has filtered down from college, in many cases so has the habit of social drinking.

School sports events, especially at night, seem to invite drinking and other problems, such as fighting. Hence some big city schools now schedule all athletic contests on weekday afternoons, with admission restricted to students. Explains one superintendent, "We have found that the culprit is often a dropout who comes to the game and shows off by drinking."

School dances can also provide an excuse for teen-age drinking. A Michigan teacher has these constructive suggestions for the prevention of drinking at school dances:

A uniformed officer standing at the entrance makes a real impression on young people. Drinking students are more hesitant about entering if they must pass such an officer.

Detection at the door can prevent a scene on the floor! Sometimes teen-agers bring liquor in their cars, enter the dance before drinking, leave during the dance, go out to their cars and drink, and then try to reenter. This situation can be averted in this way: Upon arrival at the dance, students can be stamped on the hand with indelible ink. Anyone who leaves and then tries to return will bear this stamp and be refused admittance.

Nearly all states have laws requiring alcohol education. The quality of teaching in such courses, however, is generally mediocre, to the best of my knowledge.

Alcohol education is sometimes taught as a separate course, rather than as a unit in an existing course. Most educators I interviewed disapproved of this approach, believing that it places undue emphasis on the subject. Instead, they favored making alcohol education part of other courses such as health education, driver and safety education, science (especially biology), social studies, family life, or homemaking.

"But schools can't afford to drop it haphazardly into the curriculum just to meet a legal requirement," warns the director of the Cleveland Center on Alcoholism. "It has to be carefully planned with no effort spared to prepare teachers adequately for the job."

In some states (Oregon for one) many teachers now receive special instruction in alcohol education through in-service workshop and summer sessions. Other states have workshops for teachers, and some have given scholarships and college credit for teachers who participate in workshops.

"We will get nowhere until we can replace the image of alcohol education as a bothersome, unimportant or embarrassing fringe item which overloads the curriculum," insists Margaret L. Clay, University of Michigan psychologist. "As long as students believe that this is all alcohol education has to offer, they won't buy it. What they want is information which will help them with their own conflicts."

One organization that educators can turn to for current materials on teaching about the effects of alcohol is the Association for the Advancement of Instruction about Alcohol and Narcotics (212 South Grand Avenue, Lansing, Michigan 48913). Another organization which has published a great deal of material is the Rutgers Center of Alcohol Studies at New Brunswick, New Jersey. Educators may also contact their community Health and Welfare Councils, chapters of the National Council on Alcoholism, Family Service associations, and other United Fund agencies which have vast experience in helping young people cope with special problems. In addition, state and local public health departments can often furnish needed resources for teaching about the effects of drinking.

With all of today's talk about teen-age drinking, people tend to forget that the overwhelming majority of high school boys and girls aren't preoccupied with alcohol even if they drink on occasion. As William J. McCord, director of the South Carolina Commission on Alcoholism, told me, "Most youth are ready and able to demonstrate responsible behavior toward alcohol use or nonuse if we give them the opportunity or choice. They might even do a better job at this than we adults, whom they are now trying to imitate."

Drug Addiction

Almost any estimate of the total number of youthful drug addicts or potential addicts must be viewed with skepticism. For instance, a New York newspaper recently estimated that there are as many as a million drug addicts in this country and that "most of them are young people." However, the Federal Bureau of Narcotics reported that in 1964 there were 2,029 persons under age twenty-one officially identified as drug addicts. Even if the total number of youthful addicts or potential addicts were ten times greater than the number of known addicts, the total would still be far short of figures quoted by the press.

Most drug users—youthful and adult—are believed to be concentrated in a few large cities, notably New York, Los Angeles, and Chicago. But the problem also exists in other metropolitan centers.

Until now the majority of known teen-age addicts have come from low-income, big city neighborhoods, such as New York's Harlem. In recent years, however, authorities have discovered widespread use of narcotics in some affluent suburbs where in their search for kicks, bored adolescents have turned to marijuana, heroin, and LSD (lysergic acid diethylamide). Indeed, among some well-to-do youngsters, experimenting with drugs has become the "in" thing to do.

Contrary to popular belief, students seldom obtain their drugs from adult peddlers or "pushers." Sociologist Alfred R. Lindesmith of Indiana University, probably America's leading authority on drug addiction problems, told me: "Adult pushers don't generally hang around schools or stand on street corners selling drugs to students. Usually, it is the student's 'best friend' or a classmate who introduces him to drugs."

"The biggest problem we have with narcotics," adds a physician for a large southwestern school system, "is with dropouts who come on our school grounds and try to sell drugs to students."

Psychotherapist Ernest Harms, who for many years has studied youthful drug addiction in New York, says: "Some of these youngsters [who sell drugs] had no high school education whatever, but they had read considerably on drugs in professional literature which they obtained in secondhand bookshops."

The greatest drug problem among teen-agers is not so much the use of narcotics as it is the indiscriminate swallowing of pep pills (amphetamines) and goof balls (barbiturates). Compared with the number of pill takers, relatively few high school students smoke marijuana or use addictive drugs.

Many youngsters do not realize that indiscriminate use of pills can be just as dangerous as marijuana smoking and even experimenting with some narcotics. Excessive use of amphetamines can possibly bring on convulsions and death. An overdose of barbiturates can likewise be fatal.

In an upper-income New Jersey community, detectives arrested a seventeen-year-old boy for handing out pep pills he had stolen from his father's medicine cabinet. Even though he received no money for the pills, he was booked as a "pusher." An outraged matron in the community protested: "I've taken those pills myself— my own doctor prescribed them. What harm could they do?"

The seeming ease with which young people can obtain dangerous drugs deeply disturbs many law enforcement agencies and school authorities. Many youngsters need look no further than their family medicine chests. Some have even obtained drugs from mail-order houses, according to an Illinois legislative committee.

A number of cough medicines which contain codeine, an opium derivative, can be purchased without prescription. Some adolescents have been known to drink several bottles of these "codeine cocktails" a day.

Student drug users seldom risk being caught in high school with pills or narcotics. Nevertheless, on occasion, some try to sneak them in. For example, a sixteen-year-old Massachusetts girl sewed pep pills into the hem of her dress, and a high school senior in Ohio brought marijuana to school concealed behind the headlights of his car.

What causes a high school youngster to take drugs nowadays, especially when the dangers have been so well publicized?

Many students experiment with drugs out of bravado, boredom, curiosity, or escapism. Others do so because they fear being called "chicken."

A California investigation found that "most of our narcotics addicts have poor school records, or have dropped out of school early and have little or no vocational skills." A New York University study concluded that adolescent addicts suffered from deep-rooted personality disorders, were cynical about life, and had a general feeling of futility.

Some students use pep pills to stay alert while cramming for exams or completing an assignment on a crash basis that requires long hours without sleep. "I was worried about a term paper I had to do," one student told me. "I thought if I took 'bennies' I could finish it in a breeze."

Although the drug problem has been widely dramatized, it has received comparatively little attention in the school curriculum. Some school administrators fear that even the slightest mention of narcotics could lead to misunderstanding and unfavorable publicity.

A former New York City Department of Health official says: "A school administrator who is really concerned about the health of his students, rather than just the reputation of his school, must be willing to admit a drug problem exists, if it does, and make the solution educational, not punitive."

Most states have laws requiring some teaching about narcotics, but these are usually vague, such as: "Instruction shall be given in

... alcohol and narcotics and their effects upon the human system as determined by science."

Some school systems "satisfy" the law with a forty-minute lecture at the end of the student's senior year—which is usually too little and too late. The problem needs to be tackled much earlier and more comprehensively.

Schools often include teaching about the dangers of narcotics, alcohol, and tobacco in a single unit. One superintendent told me: "Because alcohol and tobacco are socially and legally acceptable, many students can easily infer from such a course that there is no difference between them and narcotics."

Many schools invite outside speakers, sometimes ex-drug addicts, but more often police officers, to lecture to students. However, some educators fear that these talks may tend to overdramatize the subject and thus possibly encourage some youngsters to experiment with drugs. "It doesn't help when police officers, in one-shot sessions, show a scare movie followed by a 'Don't Use Drugs' talk," insists one health expert.

Most educators I talked with believe that facts about drug usage and narcotics addiction should be included naturally in some regular course such as health or science. "Any course is worthless that begins with, 'Today we are going to talk about narcotics,'" one outspoken educator told me.

A Westport, Connecticut, report last year recommended that curriculum materials on the dangers of drug addiction be updated and that communications be improved between school officials, police, health officers, doctors, and parents—all of whom tend to keep information about teen-age narcotics usage to themselves.

In some communities, teachers have been urged to look for danger signals which might indicate a student is on drugs: Is he suddenly slipping in his schoolwork? Has he become secretive? Does he suddenly wear long sleeves? Has he stopped being interested in sports or the opposite sex? Has he a new set of friends? Has he lost interest in his appearance? Does he have sudden fits of anger followed by depression?

There are limits, however to detective work of this sort. As one principal pointed out. "I don't want my teachers rushing students to me or the school doctor just because he appears drowsy or listless."

The New York City Board of Education gives this advice to teachers. "When suspicions are aroused, it is best to avoid direct accusations. The wiser course is to refer the matter to the school principal, whose responsibility it is to take the next step—referral to the School Health Service."

The Chicago Board of Education warns school personnel to "avoid becoming involved in any way other than to report recognized or suspected incidents or drug users or sellers."

Since the beginning of time, young and old people have searched for euphoria with pills, herbs, and all sorts of weird concoctions. Is it any wonder, then, that today a small percentage of America's youth are experimenting with drugs? The problem, nevertheless, must be taken seriously.

As one superintendent of schools in New York said in a letter to parents: "Let us not seek comfort in the fact that many other communities have a similar problem, probably worse than in our community. Nor should we allow ourselves to be complacent because it now affects only a small hard core of our youth. Drugs and narcotics use by *any* portion of our teen-agers is a potential danger to the entire community."

YOUTH AND NARCOTICS [5]

"It's the big thing, the hip thing to do. A friend of mine, we were talking one day and the subject of marijuana kept coming up. It ended up we got together and I turned on for the first time."

The speaker, David, a tall, nineteen-year-old student at the Juilliard School of Music, is not a narcotics addict, but he is representative of the increasing number of young people from the substantial, the sophisticated and the educated families of the city and its suburbs who are using marijuana, barbiturates and addictive narcotics.

[5] From "Narcotics a Growing Problem of Affluent Youth," by Martin Arnold, staff reporter. New York *Times*. p. 1+. Ja. 4, '65. © 1965 by The New York Times Company. Reprinted by permission.

This affluent narcotics user, who starts as a teen-ager with marijuana or "goof balls" (barbiturates) and later becomes "hooked" on heroin, has complicated even further what the Police Department says has become its No. 1 problem—the use of and traffic in narcotics.

He does it not to flee the misery of the slums, but because he wants kicks, because experimenting with narcotics is "in," is "hip," is even more challenging than the sex and liquor parties of a generation ago. . . .

Unofficially, the police estimate that about 35 per cent of the marijuana smokers like David will eventually become addicted to narcotics. Of the other 65 per cent, some will seek, and be helped by, psychotherapy; some will pull out of the habit on their own, dismiss it as a youthful phase; and many will settle into a rootless, goalless existence in which marijuana will be a vague but basic element, like changing partners, lodgings and jobs.

The use of marijuana and other narcotics, which began spreading years ago from the city's slum areas, has during the last five years increased considerably in Greenwich Village, the new Bohemia of the Lower East Side, the neighborhoods surrounding the city's universities, and the suburbs, according to the police.

Because the world of the drug user is a subterranean one, there are no accurate statistics available on the number of people using narcotics. Most of the figures are based on observations and inferences by the police and by medical and social agencies.

The estimates of the number of addicts in the city, those who are hooked on heroin (horse) or other narcotics, range from an avowedly conservative 23,000 persons to a possibly exaggerated 100,000 persons. These figures do not include the marijuana users. . . .

Marijuana has not been proved to be medically harmful or addictive. But it can become as habit-forming as cigarettes, and its possession is illegal because it has proved to be a first step, in many cases, to heroin and other narcotics.

Marijuana is one of the three general classifications of narcotics covered by the state health and penal laws and by the City Police Department Narcotics Bureau. The others are the cocaines, which are nonaddictive, and the opiates, such as heroin and opium, which are addictive.

But the marijuana user tends to slip into a milieu in which drugs and the kicks they supply become the focal point of his social activity. The smoker is casual about—indeed proud of— the fact that some of his friends have gone beyond marijuana to heroin.

And because the continual smoker is often deeply disturbed emotionally—using marijuana to release his tensions and brighten his world—he often comes to the psychological crossroads where he seeks help or flees further from reality with the addictive drugs, such as heroin.

The police files are filled with cases of young women from well-to-do families who have turned to prostitution and well-educated young men and women who commit crimes against person and property as their addiction requires more and more money.

Dr. Graham B. Blaine Jr., psychiatrist to the Harvard and Radcliffe Health Service, describes the social phenomenon of the affluent addict as an "unconscious" hunt for "danger—playing with fire."

It springs from affluence [Dr. Blaine says]. We give young people a lot. When a young man can raise his finger and mama gives him a Jaguar, things are too easy. He has never been tested in real danger.

Never having been tested they are distasteful of themselves and are trying to alter with drugs their personalities. . . . They have a lack of hope with the world at large and themselves in it.

Dr. Blaine says marijuana and cocaine users often have the psychological "tendency and motivation to go on to heroin if given the opportunity, and they can usually get heroin from the same suppliers who sell marijuana."

And because most of these people who become addicts do so in their late twenties and early thirties, the inference is that they were usually on marijuana or some nonaddictive drug for a long time before they yielded to the desire for the greater sensation of heroin. . .

So far as the individual is concerned the marijuana smoker and the narcotics addict are more a medical than a police problem; and thus, many experts believe, society in attempting to deal with the problem of addiction perhaps runs into a contradiction.

It is that while many smokers and addicts indulge first as an act of rebellion, they also do so with the mental cushion that society is now more understanding and permissive about the use of drugs. (In Britain, for example, addicts are often legally maintained on their addiction.)

Marijuana, among the better educated, has a mystique all its own. It and heroin and other drugs also are the subject of a number of myths, the fundamental ones being that there is a cure for addiction and that marijuana cannot become a harmful habit.

Marijuana is classified by the experts as an excitant, although with continual use it can become a depressant. For some persons, it is always a depressant.

It distorts time and space, and the user often has a slight floating sensation. At the same time, he feels that he is functioning in slow motion.

Marijuana generally releases inhibition and makes one susceptible to suggestion. Some people say it is a sex stimulant, but others find it has the opposite effect, deadening all sexual desire.

Most young people who smoke marijuana start at a party. Either they have gone to the party because they have heard that marijuana would be smoked and wanted to try it, or they have been dared to smoke it once they were there; or they did not want to feel left out.

In case after case, among an increasing range of people, an observer found that the smoking of marijuana had become a status symbol. The young adults who smoked it considered themselves pace-setters and disdained people who would not try it.

At some parties it was done casually. Several people would light up—either a cigarette or a pipe—and then hand it around. The conversation for most part was about the sensations. Those who declined, more often girls than men, were considered "square," out of things. . . .

A marijuana cigarette is called a "joint" by a user. The butts are called "roaches," and are saved to be smoked after the effect has nearly worn off and the user wants to get back a slight glow.

The music student, David, first started on marijuana when he was a senior in the High School of Music and Art. "A kid starts the same way he starts cigarettes," David said. "He whips behind the shed or door and whips out a butt and starts choking with it at first, but keeps it up—keeping up with the Joneses sort of thing.

"There comes a point where I can channel my thoughts more clearly. I can separate that which is really bothering me from the trivial. When I'm really bugged I smoke heavily, and there are days when I'm completely stoned."

David lives with his parents, both successful classical musicians. One or both are often away from home.

"Maybe I feel pressure because I'm not yet successful. My mother is a little high-strung and I'm high-strung. My throat gets scratchy, and I turn on."

He speaks in contradictions.

First he may say: "In two years on pot I've had enough time to get a preliminary judgment of myself. I really don't foresee becoming too dependent on it. That's why I know I'll never get hooked on heroin."

But a minute later he will say: "I don't smoke it any more often because I've become quite afraid that I'll soon need even far more. I can go weeks and months without pot, but I don't expect to because I'm in control, so why worry?"

A smoker rarely indulges alone. He almost always smokes in social situations, often at so-called "pot parties." He does not hoard his marijuana but shares it. It is this way with David, who smokes marijuana often during sessions with fellow students.

The same is most often true for those who begin their drug experiments with cough medicine high in codeine, the barbiturates and Benzedrine, referred to as pep pills and bennies. These have become particularly popular at teen-age suburban narcotic parties in private homes and parked automobiles on secluded streets.

In fact, so smart has the smoking of marijuana become that an organization, known as Lemar, has been founded in San Francisco to fight the legal restrictions against it. Allen Ginsberg, the poet, is a leading New York member of Lemar, which stands for "Legalize Marijuana."

But the sociability factor is not true of the "junkie" who is on heroin. Heroin, and the pursuit of it, becomes the junkie's whole life. He will more than hoard; if forced, he will kill for it.

The use of heroin becomes an addiction. The addict is physiologically and psychologically hooked on heroin and other drugs such as opium. A "mainliner"—an addict who injects heroin directly into the bloodstream—for example, will eventually reach the point that the drug no longer provides him with euphoria and grandiose dreams.

Rather, he needs it simply to function. That is why some addicts will voluntarily enter hospitals, not to be cured, but to bring their tolerance of heroin back to a point where they get their kicks and can afford the habit. . . .

The connection between marijuana and heroin is often as straight as a railroad track. But in recent years a number of stopovers have become popular. They are the so-called mind-expanding drugs (psilocybin, mescaline, peyote, ground morning-glory seeds and LSD); the opiates and synthetics (codeine, Dilaudid, paregoric, Demerol and Methadone); and the addicting but nonnarcotic barbiturates (Seconal, Nembutal and the sleeping pills or goof balls).

The mind-expanding drugs are hallucinogens, as are the pep pills and the bennies. Most other drugs, like heroin, produce euphoria, stupor, intoxication, slovenliness and lethargy. Popular now is amyl nitrate, which comes in phials and is used to treat artery-disease patients.

One sniff and the user has an hallucination that lasts perhaps thirty seconds.

All of these, but particularly heroin, present an unusual problem for the police in a city like New York, which is believed to have at least one half of the addicts in the country. To sell heroin, marijuana or other narcotics is a felony, punishable by a possible, but rarely pronounced, fifteen-year prison sentence. To possess these narcotics can be a felony or a misdemeanor, depending on how much one has.

The Police Narcotics Bureau is the largest such unit operating in a single place in the world. It has two hundred men and women headed by Inspector Ira Bluth, an articulate City College graduate, who has been a policeman since 1940.

Police work in narcotics is subtle and difficult. There is seldom a beginning to a case, except as it is developed by the bureau itself. Unlike a robbery, for example, the victim in the narcotics case—the addict—is never a complainant.

The informant is nearly always a user who has been arrested and who informs rather than go to jail.

Inspector Bluth sums up the narcotic problem this way:

"One woman, whose son is an addict, came in recently and told me that she hopes there will be a day when 'I come home from work and am notified that my son is dead. Tell me he's dead. I have a daughter. She's still OK, but I'm afraid for her. Tell me he's dead.' "

III.   YOUTH IN REBELLION

EDITOR'S INTRODUCTION

Juvenile delinquency is a term which refers to crime and other offenses among the young. The youthful offender is singled out and put in a special category. He is a law-breaker. But because of his youth he is not always judged by the same standards as adults. This reflects the fact that we look upon juveniles differently. We do not even see them as young adults. Instead, they are categorized as teenagers, young people, or adolescents. Whether we admit it openly or not, we implicitly recognize that the world of the adolescent is different from the world of the adult. Young people do not understand their elders any better than their elders understand them. What the sociologists call a "youth culture" has been created—a system of values that runs parallel to the adult world, but is nonetheless outside it. This process has been going on longest in the United States, and thus can be found at its most extreme in this country. But it is happening everywhere. The phenomenon of juvenile delinquency cannot be understood without coming to terms with the psychology of the teen-ager. Only when we recognize how the teen-ager sees the adult world and what he wants from society, can we understand why young people are so often in a state of rebellion.

This section attempts to put the phenomenon of the teen-age society into focus and to explain why young people revolt against the standards of their elders. This revolt is what adults call "delinquency." But for the young it is often a form of self-assertion, or even of survival. The first selection, by Samuel Grafton in *Look* magazine, describes tensions and antisocial violence among young Americans. The second selection, from a United States Department of Health, Education, and Welfare pamphlet by Marvin E. Wolfgang, is an illuminating inquiry into the world of the adolescent. Next, the playwright Arthur Miller considers why young people turn to violence as a means of expressing their rejection of society. The final selection from *Time* urges adults to keep a sense of proportion about the perennial rebellion of the young.

THE TENSE GENERATION [1]

Across the country, from cities down to small towns, a novel note of tension, even of danger, has lately been added to the normal strains of life. It is as if a new population element had seeped into residential America, at odds with the old settlers and implacably determined to show its malice. If you have a teen-age son, and live in any one of a large number of suburbs, you have noticed that he shows a certain hesitancy, perhaps even fear, about going out alone at night. On the way to the office any morning, you may have heard how the windows of all the cars on a certain block were smashed, the night before, with baseball bats. Your local school may have been invaded over a weekend, its furnishings broken, its rooms doused with water. Even without putting all these items together, you may have had a chill, dismal feeling that something strange is going on.

But it is time to put all these items together. There is a new force in American life, which has to be understood and handled before it is too late. There are regional variations in the way this new power factor in our culture behaves. In some areas, the touch may be relatively light: hubcaps snatched off your parked car and the radio antenna snapped. In others, say, in some of the harbor districts south of Los Angeles, when you stop for a light, your car door may open and a hand reach in to grab parcel or purse from the seat beside you. Whatever the local manifestation, it is marked by hostility, daring and senseless destructiveness. In Miami, a few weeks ago, a resident who had left his sixteen-foot outboard moored at a yacht club for a few hours, returned to find that everything removable had been removed, including spare engine parts, extra propellers and life jackets—and that the boat had then been quietly sunk.

[1] From an article by Samuel Grafton, free-lance writer. *Look*. 27:17-23. Ag. 27, '63. Reprinted by permission of the Editors of *Look*. Copyright © Cowles Communications, Inc., 1963.

To describe those who engage in these and many similar activities, it is necessary to use a terrible judgment: They are the sixteen-year-old failures in American life. Their command posts are street corners and sidewalks in front of selected drugstores, restaurants and bowling alleys. Take a short drive tonight in almost any city or town, and you may observe, outside one of these places, six, eight, or up to two dozen boys and young men. They just stand, staring emptily ahead. Sometimes, they will jiggle a little, as if remembering a dance. They will be dressed rather alike—jackets, short pants and white socks, which are a badge this year. Many will have high, crested hairdos, made up of intricate swirls and reverse combings. It is as if they had deliberately made themselves identifiable and posted themselves in public, to shock onlookers and attract attention. There are psychologists who think that is exactly the motive involved.

Boys have stood on street corners ever since there have been boys, and corners. But to Look researchers, studying these groupings in Westchester County, New York, in a St. Louis suburb, on South Gate Avenue in Los Angeles, on the peninsula below San Francisco—and in Chicago and Cleveland and Boston and Miami—it became clear that a subculture is forming in the United States and that these are no accidental street-corner gatherings. Anger flares out of these jiggling, humming lines backed up against the convenient buildings, and shows itself in flashing bursts of characteristic activity.

There is a search for victims. A boy sitting quietly on a street bench . . . will be suddenly, terribly beaten. Parents become numbly aware that there is a certain danger in the streets. They talk about it, but they see only the more conspicuous manifestations, not the subculture, not the underlying pattern. Give a party for your teen-age son or daughter, and you may meet the new subculture in person. As many as a hundred or more of these young men may show up, to force their way into your house, seize everything that can be eaten or drunk, and perhaps beat some of the invited guests. . . . As a result, people talk and journalists write about "party crashing" as if it were a single, separate problem, instead of seeing it for what it is: one brutal onslaught, out of hundreds, against peace and dignity—all stemming from the same source and clamoring for our understanding.

Around Miami, these same young men pick up the round, white-painted cement "mushrooms" used to designate traffic lanes and heave them out of their cars at mailboxes. A variation of this sport is called "dynamiting"—using giant homemade firecrackers to blow up mailboxes. Near St. Louis, the youngsters' war against the world takes the form of a sudden wheeling out of a drive-in-restaurant lot and a dash down Lindbergh Boulevard at 70 or 80 miles per hour, to the terror of other motorists. . . .

Mrs. Katherine Ambrose, caseworker for the Family Service Agency of San Francisco, describes the boredom, tension and loneliness of a group of boys in the low-income San Francisco suburb of Hunter's Point: "They go to a bowling alley, but it costs 75 cents a line. The kids hang around, smoke, laugh, and the bowling alley kicks them out. So they go to a corner grocery store and hang around there. The owner throws them out, and finally the police come and chase them. Fighting back, they put on leather jackets, to look alike, to be something." In the pleasant land above San Francisco, Celia Walker, social worker for the Family Service Agency of Marin County, says, "Even before the unsuccessful ones drop out of school, you can see the boredom and anxiety setting in. . . . We ask them what their routine is. They tell us they watch TV. What do they watch? They don't know. They just watch. They can't tell you the next day what they've seen." She adds, "Drinking is almost obligatory; it's as if they haven't arrived, if they don't drink."

Nicholas Suntzeff, executive director of this small, highly competent agency, says, "A lot of things happen on our main road, Highway 101, that the kids know about and most adults don't. It's an entire separated life. The kid with a new cutout or exhaust will cruise up and down, showing off the gadget; he'll slow down, then rev up and promote a drag race. You could drive along and not know what's happening; it's a mobile world. They'll chase a convertible with girls in it and try to get them to drag. There's a kind of grapevine up and down the road; the kids will hear about something going on fifteen miles away and tool off to get there. Adults will vaguely note something going on, without understanding. A car means something special to a boy in late adolescence, particularly one who is being defeated in schoolwork or in getting a job. It is power. It is control. It is speed. It means he can go faster than those who think they are better than he is. A gun gives him the same feeling. So, sometimes, the police pick up a boy speeding with a gun beside him."

Sex, of course, is part of this subculture. "Look for the boys, and somewhere nearby you'll find the girls," say social workers. They won't always be visible on the street corners, but can often be seen in the backs of cars near at hand. Sometimes, observers find a group of boys, with just one girl hanging around them and even spurring them on. "A girl can be a queen in such a group, and this kind of social power is her motivation," says a Los Angeles expert. Not as many girls go off the track during adolescence as do boys—one estimate is one socially disoriented girl to about every four disturbed boys—but the number is significantly large. . . .

Who are the young people that make up the cast of characters of this strange juvenile night life? A short and shocking answer comes from Chief Judge Albert A. Woldman of the Cuyahoga County (Cleveland) Juvenile Court. "They're the excess baggage of society," he says. They are not good enough academically to feel that they belong in school, and business doesn't want them or need them. Judge Woldman feels they are a new group, not the familiar hard-core juvenile delinquents. Many come from middle-class or even well-to-do homes. Their common denominator is that they have lost their way. The stiffening of academic requirements since the first Sputnik flew in 1957 has made school pressures intolerable to them. And the same scientific upsurge has produced automation, which has wiped out the jobs they might normally have turned to. They're not needed anymore, even as pinboys in bowling alleys or as elevator operators. "This is a social disease of progress," says the Judge. . . .

Every income level contributes to the tense generation. (It isn't a race problem, either; respectable white neighborhoods are as plagued as respectable Negro areas.) In a downtown Cleveland district where steelworkers live, the amusements are different, but the spirit is the same as in many a plush suburb. Shig Ogata, a Japanese-

American settlement-house worker in the steel area, finds that the neighborhood groups hang around the parks and intentionally hit baseballs at groups of old men playing cards, or vandalize playground equipment so that it falls apart when a child climbs on it.

A typical day's routine for boys in this subculture was described in Chicago by some of the youngsters themselves. The idea is to sleep late each morning, so that their fathers will have left for work by the time the boys gets up. They loaf around the house, perhaps watch a ball game on television during the afternoon. In the later afternoon, they hunt up other jobless youths and plan a night of partying, or just roaming. If an older person approaches them, the boys usually lapse into monosyllables. They consider anyone over thirty impossibly ancient.

They frequently use girls to make liquor purchases for them, since girls can dress to look older than their ages and thus circumvent the twenty-one-year-old rule. Many of the boys resort to phony draft cards, with false ages inserted, to solve the liquor-buying problem. (Apparently, the art of forging draft cards is known to thousands of boys all over the country.) Drinking is a big part of the total picture, and many of the actions of the tense generation can be understood more easily if one realizes that they are the work of drunken youngsters. Desire to get liquor is a chief motive for party crashing. "We don't go looking for trouble," said a habitual Chicago party crasher naïvely. "We just want to drink their booze and take their broads."

For all the furious bravado of their actions, there is evidence that the wild young men of the street corners are frequently aware they are off the track. They quite often sense that something is wrong with them. One corner lounger burst out recently to the Reverend Lorence Long: "Why aren't we accepted like the collegiates? Why can't we go where they go?" Long says, "They feel their isolation. Party crashing is really directed against the 'in' group. These kids know they need help. But they can't talk to anybody, so they get their 'help' out of kicks—a fight, getting drunk, getting hopped up on pills or on narcotics." . . .

A number of boys don't join any group. They retreat into themselves. One, in the San Francisco area, wanders down into southern

California and Mexico by himself, looking for others like him and never finding a friend. A motorcycle may become all that's worthwhile in life to such a boy. Others will retreat in a different way, swallowing capsules from inhalers and sitting at home, sometimes for years, doing nothing. . . . Seen at a distance, the high school "hood," with his fancy hairdo and his wolfish look of disdain, is a repellent figure. Get a little closer to him, become involved with him, and you may get your heart broken. . . .

The situation in all of the communities *Look* studied cried out for more jobs for youth. Close to a million out-of-school youngsters under twenty today have literally nothing to do. One sixth of all the unemployed in the country are youngsters—although this age group makes up only one fourteenth of the labor force. The unemployment problem is rapidly getting worse, because the "war babies" are now reaching their late teens and looking for work. There are a million more sixteen-year-olds this year than last. Teen-age unemployment, says Secretary of Labor W. Willard Wirtz, "could develop into one of the most explosive social problems in the nation's history."

"In certain big-city neighborhoods, four out of five youths are idle," says Chicago's Commission on Youth Welfare. More keep pouring into the job market. The annual rate at which students leave school for work, now approaching 2.3 million, will hit 3 million by 1970. But the kind of jobs youngsters traditionally used to find—such as shipping boys or untrained clerks—are vanishing at the rate of 250,000 a year, partly because of automation.

Jobs alone are not the entire answer. It is tough to need a job and not be able to find it. But a youngster who has been raised with a decent set of values does not, for that reason, hit other people on the head, sniff glue, knock over gravestones (an increasingly popular juvenile diversion), or seduce young girls. Evidence suggests that many of the youngsters who spend their evenings decorating street corners don't want jobs badly enough to do very much to get them. Businessmen have testified at Washington conferences that they frequently do have jobs, but can't give them to boys who don't look right or dress right or know how to spell. It would seem reasonable to suppose that a young man so desperately anxious for a job that he is willing to ruin his life by barbiturate addiction in sheer frustration over not getting one might first experiment with cutting his hair, wearing a necktie and learning to spell two hundred common English words. Many will not go to this trouble.

Unemployment is as explosive an issue as Wirtz says it is, but many experts in this field feel that other difficulties are involved, including profound problems of motivation. Ever since the first Sputnik, the American middle class has apparently decided that the only conceivable happy life for its children lies in intellectual activity, preceded by years of academic distinction. No academic innovation has been too daring for our schools to adopt, but few middle-class parents have worried very much about whether the schools are providing vocational training. Our youngsters have caught this national attitude and often share the feeling that there is something shameful about any work with one's hands (except, maybe, brain surgery). Middle-income-group boys who would like to do manual work are made to feel as declassed as India's untouchables. (One West Coast professional man whose son had been in difficulties and was under psychiatric treatment, was horrified when told that his boy wanted to be an auto mechanic. When he gave in and bought his son an old car to repair, the youth stayed out of trouble from then on. He spent the better part of a year happily repairing the vehicle after school hours.)

The emphasis on academic success makes the youngster who is unable to achieve it feel like a failure in life at fifteen or sixteen. We have succeeded in creating a class of half-grown rejects of society.

In a world as complicated as ours, and as filled with stresses, what children need most of all, obviously, is the closest possible kind of continuous communication with their parents. It is here that we are scoring our greatest failures.

Almost everybody who works with troubled youths believes that the only approach that offers any hope is opening up of lines of communication with them. Even the worst big-city gang improves when a "street worker" manages to make contact with it and to win its attention and respect. But there never was a time when genuine communication with the young seemed harder to achieve. Parents want their children to be busy and "popular." They regard hyperactivity as success, though it leaves little time for the uneventful being together and casual conversation that add up to human relationships.

So organized is juvenile life today, with dancing, music lessons, language clubs, sports and classes, that, says Nicholas Suntzeff. "I find kids of twelve carrying date books, with every half hour of the week filled in." Parents themselves are busy and preoccupied, often in organizing the very activities that keep their children busy, thus making sure that hardly anybody ever gets to be with anybody else. The successful suburban father is likely to be in such demand in his town for club, committee and board meetings that he ends up with only hearsay information about what his children are doing. (In one California town, a local outdoorsman makes a good income taking boys up into the mountains for camping trips; mothers eagerly engage his services in order to "provide their sons with a masculine image," father being too busy to do it himself.)

A probation officer in the Beverly Hills area comments that the too-busy father tends to give his children money instead of time, because he has more money than time. Thus, by a single act, he distorts both their sense of practical values and family values. Social obligations, themselves a sign of success and personal progress, are heavy. It takes a dedicated parent to cancel golf, cocktail parties and trips to the city to spend time in ordinary talk with his young. In a pressurized world, engagements with one's own children are the most easily postponable. "Many youngsters really don't understand what their fathers do, because they see them so seldom, and actually have no clear idea of a man's role in life," comments a youth worker.

Psychologists say that the worst thing a time-pressed parent can do is to give up his own standards. With a helpless shrug, a father OK's beer at a teen-age party because he wants the youngster to have a good time, to be popular, and because he's too busy to handle the situation positively and constructively. But when a father surrenders his own standards, the kids know it, and the image they have of Pop grows dimmer and more confused. Children may become annoyed at discipline, but they know it means that their parents are concerned about them. They take lack of concern as lack of love, even while they may seem to be enjoying this easy freedom. "They need limits. They need someone in authority," says Freda Mohr, executive director of the Jewish Family Service of Los Angeles. Freedom, in fact, say psychologists, can be frustrating to youngsters, for adolescence is a time in which they have to do battle against authority, to test out their emerging adulthood. But if there is no authority, there is nothing to do battle against; the world becomes confused and uncertain, and the sign posts dissolve. Sometimes, children literally don't know what is allowed and what is not. . . .

Many observers do not place the full blame on parental inattention. They declare that often values that are bad in themselves are directly communicated by parents to children. "Parents will make an excuse for a boy who takes a car without permission," says Miss Mohr. "When he is picked up for doing something of this sort, parents will write a false note to the school, to explain his absence. As the kids act up, parents learn to 'go along' with them." Rabbi Morris N. Kertzer of Larchmont, New York, finds that the "affluent society" creates a moral tone of its own that is not altogether good. "We live in an age of matchless extravagance," he says. "But almost all religious virtues are based on poverty: thrift, unostentation, thinking about the future, giving to the poor, instead of wasting." Youngsters pick up other questionable values, adds Rabbi Kertzer. Ours is an age of violence, and they hear much talk of "megadeaths." It is an age of great mobility and rootlessness, in which children rarely plan to stay in the home community. "It is an age," the Larchmont clergyman notes, "in which juvenile offenses can be committed with impunity, because of the great protections which the law, custom and the press throw around juvenile wrongdoers." It is a very complex age, in which there is little family cohesion. "Almost invariably," according to Rabbi Kertzer, "when a boy is picked up by the police, and the police call his home, the parents are out. Stability is lost when the parents are not at home. When police do reach the parents, parental capacity for self-deception can be enormous. Sometimes, they will turn on the arresting officer, challenge his identification of their boy, accuse him of false arrest and threaten action."

Larchmont and many other communities have been conducting meetings to study the problem. That this kind of agonizing reappraisal is spreading is perhaps the best sign uncovered by *Look* researchers. . . .

In hundreds of towns, teen-age job programs are under way. If the number of such programs were multiplied by ten, there would still not be nearly enough. Such efforts, plus parental self-study—plus counseling by groups like the member agencies of the Family Service Association of America and others—are the only way out.

Time is short, because human wreckage piles up fast in this area. Each boy is different and reaches the street corner through a route of his own. Among those encountered by *Look,* one boy was a victim of a hard-driving mother, who had visionary ideas of his quite-average abilities. Another had a father who alternated between alcoholic binges and wild preaching of success-sermons. For many a youngster, no matter what the causes that have landed him on the corner, after a couple of years not even a job is a solution.

Experience shows that once normal middle-class values are relaxed, the descent is rapid. The National Education Association has noted that there is a curious tendency these days for middle-class youths to imitate the slum dweller, to speak his language, to wear his clothes, to act as they imagine he acts. Perhaps they envy his supposed freedom of choice as to how to live. Whatever the mechanism, something new and rougher than we have ever known before has crept into misbehavior among the young, even among such certified and selected specimens of youth as students at Princeton University, one thousand of whom, in a recent riot, started fires, tried to overturn a train, tore down iron fences, set up a barrage of "cherry bombs" and damaged property at the home of Princeton's president, Robert E. Goheen. Eleven students were suspended for an academic year; two were sentenced to five days in jail. The student editors of the *Daily Princetonian* admitted that the affair "passed beyond the realm of prankishness to that of crime." Those words sound like an exact description of the change now taking place among the young people of a thousand cities. Clearly, none of us can afford to lose any time in altering this situation, starting first within our own hearts, then working outward to our communities.

THE CULTURE OF YOUTH [2]

Gertrude Stein is alleged to have said that the United States is the oldest country in the world because it has had the most experience with modern industrial society and its complex consequences. With similar perception, Dwight Macdonald has said that the United States was the first to develop the concept of the teen-ager, a concept which is still not well accepted in Europe, and that we have had the longest experience with the subculture of youth. The way we handle a nearly "overdeveloped" society with transportation, bureaucratization, impersonal, automated living, and the way we learn to understand the new problems of youth and the existence of poverty to remind us of our social imperfection, will be lessons of value to underdeveloped or newly developed countries. Despite our longer experience with modernity and the teen-age subculture, we still have lessons to learn about the problems created by both, and the particular interrelation of modern youth and modern poverty is especially important and striking in many ways.

Our youth in general are richer today than they have ever been and have more alternatives of action and more privileges. The list of privileges usurped by youth has not only increased but has shifted downward in age. The high school student of today has the accouterments of the college student of yesteryear—cars, long pants, money, and more access to girls. This downward shift in privileges, precocious to younger ages, is a phenomenon well known to every parent whose own youth subculture was devoid of them.

Not only are our youth more privileged and richer, but they have for some time constituted an increasingly significant portion of American purchasing power. The statistics of consumption of lipsticks and brassieres, even by twelve- and thirteen-year-olds, are well known, as are those of records, used cars, popular magazines, and transistor radios. The magnified purchasing power of young teen-agers is one of the factors that tends to make them want to grow up faster or not at all, which is suggestive of Reuel Denney's credit-card viewpoint of "grow up now and pay later."

[2] From pamphlet by Marvin E. Wolfgang, Department of Sociology, University of Pennsylvania. United States Department of Health, Education, and Welfare. Office of Juvenile Delinquency and Youth Development. Supt. of Docs. Washington, D.C. 20402. '67.

The ambivalence of the analyzers regarding whether our youth become adultlike too early or behave as adolescent children too long is a scholastic debate that has not yet been resolved by empirical data. Moreover, a valid appraisal of the "youth problem" is also made difficult by the existence of conflicting cultural prescriptions for youth. We appear to want teen-agers to act like young adults in our society, yet we are increasingly stretching the whole socialization process from childhood to adulthood. And the number of people involved in the subculture stretch is increasingly large. There are nearly seventy million persons in the United States under eighteen years of age, or nearly one third of the nation's population.

The number reaching age eighteen each year has, however, doubled within a decade. There were two million in 1956 and four million in 1965, the result of the "baby boom" of the late forties. Of the more than 1.5 million who graduate from high school, about half will register for college, and the 25 per cent of the sixteen—twenty-four age group now in college will increase. One could say with Denney that the age of extended socialization is already in full swing.

It is of correlative interest that the public has become disturbed by the announced figure of 7.5 million school dropouts during the 1960's, despite some queries about whether we really want to or can prevent all school dropouts. The middle-class and middle-aged producers of prescriptions for youth want to keep them in, or return them to school for reasons that extend from a genuine belief that all youth should benefit from more formal education to fears that dropout youths inundate the labor market and thereby contribute to delinquency and crime. Our society would apparently like more children to go to college, often without commensurate concern for how the extended period of dependency, socialization, and an indiscriminate density of college population may contribute to producing mediocrity of educational standards. Yet, without continued education, the dropouts are commonly dependent in other ways. As Lucius Cervantes has very recently pointed out, although the dropout group cuts across social class, ethnic, and geographic lines, most come from the blue- and lower-white-collar economic classes. In summarizing, he says:

The dropout rate nationally is between 30 and 40 per cent. The rate is higher in the South than in the North; higher among boys than girls (53 per cent versus 47 per cent); higher in the slums than in the suburbs. Most dropouts withdraw from school during or before their sixteenth year. There is ten times the incidence of delinquency among the dropouts as there is among the stayins. In view of society's educational expectations for modern youth and dropout youth's inability to get a job while "just waiting around for something to happen," the very state of being a dropout has all but become by definition a condition of semidelinquency.

On the one hand, then, the privileges and age roles are being extended by being lowered, and young teen-agers are as sophisticated or cynical, as fantasy-filled and joyriding as our older teen-agers used to be. On the other hand, and at the other end of the range of the youth age, the period of their not moving into adult roles is also being extended.

This extended socialization is accompanied by the problem of poor adult models. Throughout the social classes, it appears that the search for the adult to be emulated is often a desperate and futile quest. Part of the reason for this futility is due to the very rapid social and technological changes occurring in our society which make it more difficult for the adult to perform his traditional role of model and mentor to youth. Social change is so rapid, says Kenneth Keniston, that growing up no longer means learning how to fit into society because the society into which young people will someday fit has not yet been developed or even, perhaps, cannot properly be imagined. Many youths feel forced into detachment and premature cynicism because society seems to offer youth today so little that is stable, relevant, and meaningful. They often look in vain for values, goals, means, and institutions to which they can be committed because their thrust for commitment is strong. Youth can be a period of fruitful idealism, but there are few of what Erik Erikson would call "objects of fidelity" for our youth; so that "playing it cool" is more than an ephemeral expression—it becomes a way of avoiding damaging commitments to goals and life styles of the parent generation which may be outmoded tomorrow. Times and viewpoints shift rapidly, and many of our children resemble world-weary and jaded adults at age fourteen. The social isolation, social distance, alienation, and retreat from the adult world are increased by many social and technological mechanisms operating to encourage a youth subculture. As the numbers and intensity of value sharing in the youth subculture increase, the process of intergenerational alienation also escalates. Parents have almost always been accused of not understanding their children. What may be new is that more parents either do not care that they do not understand, or that it is increasingly impossible for them to understand. Perhaps, then, it is not that parents are poor models for the kinds of lives that the youths will lead in their own mature years; parents may simply be increasingly irrelevant models for their children. So rapid is current social change that the youth of today have difficulty projecting a concept of themselves as adults. . . .

The Masculine Protest and Its Transformation

Social scientists have long stressed the importance of the theme of masculinity in American culture and the effect that this image of the strong masculine role has had on child rearing and the general socialization process. The inability of the middle-class male child to match himself to this masculine model and the neuroticism that is the consequence of this increasingly futile struggle was vividly brought to our attention years ago by Arnold Green. . . . There is reason to believe, however, that this once dominating culture theme is dissipating, especially in the central or middle-class culture, and that this dissipation is diffusing downwards through the lower classes via the youth subculture. It may be argued that in the United States, while the status of the sexes in many social spheres of activity has been approaching equality, there has been an increasing feminization of the general culture. Instead of females becoming more like males, males have increasingly taken on some of the roles and attributes formerly assigned to females. It is not so much that maleness is reduced as a goal motivating young boys; rather, physical aggressiveness, once the manifest feature of maleness, is being reduced and the meaning of masculinity is thereby being changed to more symbolic forms. The continued diminution of the earlier frontier mores which placed a premium on male aggressiveness has been replaced by other attributes of masculinity. The gun and fist have been substantially replaced by financial ability, by the capacity to manipulate others in complex organizations, and by intellectual talents. The thoughtful wit, the easy verbalizer, even the striving musician and artist are, in the dominant culture, equivalents of male assertiveness where broad shoulders and fighting fists were once the major symbols. The young culture heroes may range from Van Cliburn to the Beatles, but Billy the Kid is a fantasy figure from an earlier history.

It may well be true that in many lower-class communities violence is associated with masculinity and may not only be acceptable but admired behavior. That the rates of violent crimes are high among lower-class males suggests that this group still strongly continues to equate maleness with overt physical aggression. In the Italian slum of the Boston West End, Herbert Gans describes families dominated by the men and where mothers encourage male dominance. On the other hand, lower-class boys who lack father or other strong male figures, as is the case with many boys in Negro families, have a problem of finding models to imitate. Rejecting female dominance at home and at school, and the morality which they associate with women, may be the means such boys use to assert their masculinity, and such assertion must be performed with a strong antithesis of femininity, namely by being physically aggressive. Being a bad boy . . . [it has been] said, can become a positive goal if goodness is too closely identified with femininity.

Whatever the reasons for this stronger masculine role among lower-class youth, its retention will continue to result in violence, because the young male is better equipped physically to manifest this form of masculinity than the very young, the middle-aged, or the very old. Because he needs no special education to employ the agents of physical aggression (fists, agility), and because he seeks, as we all do, reinforcement from others for his ego and commitment, in this case to the values of violence, a youth often plays violent games of conflict within his own age-graded violent subcultural system. So do others play games, of course; the artist when he competes for a prize, the young scholar for tenure, the financier for a new subsidiary, and a nation for propaganda advantage. But the prescribed rules for street fighting produce more deadly quarrels with weapons of guns and knives than do competitions among males who use a brush, a dissertation, or a contract. . . .

Should the lower classes become more like the middle class in value orientation, family structure, and stability, there is reason to believe the emphasis on masculine identification through physical prowess and aggression will decline. . . . As the disparity in life style, values, and norms between the lower and middle classes is reduced, so too will be reduced the subculture of violence that readily resorts to violence as an expected form of masculine response to certain situations.

If this social prognosis proves correct, there may not always be functional and virtuous expertise in the masculine symbolism. We could witness, for example, a shift from direct physical violence to detached and impersonalized violence or to corruption. The dominant, middle-class culture has a considerable tolerance for distant and detached violence expressed in ways that range from dropping heavy bombs on barely visible targets, to the stylized, bloodless violence of film and television heroes, and to the annual slaughter of 50,000 persons on our highways. This same culture, for reasons too complex to detail here, not only tolerates but sometimes creates structural features in its social system that seem to encourage corruption, from tax evasion to corporate crime. To transform the theme of male aggressiveness may mean assimilation with the larger culture, but this may merely increase the distance between the user and consumer of violence, and increase the volume of contributors to corruption. It may be hoped, of course, that changes in the current direction of the dominant culture may later produce a more sanguine description of this whole process.

Youth and Violent Crime

There is little more than faulty and inadequate official delinquency statistics to answer basic questions about the current extent and character of youth crime. Recording techniques have changed,

more juvenile police officers are engaged in handling young offenders, more methods are used for registering such minor juvenile status
offenses as running away from home, being incorrigible, or truant.
For over a decade most city police departments have used a dichot-
omy of "official-nonofficial arrest" or "remedial-arrest" or "warned-
arrest" for apprehending juveniles, but not for adults. Yet both
forms of juvenile disposition are recorded and rates of delinquency
are computed in the total. . . .

The public image of a vicious, violent juvenile population producing a seemingly steady increase in violent crime is not substan-
tiated by the evidence available. There may be more juvenile delinquency recorded today, but even that is predominantly property offenses. Rather consistently we are informed by the Uniform Crime
Reports, published by the Federal Bureau of Investigation, that two
thirds of automobile thefts and about one half of all burglaries and
robberies are committed by persons under eighteen years of age.
Among crimes of personal violence, arrested offenders under age
eighteen are generally low: for criminal homicide they are about
8 per cent; for forcible rape and aggravated assault, about 18 per
cent.

What this actually means is not that these proportions of these
crimes are committed by juveniles, but that among persons who are
taken into custody for these offenses, these proportions hold. Most
police officers agree that it is easier to effect an arrest in cases involving juveniles than in cases involving adults. Most crimes known
to the police, that is, complaints made to them or offenses discovered
by them, are not "cleared by arrest," meaning cleared from their
records by taking one or more persons into custody and making
them available for prosecution. The general clearance rate is roughly 30 per cent. Thus, the adult-juvenile distribution among 70 per
cent of so-called major crimes (criminal homicide, forcible rape,
robbery, aggravated assault, burglary, larceny over $50, auto theft)
is not known and cannot safely be projected from the offenses
cleared or the age distribution of offenders arrested.

In addition, very often the crude legal labels attached to many
acts committed by juveniles give a false impression of the serious-

ness of their acts. For example, a "highway robbery" may be a $100 theft at the point of a gun and may result in the victim's being hospitalized from severe wounds. But commonly, juvenile acts that carry this label and are used for statistical compilation are more minor. Typical in the files of a recent study were cases involving two nine-year-old boys, one of whom twisted the arm of the other on the school yard to obtain twenty-five cents of the latter's lunch money. This act was recorded and counted as "highway robbery." . . .

The data needed to describe the volume of youth crime are inadequate at present, but an alarmist attitude does not appear justified. Age-specific and weighted rates are required before trends can be validly presented and analyzed, but because of the known rise in the present adolescent population due to high fertility rates of the late 1940's, there is reason to suspect that any over-all increase in juvenile delinquency can be largely attributed to the population increase in the ages from fourteen to eighteen. The absolute amount of delinquency can be expected to increase for some time, for this same reason, but there is no basis for assuming that rates of juvenile violence will increase.

Moreover, as the suburban population increases, the amount of juvenile delinquency can be expected to rise in these areas even without a rate increase. In addition, as the social class composition of suburbs changes, as it has been, from being predominantly upper class to containing more middle- and lower-middle-class families, the rates of delinquency of the last migrating class will travel with them. . . . What is often viewed as middle-class delinquency is not middle class in the sense of the traditional middle-class value system or life style but only in terms of a middle-income group. . . .

Finally, with respect to delinquency, it might be said that a certain amount of this form of deviancy has always existed, will continue to exist, and perhaps should exist. . . . Not only does the existence of delinquency provide the collective conscience an opportunity to reinforce its norms by applying sanctions, but the presence of deviancy reflects the existence of something less than a total system of control over individuals. Moreover, there appear to be personality traits among many delinquents that could be viewed as virtues if behavior were rechanneled. For instance, Sheldon and Eleanor Glueck noted, in *Unraveling Juvenile Delinquency,* that among five hundred delinquents compared to five hundred nondelinquents, the delinquent boys were characterized as hedonistic, distrustful, aggressive, hostile and, as boys who felt they could manage their own lives, were socially assertive, and defied authority. The nondelinquents were more banal, conformistic, neurotic, felt unloved, insecure, and anxiety-ridden. The attributes associated with the delinquents sound similar to descriptions of the Renaissance man who defied the authority and static orthodoxy of the Middle Ages, who was also aggressive, richly assertive, this-world rather than other-world centered, and was less banal, more innovative, than his medieval predecessors. The Glueck delinquents also sound much like our nineteenth century captains of industry, our twentieth century political leaders and corporation executives. The freedom to be assertive, to defy authority and orthodoxy may sometimes have such consequences as crime and delinquency. But it is well to remember that many aspects of American ethos, our freedom, our benevolent attitude toward rapid social change, our heritage of revolution, our encouragement of massive migrations, our desire to be in or near large urban centers, and many other values that we cherish, may produce the delinquency we deplore as well as the many things we desire.

The Search for Power and Participation
Youth, Negroes, and the Poor

We have said that to speak generically of youth overlooks variability in a pluralistic society, and we have drawn attention to some notable variations between middle-class and lower-class youth. There are, however, many more versions of the concatenation of variables that differentiate youth. Being young, middle class, white, and from an economically secure family generates a quite different image from being young, lower class, poor, and Negro. In sheer absolute numbers, more young people are located in the former group than in the latter and probably suffer fewer strains from culture contradictions . . . and psychological deprivation than do the latter. There is likely to be greater conformity to parental prescriptions in the former, more familial transmission of group values, more cohesiveness of the family. The Negro, lower-class youth drop out of school and drift into delinquency in greater proportions than do white middle-class youth. Class is probably a stronger factor contributing to value allegiance and normative conduct than is race, which is to say that Negro and white middle-class youth are more alike than are Negro middle- and lower-class or white middle- and lower-class youngsters.

Yet, . . . there are characteristics of the life stage, status, and style of youth in general which are shared by the status of poverty and the status of being Negro in American society. All may be described as possessing a kind of structural marginality that places them on the periphery of power in our society. When the multiple probabilities of being young, Negro, and poor exist, the shared attributes are more than a summation. The force of whatever problems they represent is more of a multiplicative than an additive function.

Youth, Negroes, and the poor have subcultural value systems different from, yet subsidiary to, the larger culture. They often share many features, such as being deprived of certain civil rights and liberties, barred from voting, and denied adequate defense counsel and equality of justice. Their current statuses are frequently subject to manipulation by an enthroned elite and their power to effect change in their futures may be minimal. They tend to have common conflicts with authority and to be dominated by females in the matriarchal structure of their own social microcosms.

All three groups know the meaning of spatial segregation, whether voluntary or compulsory. For youth, it is in schools, clubs, seating arrangements, occupations, forms of entertainment, and leisure pursuits. For the poor and for Negroes, it may be all of these as well as place of residence and other alternatives of work, play, and mobility opportunities. There are similarities in their subordinate and dependency status, and in having poor, inadequate, or irrelevant role models. The values and behavior of the dominant culture and class in American society, as adopted by Negroes, often reveal a pathetically compulsive quality; the poor have been denied access to the ends to which they subscribe, and youth is, at best, a power-muted microculture. For all three, norms seem to shift and change with more than common frequency or are not clearly designated. All three groups tend to be more romantic, nonrational, impulsive, physically aggressive, more motivated toward immediacy and directness than their counterparts in the dominant culture. There is among youth, Negroes, and the poor more deviant and criminal behavior, and a greater disparity between aspiration and achievement. At times their revolt against authority erupts into violence for which they feel little guilt or responsibility.

Increasingly they are self-conscious, aware of their own collectivities as subcultural systems, partly because their revolt is today a greater threat to the systems which have been established to control, govern, or manipulate them. The poor are being asked for the first time what they want and what they would like to do to help themselves or have done for them. Negroes are acting as advisers and consultants on Federal policy, and young people are being heard when they speak about Vietnam, restrictions on passports, college curricula, faculty appointments, and new notions of freedom and sexual morality.

With more clarity and conscience, the three groups are searching for meaningfulness, identity, and social justice. They are articulating their protest against powerlessness, are seeking participation in decision-making processes that affect their own life conditions. That some retreat into drugs, alcohol, and other symptoms of alienation is now viewed as dysfunctional by their own majorities as well as by the establishment. That some resort to violence, whether in Watts or in Hampton Beach, is episodic, meant to display boredom with their condition, blatant protest, and latent power. . . . But their use of violence is end-oriented and cannot be viewed as a cultural psychopathology. They desire to be recognized, not to be forgotten, because they now see themselves for the first time. They are seeking . . . to be taken seriously, to be listened to.

One of the interesting things about American youth today, especially the older student segment, is its activistic character and increasing identification with the poor and with the civil rights movement. There is an intense morality and a demand for clear commitments. In many cases young people are directly involved in working in neighborhoods of poverty or in the Negro struggle in the South, whether in song, march, or litigation. Moreover, the idealism of youth and this identification with the process toward participation in power [is] being fostered by Federal support of the Peace Corps program, both foreign and domestic, and by much governmental concern and protection of young civil rights workers in the South. But the reference here to identification is not to these overlapping involvements; it is to the means for communicating their lack of participation in formulating the rules of life's games. Impatience, discontent, and dissatisfaction with the state of American society become healthy reflections of a new commitment, a commitment to the desire for change and for participating in the direction of change. . .

Obviously, there are also differences among the three groups, the most striking of which is the fact that youth is a temporary stage in a life cycle and that ultimately the structural marginality and status deprivation are overcome for many by the passage of time. The representatives of the subculture of youth are mobile, eventually leave the subculture. . . . But the status designation of Negro is, except for race crossings, permanent, and the poor commonly have oppressive generational continuity. That youth in its temporariness shares with the major minority groups certain attributes of being and of the struggle for becoming is itself noteworthy, even if the youth were less affected by and conscious of their mutual interests, means, and goals. Perhaps the short sample of time represented by youth will one day be viewed in the long perspective as symbolic of the longer, but also temporary, state of deprivation and disenfranchisement of being poor or of having the status of Negro in American society.

The identity of youth with the protestation process, whether similar to or in common with the poor and the Negro, is, of course, not universal. . . . Its expression is, nonetheless, vigorous and viable. It has entered the arena of public attention and functions as a prodder for its concepts of progress. With this identity, the youth of today are unlike the "flaming youth" in the frenetic milieu of the twenties, the youth associated with the political left and the proletarian cult of the thirties, the uniformed youth of the forties, or the passive youth of the fifties. And yet, even with this identity they are without a systematic ideology. Despite the fact that they have come to realize the advantages of collective drives that prick the giants of massive and lethargic organization into action, they have developed no political affiliation. Perhaps the closest these young groups come to a focal concern is in their alerting their peers and adults to the ethical conflicts and issues embraced by society's increasing ability to reduce individual anonymity and to manipulate lives. In one sense it could be said that they jealously guard the constraints a democratic society ideologically imposes on overcontrol, invasion of privacy, and overreaction to deviancy.

There are fringes to most movements, and there are parasites attached to the youth we have been describing as healthier segments of society. Frequently the fringe looms larger than the core in the public image of youth and an excessive degree of rebelliousness is conveyed. The bulk of our youth are not engaged in a rebellion against adults, and the degree of dissimilarity between the generations has often been overstressed, as some authors have recently asserted. Rather than rejecting most parental norms, the majority of those in the youth subculture are eager to participate in the larger society. Individuals resisting specific authority patterns do not constitute group rejection of dominant social norms.

Moreover, except for those suppressed beyond youth by their status of being poor or being Negro, achievement comes with aging and that convergence often leads to the collapse of a once fiery, romantic drive. . . . With success prophets become priests and revolutionaries become administrators. The gravity of time pulls hard on our muscles and ideals and too often the earlier triumph of principle gives way to the triumph of expedience. The once lambent minds of youth are frequently corroded by conformity in adulthood and a new flow of youth into the culture is needed to invoke their own standards of judgment on our adult norms.

THE BORED AND THE VIOLENT [3]

If my own small experience is any guide, the main difficulty in approaching the problem of juvenile delinquency is that there is very little evidence about it and very many opinions as to how to deal with it. By evidence I do not mean the news stories telling of gang fights and teen-age murders—there are plenty of those. But it is unknown, for instance, what the actual effects are on the delinquent of prison sentences, psychotherapy, slum-clearance projects, settlement-house programs, tougher or more lenient police attitudes, the general employment situation, and so on. Statistics are few and not generally reliable. The narcotics problem alone is an almost closed mystery.

Not that statistical information in itself can solve anything, but it might at least outline the extent of the disease. I have it, for instance, from an old and deservedly respected official—it is his opinion anyway—that there is really no great increase in delinquent acts but a very great intensification of our awareness of them. He feels we are more nervous now about infractions of the social mores than our ancestors, and he likes to point out that Shakespeare, Boccaccio, and other writers never brought on stage a man of wealth or station without his bravos, who were simply his private police force, necessary to him when he ventured out of his house, especially at night. He would have us read *Great Expectations, Oliver Twist, Huckleberry Finn,* and other classics, not in a romantic mood but in the way we read about our own abandoned kids and their depredations. The difference lies mainly in the way we look at the same behavior.

The experts have only a little more to go on than we have. Like the surgeon whose hands are bloody a good part of the day, the social worker is likely to come to accept the permanent existence of the delinquency disease without the shock of the amateur who first encounters it. . . .

[3] From an article by Arthur Miller, playwright and author. *Harper's Magazine.* 225: 50-2+. N. '62.

Unlike most problems which sociology takes up, delinquency seems to be immune to the usual sociological analyses or cures. For instance, it appears in all technological societies, whether Latin or Anglo-Saxon or Russian or Japanese. It has a very slippery correlation with unemployment and the presence or absence of housing projects. It exists among the rich in Westchester and the poor in Brooklyn and Chicago. It has spread quickly into the rural areas and the small towns. Now, according to Harrison Salisbury, it is the big problem in the Soviet Union. So that any single key to its causation is nowhere visible. If one wants to believe it to be essentially a symptom of unequal opportunity—and certainly this factor operates—one must wonder about the Russian problem, for the Soviet youngster can, in fact, go right up through the whole school system on his ability alone, as many of ours cannot. Yet the gangs are roaming the Russian streets, just as they do in our relatively permissive society.

So no one knows what "causes" delinquency. Having spent some months in the streets with boys of an American gang, I came away with certain impressions, all of which stemmed from a single, overwhelming conviction—that the problem underneath is boredom. And it is not strange, after all, that this should be so. It is the theme of so many of our novels, our plays, and especially our movies in the past twenty years, and is the hallmark of society as a whole. The outcry of Britain's so-called Angry Young Men was against precisely this seemingly universal sense of life's pointlessness, the absence of any apparent aim to it all. So many American books and articles attest to the same awareness here. The stereotype of the man coming home from work and staring dumbly at a television set is an expression of it and the "New Wave" of movies in France and Italy propound the same fundamental theme. People no longer seem to know why they are alive, existence is simply a string of near-experiences marked off by periods of stupefying spiritual and psychological stasis, and the good life is basically an amused one.

Among the delinquents the same kind of mindlessness prevails, but without the style—or stylishness—which art in our time has attempted to give it. The boredom of the delinquent is remarkable mainly because it is so little compensated for, as it may be among the middle classes and the rich who can fly down to the Caribbean or to Europe, or refurnish the house, or have an affair, or at least go shopping. The delinquent is stuck with his boredom, stuck inside it, stuck to it, until for two or three minutes he "lives"; he goes on a raid around the corner and feels the thrill of risking his skin or his life as he smashes a bottle filled with gasoline on some other kid's head. In a sense, it is his trip to Miami. It makes his day, it is his shopping tour. It gives him something to talk about for a week. It is *life*. Standing around with nothing coming up is as close to dying as you can get. Unless one grasps the power of boredom, the threat of it to one's existence, it is impossible to "place" the delinquent as a member of the human race.

With boredom in the forefront, one may find some perspective in the mélange of views which are repeated endlessly about the delinquent. He is a rebel without a cause, or a victim of poverty, or a victim of undue privilege, or an unloved child, or an overloved child, or a child looking for a father, or a child trying to avenge himself on an uncaring society, or whatnot. But face to face with one of them, one finds these criteria useless, if only because no two delinquents are any more alike than other people are. They do share one mood, however. They are drowning in boredom. School bores them, preaching bores them, even television bores them. The word rebel is inexact for them because it must inevitably imply a purpose, an end.

Other people, of course, have known boredom. To get out of it, they go to the movies, or to a bar, or read a book, or go to sleep, or turn on TV or a girl, or make a resolution, or quit a job. Younger persons who are not delinquents may go to their room and weep, or write a poem, or call up a friend until they get tired talking. But note that each of these escapes can only work if the victim is sure somewhere in his mind, or reasonably hopeful, that by so doing he will overthrow his boredom and with luck may come out on the other side where something hopeful or interesting waits. But the delinquent has no such sense of an imminent improvement. . . .

The word rebel is wrong, too, in that it implies some sort of social criticism in the delinquent. But that would confuse him with the bourgeois Beatnik. The delinquent has only respect, even reverence, for certain allegedly bourgeois values. He implicitly believes that there are good girls and bad girls, for instance. Sex and marriage are two entirely separate things. He is, in my experience anyway, deeply patriotic. Which is simply to say that he respects those values he never experienced, like money and good girls and the Army and Navy. What he has experienced has left him with absolute contempt, or more accurately, an active indifference. Once he does experience decency—as he does sometimes in a wife—he reacts decently to it. For to this date the only known cure for delinquency is marriage.

The delinquent, far from being the rebel, is the conformist par excellence. He is actually incapable of doing anything alone, and a story may indicate how incapable he is. I went along with Riccio and the gang in his book [*All the Way Down,* by Vincent Riccio and Bill Slocum] to a YMCA camp outside New York City for an overnight outing. In the afternoon we started a baseball game, and everything proceeded normally until somebody hit a ball to the outfield. I turned to watch the play and saw ten or twelve kids running for the catch. It turned out that not one of them was willing to play the outfield by himself, insisting that the entire group hang around out there together. The reason was that a boy alone might drop a catch and would not be able to bear the humiliation. So they ran around out there in a drove all afternoon, creating a stampede every time a ball was hit.

They are frightened kids, and that is why they are so dangerous. But again, it will not do to say—it is simply not true—that they are therefore unrelated to the rest of the population's frame of mind. Like most of us, the delinquent is simply doing as he was taught. This is often said but rarely understood. Only recently a boy was about to be executed for murder in New York State. Only after he had been in jail for more than a year after sentencing did a campaign develop to persuade the governor to commute his sentence to life imprisonment, for only then was it discovered that he had been deserted by his father in Puerto Rico, left behind when his mother went to New York, wandered about homeless throughout his childhood, and so on. The sentencing judge only learned his background a week or two before he was to be officially murdered. And then what shock, what pity! I have to ask why the simple facts of his deprivation were not brought out in court, if not before. I am afraid I know the answer. Like most people, it was probably beyond the judge's imagination that small children sometimes can be treated much worse than kittens or puppies in our cities.

Gangs in Suburbia

It is only in theory that the solution seems purely physical—better housing, enlightened institutions for deserted kids, psychotherapy, and the rest. The visible surfaces of the problem are easy to survey—although we have hardly begun even to do that.

More difficult is the subterranean moral question which every kind of delinquency poses. Not long ago a gang was arrested in a middle-class section of Brooklyn, whose tack was to rob homes and sell the stuff to professional fences. Many of these boys were top students, and all of them were from good, middle-class backgrounds. Their parents were floored by the news of their secret depredations, and their common cry was that they had always given their sons plenty of money, that the boys were secure at home, that there was no conceivable reason for this kind of aberration. The boys were remorseful and evidently as bewildered as their parents.

Greenwich, Connecticut, is said to be the wealthiest community in the United States. A friend of mine who lives there let his sons throw a party for their friends. In the middle of the festivities a gang of boys arrived—their own acquaintances who attend the same high school. They tore the house apart, destroyed the furniture, pulled parts off the automobile and left them on the lawn, and split the skulls of two of the guests with beer cans.

Now if it is true that the slum delinquent does as he is taught, it must be true that the Greenwich delinquent does the same. But obviously the lines of force from example to imitation are subtler and less easily traced here. It is doubtful that the parents of this marauding gang rip up the furniture in the homes to which they have been invited. So that once again it is necessary to withhold one's cherished theories. Rich delinquency is delinquency but it is not the same as slum delinquency. But there is one clear common denominator, I think. They do not know how to live when alone.

Most boys in Greenwich do not roam in gangs but a significant fraction in both places find that counterfeit sense of existence which the gang life provides.

Again, I think it necessary to raise and reject the idea of rebellion, if one means by that word a thrust of any sort. For perspective's sake it may be wise to remember another kind of youthful reaction to a failed society in a different era. In the thirties, for instance, we were also contemptuous of the given order. We had been brought up to believe that if you worked hard, saved your money, studied, kept your nose clean, you would end up made. We found ourselves in the Depression, when you could not get a job, when all the studying you might do would get you a chance, at best, to sell ties in Macy's. Our delinquency consisted in joining demonstrations of the unemployed, pouring onto campuses to scream against some injustice by college administrations, and adopting to one degree or another a Socialist ideology. This, in fact, was a more dangerous kind of delinquency than the gangs imply, for it was directed against the social structure of capitalism itself. But, curiously, it was at the same time immeasurably more constructive, for the radical youth of the thirties, contemptuous as he was of the social values he had rejected, was still bent upon instituting human values in their place. He was therefore a conserver, he believed in *some* society.

Gide wrote a story about a man who wanted to get on a train and shoot a passenger. Any train, any passenger. It would be a totally gratuitous act, an act devoid of any purpose whatever, an act of "freedom" from purpose. To kill an unknown man without even anger, without unrequited love, without love at all, with nothing in his heart but the sheerly physical contemplation of the gun barrel and the target. In doing this one would partake of death's irreproachable identity and commit an act in revolt against meaning itself, just as death is, in the last analysis, beyond analysis.

To think of contemporary delinquency in the vein of the thirties, as a rebellion toward something, is to add a value to it which it does not have. To give it even the dignity of cynicism run rampant is also overelaborate. For the essence is not the individual at all; it is the gang, the herd, and we should be able to understand its attractions ourselves. It is not the thrust toward individual expression but a flight from self in any defined form. Therefore, to see it simply as a protest against conformism is to stand it on its head; it is profoundly conformist but without the mottoes, the entablature of recognizable, "safe" conformism and its liturgy of religious, patriotic, socially conservative credos.

The Greenwich gang, therefore, is also doing as it was taught, just as the slum gang does, but more subtly. The Greenwich gang is conforming to the hidden inhumanity of conformism, to the herd quality in conforming; it is acting out the terror fury that lies hidden under father's acceptable conformism. It is simply conformity sincere, conformity revealing its true content, which is hatred of others, a stunted wish for omnipotence, and the conformist's secret belief that nothing outside his skin is real or true. For which reason he must redouble his obeisance to institutions lest, if the act of obeisance be withheld, the whole external world will vanish, leaving him alone. And to be left alone when you do not sense any existence in yourself is the ultimate terror. But this loneliness is not the poet's, not the thinker's, not the loneliness that is filled with incommunicable feeling, insufficiently formed thought. It is non-existence and must not be romanticized as it has been in movies and some of the wishful Beat literature. It is a withdrawal not from the world but from oneself. It is boredom, the subsidence of inner impulse, and it threatens true death unless it is overthrown.

All of which is said in order to indicate that delinquency is not the kind of "social problem" it is generally thought to be. That is, it transcends even as it includes the need for better housing, medical care, and the rest. It is our most notable and violent manifestation of social nihilism. In saying this, however, it is necessary to short-circuit any notion that it is an attempt by the youth to live "sincerely." The air of "sincerity" which so many writers have given the delinquent is not to be mistaken as his "purpose." This is romanticism and solves nothing except to sentimentalize brutality. The gang kid can be sincere; he can extend himself for a buddy and risk himself for others; but he is just as liable, if not more so than others, to desert his buddies in need and to treat his friends disloyally. Gang boys rarely go to visit a buddy in jail excepting in the movies. They forget about him. The cult of sincerity, of true human relations uncontaminated by money and the social rat race, is not the hallmark of the gang. The only moment of truth comes when the war starts. Then the brave show themselves, but few of these boys know how to fight alone, and hardly any without a knife or a gun. They are not to be equated with matadors or boxers or Hemingway heroes. They are dangerous pack hounds who will not even expose themselves singly in the outfield.

Flight from Nothingness

If, then, one begins to put together all the elements, this "social problem" takes on not merely its superficial welfare aspects but its philosophical depths, which I think are the controlling ones. It is not a problem of big cities alone but of rural areas too; not of capitalism alone but of socialism as well; not restricted to the physically deprived but shared by the affluent; not a racial problem alone or a problem of recent immigrants, or a purely American problem. I believe it is in its present form the product of technology destroying the very concept of man as a value in himself.

I hesitate to say what I think the cure might be, if only because I cannot prove it. But I have heard most of the solutions men have offered, and they are spiritless, they do not assume that the wrong is deep and terrible and general among us all. There is, in a word, a spirit gone. Perhaps two world wars, brutality immeasurable, have blown it off the earth; perhaps the very processes of technology have sucked it out of man's soul; but it is gone. Many men rarely relate to one another excepting as customer to seller, worker to boss, the affluent to the deprived and vice versa—in short, as factors to be somehow manipulated and not as intrinsically valuable persons.

Power was always in the world, to be sure, and its evils, but with us now it is strangely, surrealistically masked and distorted. Time was, for example, when the wealthy and the politically powerful flaunted themselves, used power openly as power, and were often cruel. But this openness had the advantage for man of clarity; it created a certain reality in the world, an environment that was defined, with hard but touchable barriers. Today power would have us believe—everywhere—that it is purely beneficent. The bank is not a place which makes more money with your deposits than it returns to you in the form of interest; it is not a sheer economic necessity, it is not a business at all. It is "Your Friendly Bank," a kind of welfare institution whose one prayer, day and night, is to serve your whims or needs. A school is no longer a place of mental discipline but a kind of day-care center, a social gathering where you go through a ritual of games and entertainments which insinuate knowledge and the crafts of the outside world. Business is not the practice of buying low and selling high, it is a species of public service. The good life itself is not the life of struggle for meaning, not the quest for union with the past, with God, with man that it traditionally was. The good life is the life of ceaseless entertainment, effortless joys, the air-conditioned, dust-free languor beyond the Mussulman's most supine dream. Freedom is, after all, comfort; sexuality is a photograph. The enemy of it all is the real. The enemy is conflict. The enemy, in a word, is life.

My own view is that delinquency is related to this dreamworld from two opposing sides. There are the deprived who cannot take part in the dream; poverty bars them. There are the oversated who are caught in its indefiniteness, its unreality, its boring hum, and strike for the real now and then—they rob, they hurt, they kill. In flight from the nothingness of this comfort they have inherited, they butt against its rubber walls in order to feel a real pain, a genuine consequence. For the world in which comfort rules is a delusion, whether one is within it or deprived of it.

There are a few social theorists who look beyond poverty and wealth, beyond the time when men will orient themselves to the world as breadwinners, as accruers of money-power. They look to the triumph of technology, when at least in some countries the physical struggle to survive will no longer be the spine of existence. Then, they say, men will define themselves through varying "styles of life." With struggles solved, nature tamed and abundant, all that will be left to do will be the adornment of existence, a novel-shaped swimming pool, I take it, or an outburst of artistic work.

It is not impossible, I suppose. Certainly a lot of people are already living that way—when they are not at their psychiatrists'.

But there is still a distance to go before life's style matters very much to most of humanity in comparison to next month's rent. I do not know how we ought to reach for the spirit again but it seems to me we must flounder without it. It is the spirit which does not accept injustice complacently and yet does not betray the poor with sentimentality. It is the spirit which seeks not to flee the tragedy which life must always be, but seeks to enter into it, thereby to be strengthened by the fullest awareness of its pain, its ultimate non sequitur. It is the spirit which does not mask but unmasks the true function of a thing, be it business, unionism, architecture, or love....

Reform of idiotic narcotics laws, a real attempt to put trained people at the service of bewildered, desperate families, job-training programs, medical care, reading clinics—all of it is necessary and none of it would so much as strain this economy. But none of it will matter, none of it will reach further than the spirit in which it is done. Not the spirit of fear with which so many face delinquency, nor the spirit of sentimentality which sees in it some virtue of rebellion against a false and lying society. The spirit has to be that of those people who know that delinquents are a living expression of our universal ignorance of what life ought to be, even of what it is, and of what it truly means to live. Bad pupils they surely are. But who from his own life, from his personal thought has come up with the good teaching, the way of life that is joy? . . . [*All the Way Down*] shows how difficult it is to reach these boys; what the country has to decide is what it is going to say if these kids should decide to listen.

KEEPING COOL ABOUT YOUTH [4]

A Russian revolutionary once suggested that everyone over twenty-five should be shot. His proposal was not adopted, but he might feel reasonably comfortable in the United States today. Nearly half of all Americans are now twenty-five or under, and the rest of the population, while not yet in danger of being liquidated, appears rather nervous and definitely on the defensive.

[4] From "On Not Losing One's Cool About the Young," a *Time* essay. *Time.* 86:16-17. D. 24, '65. Reprinted by permission from *Time* The Weekly Newsmagazine; copyright Time Inc. 1965.

The situation is not exactly new. The man who first said "I don't know what the younger generation is coming to" probably died several thousand years ago. But Americans in the mid-1960's seem to have more reason than ever to lose their cool about the young. FBI statistics tell them that youngsters under twenty-five account for 73.4 per cent of the arrests for murders, rapes, larcenies and other major crimes, and cause 31.5 per cent of all traffic fatalities. Youth stages demonstrations in support of the country's enemies. Youth parades with placards of four-letter words. Youth scandalizes proud suburbs with grass parties—grass being one of the hippiest synonyms for marijuana. The latest campus fad seems to be underground "antiuniversities" with courses in such subjects as revolution, "Search for the Authentic Sexual Experience," and hallucinogenic drugs. Boys look like girls, girls look like boys, and the songs they sing are not of love and laughter, but sour, self-pitying whines about how awful things are in a culture that supplies them with about $12 billion worth of such essential equipment as cars, clothes, acne lotions and hair sprays. The blaring jukebox message to the adult world seems to be: "Get off of my cloud. . . ."

The youth that makes the noise sets the tone, and the tone remains significant—and unique in comparison with the rest of the world. The noisy, "alienated" young are an American monopoly at the moment.

The youth of Britain and France have the same blue-jeaned bottoms and fright-wig haircuts as their U.S. contemporaries, and they dig the same big beat and atonal balladry. Still, the Teen-Age International is largely confined to matters of style; underneath, European youth today seems less discontented and considerably more cowed by the adult world. In Germany and Italy, the young are just too busy cashing in on their new prosperity to protest against much of anything. In Soviet Russia, while society is changing and the young show signs of restlessness, youth by and large remains earnestly conformist. In Japan, despite occasional student riots organized by the left, the students' competitive drudgery makes even the American race for college seem relaxed by comparison; a Japanese youngster who fails to get into a university is called a *ronin,* the term for the pathetic samurai who wandered about without a master.

U.S. parents and teachers who may hanker for a bit more obedience and less obstreperousness from their own young should take comfort in the recollection that things have been worse. Riot and rebellion are a student tradition in the Western world; university records from the Middle Ages abound in accounts of pitched battles, rapes and homicides. A proclamation of 1269 denounced the scholars of Paris who "by day and night atrociously wound and slay many, carry off women, ravish virgins, and break into houses."

Britain's illustrious public schools suffered repeated student rebellions in the eighteenth and nineteenth centuries. At Winchester in 1793, after stoning the assistant headmaster with marbles, the boys locked him up overnight in the dining hall with the warden and a teacher. When the high sheriff was appealed to the next day, he refused help because the boys had firearms and were getting ready to defend the Outer Gate by flinging flagstones down on the police. Harvard and Princeton experienced numerous such episodes. In 1788 the situation at Harvard was so bad that Professor Eliphalet Pearson kept what he called a Journal of Disorders. "In the hall at breakfast this morning," he recorded on December 9, "bisket, tea cups, saucers & a *knife* thrown at tutors. At evening prayers the lights were all extinguished by powder and lead." A partial list of college casualties during this period includes one undergraduate dead in a duel at South Carolina College and another at Dickinson, several students shot at Ohio's Miami University, a professor killed at the University of Virginia, and the president of Mississippi's Oakland College stabbed to death by a student.

All this past history suggests that Americans, in their tendency to idealize youth, often forget what it is really like.

The Invention of Youth

Society's important political, moral and intellectual changes, according to UCLA historian Eugen Weber, have always been brought about by that section of the population that was "most available." Sometimes it was the nobility, as in the curbing of absolute monarchy, sometimes the rich, as in the rise of mercantilism, sometimes the bourgeois intellectuals, as in the French Revolution. In recent times, Weber holds, the most available group for rebellion has been the young, with more time—and certainly more energy—than anyone else.

Before the industrial revolution, "youth" could hardly be said to exist at all. In primitive societies, children become full-fledged members of the tribe in one painful and often hazardous initiation, which compresses—and purges—the terror of entering adult life. In Europe until well into the eighteenth century, children were both indulged and ignored. Medieval artists even seemed ignorant of what a child looked like: they habitually painted them as small adults. A twelfth century miniature illustrating Jesus' injunction to "suffer the little children to come unto me" shows Christ surrounded by eight undersized men. Before the seventeenth century, a child passed directly into the adult world between the ages of five and seven. Schoolchildren carried weapons, which they were supposed to check at the schoolroom door. Marriages often took place in childhood. Youngsters drank heavily and even wenched according to their abilities. . . .

At the same time, society firmly kept the young in their place. In times when life as well as education was far shorter than today, they often made history at an age when the modern young are still working for their degrees; Edward the Black Prince was sixteen when he won the battle of Crécy, Joan of Arc was seventeen when she took Orléans from the English, and Ivan the Terrible was the same age when he hounded the boyars to death and had himself crowned czar. But for ordinary people, particularly under the long-prevalent guild system of apprentices and journeymen, life was a slow progression toward experience and eventual reward.

In the seventeenth century came the beginnings of the modern idea of the family with the child at its center. With greater concern for children and more schooling came a new stage of life between childhood and adulthood: adolescence, a new combination of weal and woe that has profoundly altered human institutions and attitudes.

If adolescence had an inventor, it was Rousseau, who was cynical about man in civilization: "At ten he is led by cakes, at twenty by a mistress, at thirty by amusements, at forty by ambition, and at fifty by avarice. When does he make wisdom his sole pursuit?" Rousseau saw wisdom in nature. Against the traditional Christian notion that children, scarred at birth by original sin, must be civilized through education, he felt that they were really innocent and that they are best educated through the emotions. In *Émile,* in 1762, he advised: "Keep your child's mind idle as long as you can."

Romantic Alienation

The young thus "educated" by the emotions took stage center in the romantic era, when the glorious dreams of the French Revolution—and their bloody, reactionary demise—turned youth toward an eccentric sentimentality. "They found satisfaction in ideals," wrote Madame de Staël, "because reality offered them nothing to satisfy their imaginations." Goethe intended his *Werther* as a warning to this mooning generation, but the young character who committed suicide for unrequited love became the hero of romanticism. The dirty speech movement of that day was suicide. It was, as Princeton historian James Billington points out, the first major appearance of alienated youth.

Just as Rousseau had provided the ideological basis for adolescence, the industrial revolution provided the practical one: the factories needed the young as workers. Compulsory education was sold to the House of Commons largely as a device to keep the growing number of unemployed agricultural workers under fifteen from "idling in the streets and wynds; tumbling about in the gutters; selling matches, running errands; working in tobacco shops, cared for by no man." The time spent in school fitted them for jobs in the new industrial world, and the young acquired greater economic importance than ever before. On the Continent, they also began to perform an entirely new political role in the liberal revolutions of 1848. They manned the barricades—against Louis Philippe in France, against King Frederick William in Prussia, against Metternich in Austria. They set up a quasi-revolutionary government at the University of Vienna, issued proclamations and organized an Academic Legion uniformed in blue coats, red-black-and-gold sashes and scarlet-lined cloaks.

Although the young rebels were brought back into line quickly enough, the European student remained a political force that reached a climax in the youth movements, both Fascist and Communist, between the world wars. Yet throughout all this, Europe refused to take the young more seriously than absolutely necessary. Until after World War II, the European social pattern closely resembled the ancient Chinese formula, according to which a man married at thirty and continued his learning, was first appointed to office at forty, promoted, if successful, at fifty, and retired at seventy. Disraeli might proclaim that "almost everything that is great has been done by youth." But the vast majority agreed instead with Lord Chesterfield, who remarked, "Young men are apt to think themselves wise enough, as drunken men are apt to think themselves sober enough."

It was different in the United States. From America's beginning, youth was not a shortcoming but a virtue, not a time of preparation to be got through but a glorious Eden to be prolonged and preserved. Americans do not really want to keep the young in their place; they expect that the young will stay there out of their own essentially good nature. America's all-time young hero is Huck Finn, but not in the role of the brave rebel which serious critics (including T. S. Eliot) have cast him in, but in the safe and comfortable role of a backwoods Penrod or Andy Hardy—the eternally lovable bad boy. Until very recently, the sheltered and privileged American young gladly went along with that role. Their hell-raising was equally far removed from Werther's despair and the political barricades. The United States was thus enabled to go on worshiping youth without really facing the traits of youth that all other civilizations have accepted as inevitable—rebelliousness, moodiness, shifting passions for shifting causes. Americans want to deny the basic conflict, not to say war, between youth and age. Thus when the young do flare up, their elders are surprised, hurt and disappointed.

In part, this situation was fostered by the immigrant nature of American society. The children of the immigrants were the path-finders in a new world, and taught their elders its ways. This contributed to the child-centered—some say childridden—nature of American life. More recently, what has caused American youth to live increasingly in a separate enclave or "subculture" is the ever-lengthening education process. In no other civilization have so many of the young been kept so long from the responsibilities of adult life. This prolongation of the school years, argues British sociologist Frank Musgrove, is partly a ploy by the adult world to keep the young out of competition as long as possible, for, he asserts, the "mature of Western society" regard the young "with hatred." With people living longer and retaining their vigor into advanced age, there is certainly less disposition by the mature to make way—although "hatred" seems overstating the case. Still, the diagnosis may yet prove accurate, unless the older generation keeps its cool about the young.

Every parent should know that his child judges him; but he should also know that the judgment is that of a child. The United States has alternated between taking the judgment of its children not seriously enough—and too seriously. What is regarded as to-day's youthful nihilism is undoubtedly much less alarming than it seems. Whatever political causes the apolitical American young managed to find before have virtually disappeared—hence the concentration on the few remaining ones, such as civil rights and Vietnam. Among the young bored by prosperity and consensus government, some observers discern a special group, the "New Puritans," who may be toting a protest placard alongside an anti-everything beatnik, but with an entirely different attitude inside.

Sociologist David Riesman agrees; he finds that service careers—schoolteaching, social work, government—are increasingly popular with undergraduates, and many of them are working at them part time while still in college, "trying to show that they are capable of human concern," says Riesman, "even while they are competing for grades." And Harvard Professor Erik H. Erikson believes that youth's main virtue and need is "fidelity"—to a worth-while cause. Until that object of fidelity is found and tested, rebelliousness may simply be "a period of delay, a moratorium."

It is difficult to do justice to the young without being alarmist about their failings, or sentimental about their charms, or condescending about their rawness. The dialogue between experience and naïveté, between "we-know-better" and "we-don't-care," is in a sense impossible, because it is eternally carried on in two different languages. In this dialogue, youth is bound to have the last word— but only by the time youth itself is no longer young. In the face of this ultimately common destiny, Robert Louis Stevenson struck perhaps the best note of loving humor when he said:

Prudence is not a deity to cultivate in youth. Youth is the time to go flashing from one end of the world to the other both in mind and body; to try the manners of different nations; to hear the chimes at midnight; to see sunrise in town and country; to be converted at a revival; to circumnavigate the metaphysics, write halting verse, run a mile to see a fire.

But it still matters where the fire is, and who set it.

IV. SOCIETY AND THE ADOLESCENT

EDITOR'S INTRODUCTION

Juvenile delinquency is generally considered to be an antisocial act—an act against society. Yet why should young people want to reject society? Are they not part of society just as much as their elders are? The answer is not so simple as it seems. Young people often do not feel that society is responsive to their needs. They feel that society is letting them down. Although their form of protest may be vague and their remedies unclear, they often do not accept adult society as their own. Part of this may be due to the fact that there is an eternal tension between youth and age that the best motives cannot overcome. Young people have always seen the world differently from their elders. Part of it, however, may also come from the fact that society has failed to persuade the young that its values are worthy, or that it can offer them hope for the future. If society fails to provide for the needs and aspirations of its younger members, it may be that society itself is at fault.

In the first selection Richard Schickel, writing in *Redbook,* explains the reasons why leading American psychologists and sociologists believe that society merits much of the contempt and anger directed against it by today's youth. The following selection, by Frank Musgrove, professor at Leeds University, England, argues that young people have been kept in an artificial "ghetto" by their elders, and that youth turns to violence in order to break out of this intolerable social prison. The third selection, by James Symington, executive director of the President's Committee on Juvenile Delinquency and Youth Crime, examines the problem of unemployment among the young. The final selection, by psychiatrist Robert Coles writing in the *New Republic,* questions whether our society offers a valid model for the young and whether its opportunities may be merely a delusion.

WHY YOUTH REJECTS SOCIETY [1]

Clearly, something is bothering a lot of young people today. The symptoms of their discontent are many and obvious. While beatniks as a type seem to be fading, they are being replaced by young men and women who are agitating in several directions. Some are extremely conservative in their views, some are radical. There are active students on campuses all over the country, picketing with regard to Vietnam, working for civil rights, joining left-wing organizations, joining right-wing organizations, and trying to figure out where the middle is as well.

Juvenile crime is up; so is youth unemployment. There are signs of rebellion—in dress, in music, in books, in painting. Cars are fast and sex seems to be even faster. The rebels of the University of California, at Berkeley, have been emulated at dozens of other universities by students eager to protest—in disorderly fashion, if necessary—the factorylike quality of much modern higher education. In the high schools, meanwhile, the number of students who quietly or noisily decide to drop out continues to rise despite the expensive and extensive national effort to convince them that school is really worth while. They seem to be making a mockery of the revolution in teaching methods that now offers so many exciting prospects in secondary education.

As a result of these alarms and agitations, attention has been focused as never before on the need for a critical examination of the ways young people grow up in the United States and of the ways society, both formally and informally, is preparing them to take their place in the world. Educators, students and parents recognize the urgent need to reexamine our theories of psychological growth, our faith in the quality of American education and even our most cherished assumptions about the nature of our society and its goals.

The number of critics offering theories, explanations and new perspectives on the problems of youth is large and growing. It is possible, however, to catch their general drift in the works of two of

[1] Article, "Why Young People Are Seeking New Values," by Richard Schickel, free-lance writer. *Redbook.* 127:73+. My. '66. Reprinted from Redbook Magazine, May 1966. Copyright © 1966 by the McCall Corporation.

the most influential and interesting critics of education and society: a poet-novelist-psychologist-gadfly named Paul Goodman, whose commentaries on youth and education have made him an ideological hero for great numbers of undergraduates and young men and women who have recently graduated; and Edgar Z. Friedenberg, author and professor of sociology at the University of California. The ideas of Goodman and Friedenberg in turn have been influenced by the theories of Erik H. Erikson, a distinguished Harvard psychologist whose work on childhood, youth and development forms an excellent starting point for a discussion of the perils and problems of growing up.

Erikson points out that the adolescent's energetic exuberance, his eager quest after new ideals and excitement for its own sake, are quite normal; they appear in all Western societies. Even when these energies sometimes spill over into criminal activity, it is not necessarily a sign that the whole younger generation is going to hell in a handcart. Nor is it a symptom of some frightening and mysterious sickness peculiar to our age. On the contrary, it is often a young person's direct statement of disgust over the current ways of the world, over being made, as Margaret Mead puts it, "scapegoats for adult apathy, indifference, lack of responsibility and lack of imagination."

To state it bluntly, Erikson believes that our society—any society—gets the kind of children it deserves, even secretly wants. If our children disappoint us, he suggests, it is because the world we create for them—and which, of course, influences their values and aspirations—disappoints us even more. Preadult young men and women are often confused. In any era they want to know what they should believe in, what they should try to become. What frightens some adults is the fact that many adolescents work at these questions with furious intensity. And adolescent frustration when the answers refuse to come easily is often terrible to behold.

In his remarkable book *Childhood and Society,* Erikson suggests one possible answer to their questions. He reminds readers that when Freud was asked what he thought a normal person should be able to do well, he replied simply, "To love and to work."

It is a simple formula, but not, in Erikson's view, an oversimplified one. To love successfully and to work successfully and to keep the demands of each in reasonable balance are, for him, universal goals to which everyone, regardless of class or natural gifts, may reasonably aspire. But Erikson does not claim that the ability to love and to work is easily attained. On the contrary, he is greatly concerned over the ways society conspires to rob us all of this ability.

A child is, naturally, dependent upon the adults around him for his image of the world, and the chances are that they will show him a distorted image. This can be critical, for as Erikson sees it, each of the child's stages of growth hinges on a major choice as to how he sees himself in relation to the world. If a wrong choice is forced upon him at one stage or another by the image he sees, his succeeding choices will be more difficult. The process may be likened to a minor navigational error that may put a plane a mile or so off course when it is made but that, if not corrected, can cause the plane to be hundreds of miles off when it should be reaching its destination.

By the time a child arrives at adolescence he will have made, according to Erikson, four momentous choices. As a tiny baby he will have learned either trust or mistrust at his mother's breast; in the course of toilet training he will have gained either a sense of autonomy or a feeling of shame and doubt; learning to walk during the period when the numerous terrors of infantile sexuality are first encountered, he will experience either a healthy sense of initiative or, if things go badly, a sense of guilt over goals and acts attempted or even contemplated. Finally, in school and on the playground he will meet for the first time the "inorganic laws of the tool world," and out of that encounter will come either a taste for the pleasure of productivity or possibly a lingering sense of inferiority if he is unable to master this stage.

In the worst of circumstances, then, a youngster may approach adolescence full of distrust, shame, doubt, guilt and inferiority—in short, in a terrible mess before life has even fairly begun. In point of fact, most people reach adolescence in a rather mixed-up state, with odd strengths and hidden weaknesses already part of their personalities. The great task of adolescence, according to Erikson, is the formation of a mature identity out of these bits and pieces; the problem is to decide who you are and what you want to be.

Obsessed with the question of "what they appear to be in the eyes of others as compared with what they feel they are," adolescents keep themselves together, Erikson says, by temporarily overidentifying with the heroes of cliques and crowds. This helps to explain the phenomenal appeal of characters like the Beatles or the uncanny influence that one particularly admired youth—whose virtues are usually quite unapparent to adults—can exert on a group of teen-agers. This overidentification also provides the basis for some social criticism. If the ideals of the day are entertainers, athletes, hucksters and hustlers, it is no wonder adolescents are confused; no wonder they are embarrassingly curious about the gap between the figures we ritualistically hold up for their admiration (ministers, teachers, professional men) and those in whom, as our popular culture makes abundantly clear, we are really most interested.

But the search for identity is not the only thing that preoccupies adolescents. There is also, in the late teens, the beginning of the search for love—or, as Erikson puts it, the struggle to master the problems of intimacy. This is a necessary prelude to love—but it seems to him that our social system in general and our educational system in particular are designed to limit the opportunities for the kinds of close friendships and inspirational teaching that help a youngster develop a capacity for love. When education is geared mainly to preparation for economic success and when success is defined mainly as learning to get along in order to get ahead, human intimacy is bound to be regarded as a dangerous distraction from the one true path.

Paul Goodman's *Growing Up Absurd* is the great text on this point. He describes our society as "an apparently closed room in which there is a large rat race as the dominant center of attention." In this closed room there is no alternative to the rat race—that is, to material values. So even if one despises the race, he cynically continues to run it. It is very hard to grow up under this condition,

Goodman says, for we share no true sense of community that might sustain, inspire and nurture young people until they can act on their own with fully developed powers.

Living in a closed room may not weigh too heavily on adults, says Goodman. They may not be very happy, but they can "fight and work anyway." But youngsters cannot do that. For them, "it is indispensable to have a coherent, fairly simple and viable society to grow up into; otherwise they are confused and some are squeezed out." In today's world, traditions are being broken constantly, and there are not yet enough new standards to affirm. Goodman is vague about where to place the blame for this situation; apparently it belongs to all of us, and our fathers and grandfathers as well; therefore it belongs to none of us. Which makes that amorphous thing, history, the villain of the piece.

That is exactly what Bruno Bettelheim argues in an anthology called *Youth: Change and Challenge*, which Erikson edited. Bettelheim says our world has changed from an individualistic, agrarian society to a mass, urban one, but our notion of what constitutes the good life remains fixed in the past. Unable to find the old satisfactions in our new world, achingly aware of the gap between ideals and reality, many frustrated parents apply "overt and covert pressures on youth to provide . . . what was lacking in their own lives."

Friedenberg declares that the problem is not that so many youths rebel against such pressures, but that so few do. The typical teenager, he says, "is enraged not at the tyranny of adults but at their blandness, their weakness, their emptiness. . . . Rebellion would be a lot cozier than this feeling that one has been gutted, that one is trapped, because there are no possibilities in humanity itself."

Thus both children and adults are victimized by society. But the burden falls more heavily on young people simply because adults have power over them. The natural parental abhorrence over the fact that they can't fully control adolescents is intensified, Friedenberg thinks, by what amounts to deep envy of youth and their "life not yet squandered." But since much of this antagonism to the young is not conscious, it festers dangerously in the dark—only to break out in the schools, to which parents have delegated the job of keeping young people in line.

Our schools, Friedenberg says, have two great responsibilities: to help the student find a meaning in life that makes sense in *his* terms, and to help him find a sense of self-esteem. The achievement of these goals is blocked, he says, by the history of public education in this country. The traditional function of our schools has been to train the children of immigrants to work docilely in factories and offices and to give them the guidelines by which they can pull themselves up into the middle class and beyond. This has led to an emphasis on smoothing off rough edges, learning to get along with the group to which one aspires and curbing one's individuality. The school has been the melting pot in a society that prides itself on its ability to assimilate all kinds of people. Thus schools and teachers are unlikely to respond happily to signs of originality, nonconformity or eccentricity on the part of students. The result is an education that narrows the world instead of opening it up.

In his latest book, *Coming of Age in America*, Friedenberg is devastatingly specific in his charges against our schools. Their spirit may be recaptured by any reader who remembers his school days' myriad rules of conduct and deportment, the ostensible function of which was to make you "a nice person" but which had as its real purpose the "infantilization" of adolescence and the ensnarement of youngsters "in the trailing remnants of childhood emotions which always remain to trap them."

To add to the problem, Friedenberg says, we have turned over to the schools functions that used to take place elsewhere, placing the schools in a position to alter the way a child grows, his values, his sense of his own worth, even his patterns of anxiety. And these, Friedenberg insists, are matters too important to be left to those whose major concern is formal education. In exercising this vast authority, the schools are quite democratic. We are familiar with the extent of the dropout problem in the slums, which many authorities believe is heightened by the ludicrous conflict between the middle-class values the school tries to enforce and the values that the students encounter every day in the school of hard knocks. To Friedenberg the wonder is that more slum kids don't drop out; for if middle-class youngsters are no longer stimulated by the prospect of carrying on a meaningless tradition, why should we expect to gain recruits for it in the slums?

But the prejudice against "different" children extends to more than just the poor. The school, Friedenberg charges, tries to break or drive out everyone who deviates from the norm—the rich, the excessively bright or imaginative or specialized—because in a mass society "the most serious threat to self-esteem is the possibility of meeting someone who really *is* qualified and does know how to do something special, thus opening . . . limitless vistas of inferiority."

The high school, then, does not help the student test various roles and identities; it does not help him to "connect" his unique gift with some suitable adult role. Instead, it attempts to force everyone into the current statistical model of normality. Any tentative step toward trying another role is frowned on or laughed at or ignored. Most likely the odd youth will simply be left behind, standing on the corner with the other dropouts, watching the swelling parade to college.

And college, according to Paul Goodman, is now organized like a model of the great rat race that students are going to enter upon graduation. Instead of a leisurely, civilized pursuit of knowledge for its own sake, the college student finds he must pursue good grades that will ensure the good job in the good, materially rich life to come. College is no longer the refreshing contrast it once was to high school; too often it is nothing but a sophisticated extension of that dreary, regulation-bound place. No wonder the colleges are hurrying to re-create some of the old atmosphere of higher learning; no wonder the student body is restless with revolt.

It can be argued, of course, that the critics, in order to make their point, overstate their case. We all know sensitive, humane and intelligent teachers who believe that the proper function of education is the cultivation of diversity and of the singular student's singular gifts—and sometimes, somehow, such teachers manage to break through the paper curtain of forms, reports and administrative edicts to touch the hearts and minds of their students. And we all know students who resist the effects of the great educational blender and emerge from it intact and, oddly enough, even enhanced by the experience.

But if even part of the critics' charges are true, it is clear that our approach to the problems of educating adolescents and young adults is wrong, that all the wondrous and expensive new educational technology, all our surveys, studies and seminars, will not accomplish what we so fervently wish of them. It is clear that our troubles lie not in the technology of education but in its very atmosphere.

According to Friedenberg, the essential first step in true reform is to end the connection in our minds between schooling and economic opportunity. We will not, he assures us, solve the dropout problem by repeating the formula that those with a high-school diploma do better economically than those without one. The kids understand perfectly well that the truly significant difference in income hinges on a college degree—and that college is not a choice available to everyone.

If that is true, it follows that the American high school itself, largely oriented toward college preparation, does not make sense for everyone. What is needed, says Friedenberg, is a wider range of alternatives than the present choice between a high-school diploma and dropping out. He contends that the public school now adequately serves "ambitious, conventional youth who accept with equanimity the commonplace folkways of their community" and who can comfortably express their talents in conventional ways. What we need is something equally comfortable for the others. He suggests two possibilities.

The first is a series of residential schools, open to all but mainly for the benefit of poor children. The idea is to lift them bodily out of the atmosphere of despair that surrounds them on their home turf. He is not urging, as some have, revivals of the semimilitary CCC camps. [The Civilian Conservation Corps was a Federal program of youth conservation projects during the 1930's and early 1940's.— Ed.] On the contrary, he believes that "generally speaking, slum children may be assumed to have received whatever virtues austerity might confer." So he proposes that these schools have a minimum of rules, provide students with pocket money and be lavish with food, care and facilities. "The youngsters . . . should be treated in a way that means respect to them, and for the deprived this must include a large measure of material and sensual indulgence." In addition to these schools he suggests a sort of GI bill of rights for youngsters, under which the government would pay the fees of students in need of experimenting with other alternatives, ranging from the upper-class eastern prep schools to first-rate private vocational schools.

If we encouraged a new diversity in education, Friedenberg believes, we would also improve the conventional high school, relieving it of the pressure created by its attempt to accommodate those students who least like it and whom it least likes.

It is a visionary proposal. But Paul Goodman goes even further. For instance, he suggests experimenting in the primary grades with no school at all for some children, to see if they might not pick up on their own the elementary essentials of education. A great many children do learn to read without formal instruction, while many are actually blocked by their encounter with a system of rewards and punishments. Goodman would also experiment with learning outside the classroom, with smaller schools, with classes of mixed age groups, with an end to compulsory attendance. He proposes at the college level immediate abandonment of the grading system by some of our more prestigious colleges to eliminate the pressures grading imposes on the student. He also thinks some colleges might insist on two years of work or travel or public service as a condition for entrance "to get students with enough life experience to be educable . . . to break the lock step of twelve years of doing assigned lessons for grades." Out in the world, young people might acquire some motivation other than future money rewards for continuing their education. He believes that "educational policy must allow for periodic quitting and easy return to the scholastic ladder so that the young have time to find themselves and to study when they are themselves ready." In short, Goodman is willing to try anything that will make education more flexible, anything that will acknowledge and emphasize individual differences in aptitudes and interests, in psychological and intellectual growth rates, in styles of life and thought.

But having said this, the argument begins to circle back on itself. There would be no need for a radical revision of education if society itself were not caught in a lock step that the schools must join. As Goodman puts it, "Fundamentally, there is no right education except growing up in a worth-while world. Indeed, our excessive concern with problems of education at present simply means that the grownups do not have such a world."

Whether Goodman and Friedenberg are practical or impractical, it can do no harm, in the midst of the current ferment over the problems of youth to be reminded that the young have a right to expect more from their schools than mere vocational training or the promise of good jobs at good pay. Education, rightly conceived, must help parents offer their youngsters a sense that the community they are being prepared to join is a worth-while place.

This is not merely an abstract question of social justice; it is a matter of vital self-interest to everyone. As Erik Erikson says, "It is the young who, by their responses and actions, tell the old whether life as represented by the old and presented to the young has meaning." Young people at the moment are withholding any such assurance. That some among us are willing to ponder these deeply disturbing questions is a good omen. But if we are to take critics like Friedenberg and Goodman seriously we must look beyond piecemeal reform, beyond nuts-and-bolts adjustments. We must do nothing less than take on the ultimate question of what constitutes a good life in a good society for all of us.

THE ADOLESCENT GHETTO [2]

The modern "problem of youth" is part of the wider population problem that confronts the world today. In advanced, industrial nations, and now increasingly in underdeveloped countries, the older generations are employing ingenious stratagems to stem the tide of adolescents which threatens to swamp their entrenched positions. After thirty, we all assume the stance of a latter-day Canute.

The mature can no longer assume with any confidence that a half of all who are born will die before puberty, that the remainder of the males will be decimated by major wars before they are

[2] From article by Frank Musgrove, lecturer in education at Leeds University, England. *Nation.* 199:137-40. S. 21, '64. Reprinted by permission.

twenty-five, and that many of the more enterprising among the residue will have scattered to far-flung frontiers of opportunity before they are thirty. Today the social, sexual and economic threat of the uprising generation must be faced head-on.

While there are thus unique aspects to the contemporary confrontation of the generations, "the problem of youth" is not new. It is simply more desperate. In the early days of the classical industrial revolution, when youthful skills and quickness of mind and limb were at a premium, the young entered early into adult earnings, responsibilities and positions of seniority. Their elders, handicapped by obsolete knowledge and skills, were often appendages to their children. Nevertheless, devices for regulating and softening the entry of the young into the world of adults were often ingenious and even ruthless. We no longer take the drastic measures which medieval and renaissance society adopted with a proportion of their young males (often those destined for long training and eventual high responsibility); but we still behave as if a large proportion of the young were eunuchs. The protracted education and theoretical continence required of our most gifted and favored young men would be tolerable only to a generation of geldings.

One of the most effective means of disabling the young and at least postponing their head-on competition with their seniors is protracted formal education. The evidence that such provision is often damaging to the personality and irrelevant to the economy is unlikely to halt the vast expansion of formal education for young people into their middle and late twenties. Our colleges are increasingly depositories for superabundant youth, agencies for neutralizing the threat of an insurgent generation.

Many of our problems today are a product of the very progress we have made. The young survive to manhood on an unprecedented scale; and they are lusty survivors, better fed, more physically fit, and probably more advanced in brain maturity than at any time in human history. But their elders also survive to an unprecedented degree, and modern welfare economics and systems of taxation make it difficult for them to drop voluntarily into early retirement. At a time when the young were never so well equipped with formal job qualifications, there were never so few voluntary or involuntary dropouts from the ranks ahead of them. Economic expansion can sometimes generate additional opportunity, so that the problem of succession is masked, but in many fields these gains are offset by automation. The extension of formal education and training for ever more adolescents and young adults may be a sign, not that society is desperately in need of their enhanced skills, but that it is suffering from a surfeit. . . .

The result of our increasingly elaborate "protection" schemes is that young people are extruded from adult society. They constitute a segregated, zoo-like population, belittled by the very measures intended for their advantage, humiliated, self-disparaging, by turns apathetic and hostile. It is often assumed that the young have withdrawn themselves from the world of their seniors, in protest against its values and authority. The evidence is not that they have withdrawn but that they have been kicked out: that in their teens their most ardent desire is to qualify as adults and engage in adult affairs. This becomes ever more difficult for them as the legal age for entry into many pursuits and occupations becomes ever higher, and as the statutory and conventional age of school leaving rises everywhere.

We are fortunate if this segregated, largely futile world—futile because, "in their own interests," its denizens can make no direct contribution to the vital and central concerns of society—is invaded by nothing worse than "beatlemania," marginal delinquency and sexual experimentation. After all, at the height of their physical and perhaps intellectual powers, the young have to do *something*.

Before the age of twenty, marriage is the major avenue of advance from the teen-age zoo into the world of adults, and this perhaps accounts for the unprecedented popularity of early marriages. . . . This remaining avenue to adulthood is vigorously though often unavailingly obstructed by parents. In England there are twice as many divorces in marriages which have lasted twenty years or more as in those which have lasted four years or less; but the myth that young marriages are particularly prone to disaster persists as one of the most useful weapons in the parental armory. In view of the grudging attitude to youthful marriage, the hostility and disparagement which surround it, and the often precarious finances of underpaid professional workers in their youth, the remarkable thing is not that some of these marriages fail but that so many survive.

The segregated world of youth is created and furnished by (adult) writers and tailors; the mass media define and perpetuate a sociocultural ghetto for subadults. Special institutions are created solely for the young. In England the famous Albemarle Report on youth of 1960 fostered the youth club movement (ages fourteen to twenty) and recommended specially trained and paid representatives of the adult world to supervise and oversee it. Adult institutions (political, social and cultural) have their youth departments with only the sketchiest liaison to the parent bodies.

It is probably true that the mature are not to be trusted; that they cannot be expected voluntarily to behave with decency and humanity toward the young; that youth must be preserved from the contamination of close contact with them. This would certainly seem to be the lesson of history. But it is one of the oddities of our day that we approve close social contact only between people of almost exactly equal age; that we regard as potentially dangerous, even immoral, any association between the young and adults except kinsmen and certified neuters such as priests, schoolteachers and youth leaders. The sociologists then make the great discovery that the young are to be found in "peer groups." At least one reason for the rejection of the young and their exile into a self-contained and if possible antiseptic limbo is our distrust *of ourselves*.

The population explosion which we have seen throughout the world since the end of World War II is aggravating the problem of transition from adolescence to adult life in countries at quite different levels of social and industrial progress. Unemployment in America and the depressed areas of Britain . . . is disproportionate among the younger age groups. America's "war on poverty" has been particularly concerned with the plight of people aged sixteen to twenty-one. In five years' time, if present trends persist, a million and a half in this age range may be unemployed. Unemployment among men of eighteen to twenty-five is already running at approximately twice the rate which obtains in the labor force as a whole.

In America and Western Europe (notably, perhaps, in southern Italy) the young men who have had least education are most often unemployed. But that is not necessarily because they are "unemployable"; it may be because we use our educational systems as gigantic grading devices which, in times of labor abundance, automatically debar the least educated from serious consideration. In the developing countries of tropical Africa young people who have enjoyed a Western-style education are often the most difficult to absorb into the economy. With some forty per cent of their people under the age of fifteen, the developing countries of Asia, Africa and Latin America recoil before a rising tide of youth. Accelerated programs of education on the Western school model have made a difficult position highly dangerous. In Ghana the Workers' Brigade was established in 1957 as an emergency measure to mop up educated young men: to place them in a segregated, controlled situation on the margins of society. As an agricultural army they could be held under a discipline which reduced their danger to the social order.

Although adolescents are willfully and skillfully excluded from adult status at least partly because they are a threat to the security of the elders, their segregated and semi-autonomous status is elaborately justified in psychological and educational terms (which often bear a striking resemblance to the terms once used to justify the exclusion, subordination and inferiority of adult women). A special "psychology of adolescence" has been developed, and it helps to create what it describes.

Many vocations in the past have called for a long and difficult preparation in youth. The knight was unlikely to master the range of military, social and administrative skills required of him before the age of twenty-one. What is relatively new is the notion that *all* the young must pass through a long period of dependency and social probation. However inappropriate or even grotesque, we have now assimilated all young people, whatever their social level or future employment, to the condition of knighthood.

The adolescent is a Franco-American invention. Rousseau drew the original blueprint in the eighteenth century; Stanley Hall added the superstructure more than a century later. But even as he wrote, Hall was acutely aware that American adolescents were refusing to conform to the theoretical specifications, that they were far more adult than in theory they could be. For the past two centuries, whenever two or three adults—particularly of the middle classes—were gathered together, they have lamented the "precociousness" of the young, the discrepancy between the theory and the facts of adolescent behavior.

The young are older than we think. And as they become ever older (a girl today menstruates ten months before her mother did), we attempt to make them ever younger. We certainly succeed in making them more irresponsible. The advanced industrial nations have been remarkably successful in ignoring biology.

The second major justification of an ever more protracted period of dependency and social probation for all is the alleged "complexity of modern society." In fact, for all their technological advance and administrative sophistication, industrial societies are ever simpler for their average members, and that is the overwhelming majority. Specialization in employment and the professionalization of local services have radically reduced the range and complexity of skills required by the average citizen. As jurors, tax assessors, men-at-arms, experts in animal and child psychology and physiology, our forebears perhaps needed a longer preparation for adult status than they commonly enjoyed. Today the individual can survive not only adequately but well with a remarkable paucity of skills and knowledge. That is not to say that his level of competence over a wide range of activities could not be raised; but it is nonsense to claim that the complexity of the modern world makes this imperative. Complexity is a subterfuge—at best a rationalization—for keeping in prolonged dependence a great and rapidly growing army of modern youth.

We have created a largely unreal division between adolescents and adults; we have propounded solutions for "the problem of youth" which only exacerbate the problems they should solve. Two things above all are urgent—a more realistic, or simply a more accurate, "psychology of adolescence" which recognizes the real competence and maturity of most young people at sixteen, seventeen and eighteen; and a generous reordering of our social institutions to recognize and reward their talents and abilities.

For the psychological health of individual adolescents, and for the greater social health of society, the young need to come into adult institutions as and when they are able, and on terms that accord with their actual capacities rather than their chronological ages. As a society we draw far too many (usually erroneous) inferences from the accumulation, or lack of accumulation, of years.

Extended higher education needs close scrutiny of its real purpose and effects. If it genuinely enhances the power of the young, it should be expanded; if it is really a device for prolonging their dependence and inducing immaturity, it should be scaled down. Too many of our educational and quasi-educational institutions are mechanisms for manufacturing adolescents where none naturally exist. And—to add disaster to disaster—academic success is thought to indicate promise in spheres where it is wholly irrelevant. An advanced education, in which success goes commonly to the somewhat neurotic and the more than somewhat introverted, should not be a prime requisite for a man whose subsequent career will involve solving the actual predicaments of real people, face to face, rather than handling ideas about people and formulas which embrace an abstracted aspect of a faceless multitude.

The young will cease to be a nuisance and a danger to their elders when they are no longer seen and treated as an outsider population, threatening and hostile. Their advance into the adult world should not be unnecessarily delayed. Many educational programs should be drastically pruned (although a minority of students destined for the learned professions and higher scientific work must endure an ever longer training. These are the future underprivileged—the men without the leisure which automation has brought to everyone else). The young should no longer be subjected to an extensive "protection" which is in fact an insult. More men in their fifties, forties and even their thirties should be able to retire on adequate pensions to make way for young people to offer their best before they have grown too old, frustrated and dispirited to give it.

DELINQUENCY AND THE GREAT SOCIETY [3]

Those of us working for the President's Committee on Juvenile Delinquency and Youth Crime daily confront the following facts and figures: The largest group of today's unemployed is between sixteen and nineteen years old. Their unemployment rate is more than three times that for the labor force as a whole. One in three of these new young workers—an estimated twenty-six million of whom are entering the labor force during the 1960's—is a high-school dropout, the last to be hired and the first to be fired. The FBI calculates that in 1964 juveniles were responsible for 37 per cent of the nation's "serious" criminal offenses. All together, some 686,000 of the 1.4 million juvenile arrests were referred to juvenile courts that year, with repeaters accounting for about a third of the cases. Although these referrals represent less than 3 per cent of American youngsters between ten and seventeen, it is estimated that 17 per cent of today's ten-year-old boys will be brought before a juvenile court by their eighteenth year. That estimate reaches 40 per cent in some urban ghetto areas. Add to this the current annual estimate of 200,000 cases of venereal disease among teen-agers and 100,000 illegitimate births to adolescent mothers, and the problem looms larger.

The relationship between unemployment and delinquency has not been precisely calibrated, but, like the predicted consequences of racial discrimination, it rests on more than a hunch. Recognition of widespread delinquency and the probability of its increase brought about the establishment in 1961 of the President's committee, consisting of the attorney general of the United States (chairman) and the secretaries of Labor and of Health, Education, and Welfare. President Johnson has reaffirmed its mandate in the strongest terms. A major Federal legislative instrument in this field is the Juvenile Delinquency and Youth Offenses Control Act of September, 1961, which provides the HEW secretary with authority to make grants to state, local, or nonprofit agencies for the purpose of testing new ways to prevent, treat, and control delinquency, as

[3] From "Youth, Crime, and the Great Society," by James Symington, executive director, President's Committee on Juvenile Delinquency and Youth Crime. *Reporter.* 34:41-3. F. 24, '66. Copyright 1966 by the Reporter Magazine Co. Reprinted by permission.

well as of training social workers, correction officers, police, co officials, and others in the field. The funds available for maki these grants have totaled less than $10 million annually.

Initially, under the 1961 act, sixteen major prevention projects were developed in urban areas involving new techniques of job development, job training, education, and neighborhood organization. When it became clear that their objectives could best be fulfilled within the larger framework of the poverty program, most of these projects were brought under the aegis of the Office of Economic Opportunity.

These early efforts had served to show that programs designed to involve large numbers of young people were not necessarily the best means of reaching those who most need help. Thus, in 1965 a "Special Demonstration" program was established to support small projects focused on this hard-core group.

Some of these Special Demonstrations are aimed at the relatively unexplored areas of middle-class and suburban delinquency, including increasing rates of illegitimacy, venereal disease, and the use of drugs. To date twenty-six grantees—juvenile courts, universities, foundations, and other organizations—have been given roughly $2 million to deal with the delinquent at various stages of society's encounter with him: as a behavior problem in school, a first or second police contact, a juvenile-court probationer, a correctional-school resident, and a parolee.

Most of these Special Demonstration projects affect urban youth. The community intervention team in Detroit works with juveniles from fourteen to sixteen who have been law violators; the YWCA project in Miami tests new methods of dealing with potentially delinquent girls from thirteen to sixteen; the University of California at Berkeley conducts a program for parolees aged thirteen to seventeen; and the Friends Neighborhood Guild runs a foster-family project for Philadelphia boys released from correctional institutions who have no approved home to go to. Programs to reach and involve gangs and gang leaders are under way in El Paso, Brooklyn, Detroit, and San Francisco. In Arizona a center for young Pima Indians is operated on the premise that those who understand and appreciate their tribal heritage do better in school and on the job than those who do not.

Strong family ties seem to offer one of the best assurances against delinquency in the young. I have spoken with directors of training schools who attribute the rarity of Jewish delinquents to the fact that "they take care of it in the home." This ancient culture, wherein the father is the undisputed head of the family and boys of thirteen are reminded in solemn ceremony that they have become men, appears to produce proportionately fewer young lawbreakers than less closely knit family groups. Neither do the sons of Oriental families in America which have retained their ancestral traditions —chiefly respect for the father—seem to feel a need to slug a cop in order to prove their manhood.

Since the patrolman is usually the first contact that youngsters in the streets have with the law, the value of any program that attempts to reach them is enhanced by police understanding and, if possible, participation. Police officials maintain that changes in requirements and available manpower limit the opportunity to engage in the kind of day-to-day relationships that characterized some neighborhoods in the "old days." Some question the value of such "non-arrest" contact, claiming it is not a "traditional" police function. I have ridden in squad cars with dedicated young policemen; and if the hostility of their reception in some slum areas is the normal response to this "traditional" function, something "untraditional" may well be warranted in the interest of public safety.

Unsatisfactory relations between some police and their communities and lack of communication between police and welfare officials are prominent obstacles to the effort to reduce delinquency. Even when distrust is broken down, problems of understanding remain. Nor are they confined to relations between the delinquent and those trying to help him....

The problem of communication between the social scientist and his colleagues in law and law enforcement is very real. But communicate they must, if they are to carry out in a meaningful way the presidential mandate to identify and combat the causes of crime and delinquency. Of course, the dialogue is one that also quite properly engages the spirited participation of parents, teachers, ministers, policemen, editors, scoutmasters, and enthusiasts of all kinds. It should be encouraging, I suppose, to find that many such citizens know exactly what to do about crime, particularly proponents of the "crackdown," "young punk," "jail the parent," and "teach them what it means to be an American" theories. Regrettably, the problem never seems as simple as the solutions advanced.

In any event, the overlay of a trained, if not overtrained, social worker's analysis of a given case on top of the simplistic outlines of the precinct-blotter profile adds up to a composite blur of doubtful value to the court. A more coherent total picture might require adjustments in training emphasis, whereby the police rookie loses an hour of traffic training and the budding welfare worker does a little reading on the practical problems of a patrolman.

But policemen, judges, bureaucrats, social workers, and ordinarily reticent professors can find themselves engaged in the liveliest, friendliest exchange in history without making a dent in delinquency if the juvenile himself is not given an active and responsible role to play. We are a young country and getting younger. Within a few years half of all American citizens will be under twenty-five. The median age is already down to fifteen in Latin America. There, teen-agers in urban and rural ghettos carry their smaller brothers or sisters on their backs for miles to the doctor or for safe drinking water. The challenge of living to help others and the effort it requires keep many such youngsters on a straight if rocky road. Our own children, rich and poor alike, want to feel involved in causes that transcend themselves, their community, and their time. For many, the chance to help develop and carry out neighborhood programs of education or recreation would provide such a cause.

If it is true that in some American slums up to 60 per cent of the children are raised in fatherless homes, who is to play the "acceptable male model" in their lives? Is it wiser to look for such a man from among professional caseworkers who live outside the neighborhood, or from among subprofessionals who could be found within the community itself?

The Hard Core

And what happens to those adolescents whom programs, however well conceived and executed, fail to sway? What of the "institutions" that receive them and the courts that send them there? James Bennett, former director of the Federal Bureau of Prisons, recalls that less than 5 per cent of the Federal judges in his time ever visited a Federal prison. How many juvenile-court judges have made a thorough investigation of the institutions to which they entrust their charges? But why stop with judges? How many mayors, aldermen, councilmen, or state legislators have really investigated the institutions to which juveniles are committed? And if they are found wanting, what higher priority could there be for the expenditure of public funds?

It is not a question of comforts. One director proudly claimed that his boys could watch television every night and see two movies a week. Undoubtedly they were doing that at home when they should have been working, studying, or listening to music that was written from the head and heart and not the midsection. We must ask what demands are being made of these kids, demands that will stretch their minds and lift their spirits. Rather than pap to dull them into sullen acceptance of their lot, they need classrooms, good teachers, and workshops. And they need protection from the disturbed in their midst, who must be more carefully supervised and, if necessary, separated.

We have some institutions that provide such services, but not nearly enough. Those I have seen which successfully receive, handle, train, and educate delinquent boys include the State Correctional Institution at Camp Hill, Pennsylvania, and the Annex to the Boys' Training Schools in New Hampton, New York (here there are 110 staff members for about a hundred boys, a ratio that is clearly relevant to the success of this operation); the National Training School for Boys, located in the District of Columbia, which is embarked on a new education-research program involving flexible rewards (one young man went from a fifth-grade level to tenth in eight months of schooling); and the Ozanam Home for Boys in Kansas City, where sixty boys attend school in the outside community and enjoy recreation, art, shop, and farm experiences at the home.

Many rewarding techniques for guidance within institutional limits have been developed. But returning the boy to his home community and enabling him to resist the old influences are more difficult challenges. The Labor Department has taken a lead in meeting them. Under the Manpower Development and Training Act of 1962 and its recent amendments, the department is engaged in experimental programs dealing with the training needs of youthful inmates of correctional institutions and their employment problems when released. In one such project at the New York City institution on Rikers Island, one hundred boys learned to operate data-processing equipment while acquiring basic literacy and self-sufficiency. After release, the boys were provided placement, counseling, and family referral services, with a high ratio of success.

A 1965 amendment to the MDTA enables the department to launch an experimental program to help young ex-prisoners meet the bonding requirements of jobs normally closed to boys with a record. There is hope that the success of these experimental Federal programs will commend them to state and local authorities responsible for the disposition of the vast majority of young offenders, and encourage the passage of enabling laws where necessary.

A re-examination of juvenile-court procedures may also be warranted. Some maintain that these courts have become inappropriately soft on the "sophisticated" young offender and want "stiffer procedures" for the sixteen-year-old and up. They would argue that, if juveniles are to have greater opportunities to act responsibly, they can expect less sympathy if they fail to do so. This approach is not inconsistent with the growing realization in legal circles that certain protections not ordinarily provided in juvenile courts may now be due. The admission of hearsay evidence and rejection of the "legalisms" that would block adult prosecution are permitted on the theory that a juvenile hearing is a civil, not a criminal or adversary, proceeding, and that its purpose is treatment, not punishment. As a result, justice may occasionally be sacrificed in the name of a somewhat illusory "mercy" whereby youngsters, possibly not even guilty as charged, are hustled off to a detention facility, the "facility" of which is simply to detain. We may be moving toward a more solemn and judicial approach to the older juvenile, whereby his treatment in court would be less avuncular, his sentence more "deterring," and his constitutional safeguards more complete. [In May 1967 the Supreme Court ruled that juvenile offenders are entitled to the legal protections guaranteed by the Bill of Rights. See "Juveniles Given Bill of Rights Protection," in Section V, below.—Ed.] ...

Our Bighearted Apathy

We wonder who the teen-ager in trouble is. He wonders who we are and what hypocrisies we conceal.

What crimes do we permit to be perpetrated on some families so as to undermine their faith in society and law? They are the quiet crimes of con men who victimize the poor, the new breed of Medicare parasites, the contractor who says he represents Urban Development and must improve the home to save it from condemnation, the bank that takes the note on such transactions. Delinquents take radios. Loan sharks take houses. Some landlords take all the rent a home-starved market will bear and provide as little as possible in return. This is what makes a job a tough one for the policeman, who is seen by the poor more often as the enforcer of laws that take rather than protect.

The journey of a conscience through the world of government can be tortuous. It may seem at times like a tightrope walk between evangelism and bureaucracy. Looking at the problems brings out the evangelist; doing something about them, the bureaucrat. The balancing pole is patience. What escapes headline attention is the fact that the great majority of government men walk the line without losing their balance.

The headlines on delinquency itself bring many a fist down on many a breakfast table. They stimulate letters to congressmen and other acts of futile indignation. In fairness, second-section reports of slum conditions and recommended community action also stimulate our bighearted apathy—not only with respect to those elements of society which prey on the less fortunate but also with respect to our own homes and the examples and standards we set for our own children. We talk about excellence and the pursuit of excellence. But how many adult Americans are growing breathless in the pursuit of excellence? Consider the shameful dross that the average adult community accepts as commonplace and be grateful, if incredulous, that the proportion of the young who lose sight of our highest standards to the extent of violating our lowest is under 5 per cent.

We permit our children to be spectators of vice and hate every day. To forbid it would be attacked as deprivation of some constitutional right on the part of the purveyors of vice and hate. Worse than that, it would require self-discipline on our part. But in permitting it, we do give our children some hard choices, and ourselves too. For we have the choice of whether or not to ignore the consequences of the double standard we so calmly observe. As long as this is the case, the teen-ager of our time is tempted to inquire what is "like so great" about our society.

OPPORTUNITY TO BE WHAT? [4]

Whatever the age of our nation and the growth of its problems and responsibilities, we as a people living now, or about to live in the next few decades, will be predominantly young. The statistics are impressive: one out of every three people in the United States was seventeen or under in 1963; by 1965 it will be two out of five. All of which means there are 70 million people in this age group, 63 per cent more than in 1947. For the last four years the number of seventeen or younger has been increasing at 6.6 per cent a year, 4.5 times as fast as the total growth of our population. . . .

Fortunately, a generation of restless observers has given us an astonishingly rich collection of information about young people as they variously live on this planet: the farflung differences that characterize their growth and development; the immensely complicated matter of how their lives are influenced not only by the hands and belts of their parents, but their beliefs and dreams; the relationship

[4] From "Youth: Opportunity to Be What?" by Robert Coles, psychiatrist and author. *New Republic.* 151:59-64. N. 7, '64. Reprinted by permission of *The New Republic,* copyright 1964, Harrison-Blaine of New Jersey, Inc.

between childhood and adolescence and the stubborn social, political and economic forces in a society which also help shape their nature and often neglect their special needs. We have, as a matter of fact, a proliferation of facts, experiments, "pilot projects" and "programs" which tell us a lot about such matters as how best to teach our children to read or learn foreign languages or mathematics. I am sure that as we put our minds to it, the general problems of a large youthful population will enlist more of such information and the "techniques" developed from it.

There is, however, an important distinction between a Great Society and a richly competent one. We can cram facts into our children, wipe out most of the diseases which weaken or cripple their bodies, even keep them busy and working as they become youths so that our unemployment figures nearly vanish (and simultaneously the crime which is related to idleness and a sense of futility) and still find a generation of young men and women with none of that spark of ethical concern which could be called "charity" in other times without embarrassment or the grim implications now attached to the word. Smug power and skill are not, I would imagine, what we have in mind when we try to reason and work our way toward a more responsible youth as a reflection of that same kind of society.

It is easy for some of us to define our goals for young people: they need more lively and daring schooling, better health than all too many of them seem likely to have, a sense of worth unqualified by the various irrelevancies hitherto so essential to it, the definite expectation of some kind of work which will be useful to all of us. Such goals are agreeable platitudes until any attempt even to begin realizing them confronts us with the tough resistance in our society to their transformation into practical realities. It is easier to talk about whether or not we should give the vote to the coming tide of young people, or debate the proper age for driving, or the locations for our modern school buildings.

Slum youths and middle-class ones both seem restless, and their lawlessness—each for its own reasons—draws an anxious, cumulative attention. We are beginning to realize that the very definition of "youth" is elastic. Whose youth? A Negro sharecropper's, which begins at ten and ends at fifteen? A college student's which at twenty-one may still have years of school days ahead? We are also beginning to realize that comfort and strength do not insure good sense in our young; and so we ask ourselves about the meaning of words like "maturity." Can we free it from its deadened, pompous abuse and give it a real meaning, describing young people who have found that leading their own lives need not demand either aimlessness or that total surrender to the past which some confuse with "growing up"?

Rigidities in our political and economic life may have prevented us from doing as much as we should for some of our youths, or enabling many others to offer their talents to some purpose, but the more kindly and level-headed of our specialists on the behavior of children have given us a storehouse of information about how children grow and what they need to feel strong and willing to take up their own lives.

We know, for instance, that individual discontent is part of growing, that rebelliousness in youth is to some extent natural, and that what is critically important is the way our society gives form to these psychological developments. A ten-year-old who at that age is a migrant farmer and a twenty-five-year-old graduate student may both be going through the turmoil of saying goodbye to their parents, the confusion of greeting their own independence, with its promises and calls of duty, but clearly each will have his separate struggle in both form and content, in thought and action.

Nor are culture and class the sole determinants of the kinds of assumptions we are allowed or denied as we grow older. We live in time and space, and what is happening in world history, or where we live, not simply our country but the region of that country, affect our habits and beliefs. The problems facing American youth are thus not all of a kind, and the solutions to them will come from different directions. Laws of the greatest urgency will help some; other young people will need from their elders a kind of ethical example all too rare if they are to survive that poverty of ideals which defies our moral laws and sometimes helps keep much-needed written ones from coming about. There is no point in setting one kind of problem against another, one class against another.

One order of problems ahead is that of the badly educated, sickly, jobless young men and women whom we call "poor" or "disadvantaged." I shudder at those words. They are so abstract. They allow us to forget the individual lives of boys and girls who must grow in those grim, cheerless tenements, those dreary rural cabins, all of them smelling and hot in summer, chilling and drafty in winter. Writers like Orwell and Agee have tried desperately to shatter their reader's, their fellow man's, natural desire to shy away from the misfortunes of the poor, only to acknowledge the near impossibility of the task. Perhaps statistics have some bit of strange and effective eloquence. If so, they are to be had in profusion: during this decade more than seven million young people will leave school without graduating, and one third of them will have an eighth-grade education or less; one third of the young men now turning eighteen would be rejected by the Selective Service System if they were examined, half of them because they couldn't pass the mental examinations, the remainder because of failure to qualify physically; a study of youths actually rejected by their draft boards showed that 80 per cent of them were school dropouts, 9 per cent had court records and 28 per cent were unemployed.

Such are the lives which go to awful waste in a nation which offers millions of its youths a kind of experience new in history: the peculiarly ironic and unsettling one of living out an impoverished life in the midst of a country actually perplexed about what to do with its agricultural and industrial capacities. Under these circumstances poverty is not an unavoidable fact of the world, a shared struggle for an entire nation, but a matter of willful carelessness or dishonorable apathy for the majority of us who are comfortable. For those living the threadbare life of migrant farmers or sharecroppers, or attempting survival in the rat-infested ghettos of our cities it is almost a matter of being singled out for condemnation.

I suppose many of us imagine that children growing up under such conditions fail to get the point of their relative shame and humiliation. It is certainly easier for us to think of these young people as not only off yonder, but unaware of how arbitrary and needless their fate is. But in my experience even children of eight or ten can fathom their comparative social and economic situation.

They see the world about them and draw the right conclusions, that they must live wastefully and meagerly, that their lot contrasts not with that of a few courtiers, but with that of most of their countrymen. A white boy of nine in the north Georgia foothills to the Appalachians said to me: "I'm sure glad I wasn't born colored, but to be rich I think I should have been born some other place." What he called rich could only be defined by the very real poverty of his family, and, for that matter, an entire region on which his town bordered. As for what I have heard these past years from Negro children, it has all been a forceful reminder of just how accurate the young can be about their world.

What is crumbling in our country today is a caste system, and though sociologists have written at length on the subject in the past, the public does not have a clear idea of the critical differences between caste and class. When I hear from a Negro child whose parents are quite well off that he would forsake all his toys, all the advantages he enjoys in a private room of a comfortable home, for a lighter shade to his skin I know I am confronted with more than a problem of past mischief visited upon Negroes. Poor youths present one order of challenge to our nation; Negro youths all that and more. . . . Since 1955 Negro youths have had to battle a steadily rising condition of unemployment, a far more intractable one than that facing our poorest whites. One penologist told me in the course of a discussion of the incidence of crime among Negro boys and girls, let alone young men and women—"it's probably the one kind of job a lot of them can get, stealing." Now, the effects of such relative hardship and idleness upon growing children are several. There is no use telling children growing up in *our* poverty that there is a tougher, more abased kind of existence in Asia or Africa, or that any bad luck here is really an impressive kind of good fortune. Children tantalized by an elusive, always present but always unobtainable abundance are children meanly treated. Additionally frustrating to jobless youth is a rhetoric constantly preached about the "freedom" and "opportunity" which our nation offers all its citizens. It offers both to many of us. Yet unemployed young people, between sixteen and twenty-four, now represent about one of every three unemployed workers in the United States; and for the past five years the number of unemployed youths has drifted constantly upward.

I have recently begun talking with random youths seeking jobs to no avail, and with some people who work in the public and private employment agencies to which they go. I followed a few of these youths about as they tracked down one possible job after another from early morning until late in the afternoon. They were earnest, well-meaning lads. They wanted to work. They were not drifters, not hoods, not violent, not in the slightest interested in public welfare. They are teen-agers, still hopeful, still determined. Underneath, though, they are tiring; and every once in a while in each of them I could see the sulky mood, the set face, the irritability that indicates rising frustration. The plain facts are that even the most menial jobs are sometimes unavailable, and good ones very hard to find for hundreds of thousands of young people all over the country. In time these youths will not only become older, but apathetic and finally inert. If they let it go at that, we will at least be unbothered by the sadness, the bafflement of their position; the hope they have surrendered, the ambition put aside, the trust lost. They will be good and law-abiding people, and if they live short, ailing lives, at least they will have the grace to stoop quietly out of our way. Only a few from the middle-class world will confront the slow wasting of such youths—teachers who will face their developing insensibility, public welfare workers who will look at their shrugged passivity, their spiritless lives at a standstill.

While some youths lose any real voice of outrage fairly quickly, others manage their despair less responsibly—tough boys and girls who become the vicious youths of our slums. Confused, scared, and nasty, at ten and twelve, they are drinking, smoking, trying an assortment of narcotics, clinging to and seizing one another with that extreme hopelessness (and its expression in surly calculation) which we call "promiscuity." They will not let us overlook them so easily. They provoke us and eventually anger us enough to want away with them.

With determination we can forget them, the ill-favored. There are so many of us who are comfortable, and clearly so out of our own efforts, our parents' efforts, that any who still lag behind must be shirkers or truants. It is certainly no empty talk which recalls how hard millions in our middle class have struggled to achieve their present life, or to hand it down, in all its improvement upon their own, to their children.

In the face of such events there is a terrible irony in the trouble-some, almost scoffing return many middle-class families seem to be getting for all that effort: a constantly rising incidence of suburban delinquency; the continued evidence in our finest suburbs of mind-less and sometimes even brutishly criminal behavior; the appear-ance of enough dulled and blasé youths to make it clear that a father's social and economic success does not automatically become his children's integrity; the widespread and bewildering outbreaks of riots—on beaches, in parks, on campuses—which in their vicious, destructive, and even carefully-planned quality have marked them-selves off from the casual and humorous "panty raids" of the past.

Any discussion of American youth must take all this into ac-count. Some critics of democratic liberalism have done so, remind-ing people who have worked for social and economic reform that they have been guilty of a naïve utopianism. After all, the proof is in—when people are no longer poor or exiled, they are still unhappy, and their children even more so. . . .

Much more important than condemnation, however, is an at-tempt to discover why people (if they do) imagine that such de-velopments as social-welfare legislation or psychoanalysis will guarantee an absence of problems or tasks in the home or the com-munity. If some liberals once had such notions, they have no doubt long since been disabused. It is, rather, many who are not so much liberal or conservative, or political in any real sense—their ideology is associated with successful membership in our uncertain and wide-spread middle classes—who continue to operate under various forms of what might better be called uneasy materialism than naïve lib-eralism. The liberals hope to vote a better kind of material life for all, hoping that such a struggle will contribute toward a more ethi-cal life as well by its very example and influence. When they are disappointed, some of them turn on those who continue to urge, for different reasons, a more decent existence for those in need of it.

The sad truth often is that . . . finally affluent but disenchanted, they fail to realize the continuing insecurity of their acquisitive success.

How About Delinquency

Crime statistics released by the FBI show that teen-agers account for 63 per cent of all arrests for car thefts—indeed 88 per cent of all such thieves arrested are under twenty-five. Then, we are told that for all criminal acts, excluding traffic offenses, the arrests of youths under eighteen increased by 4 per cent in 1963. In suburban areas the increase in general teen-age criminality was 15 per cent. That is not all. For the crimes of homicide, forcible rape, robbery, aggravated assault, burglary, larceny and auto theft, young people of eighteen or under accounted for 46 per cent of all arrests in 1963. In the suburbs the rate was 51 per cent. Finally, in the first six months of 1964 serious crime increased 15 per cent over the same period of 1963; but in the suburbs the increase was 23 per cent.

What are we to do with such information? Scream that all those children are spoiled, that they have failed us? Or look more closely at ourselves and what has happened in too many homes between us and our children? Amid the din of parents telling themselves and one another how very much they give, and work hard to give, their children, how pivotal the concern they have for their children's welfare, the ungracious response of those children seems like an incredible betrayal indeed; until, that is, one begins to listen to some of these parents—and their children—in courts, child guidance clinics, school counseling offices, or the deans' and doctors' offices of some of our colleges. I have treated some of these parents and some of their children, and a sad spectacle it sometimes is by the time some delinquency or symptom in one or the other forces the issue to a crisis. There are the parents who have spent their lives accumulating money, property, fine homes in the "best" neighborhoods (with, of course, excellent schools) and all of it "for the sake of the children." Many of them are quite helpless before their children, quite afraid to say no to them on any count. Frankly, some of the stories are at once chilling and tragic, instances as they are of how adults can use children to rationalize their own worries and greed.

The reactions of the children to such parents are, of course, various. It may sound incredible to your ears, but I have heard some white youths from our most exclusive towns on the eastern seaboard wish that they were Negro students in the civil-rights movement. Their envy is directed toward those who have infinitely less, but apparently more.

One of the real troubles—apart from space—with any case presentation to illustrate some of these problems is the near-impossible task of doing justice to behavior as it develops over time. There we sit, in those staff conferences, talking about a good deed by a youth or his parents, but the truth of how our lives are lived (and problems brought about) often defies the generalizations and explanations we summon. We can all scorn blundering parents in their last desperate indulgences with their children before the onset of trouble. Yet in listening to these cases unfold in their knotty untidiness, one more likely than not discovers that a final, alien offense done by a youth may crown years of subtle handiwork by parents aided by an entire society in the sense of the doctrines and values it may teach to those parents. We all look for specific wrong-doing—it is easier for us to live with that kind of explanation—but the drift of a nation and its individual mothers and fathers accounts for a good deal of what happens to our youth.

No people should know this better than we who have lived in this century, who have witnessed millions of youthful minds and bodies become willing, heroic cannon fodder for the cruelest of political systems and the weirdest of ideologies. Totalitarianism has not merely exploited the vulnerability of youth, but used youth's search for ideals to elicit a passionate kind of zeal from it. Young people hunger after their birthright, a visible future, and they are keen to sense from their parents and the world around them the possibilities and desirabilities of that future. We have seen that other youth are not immune to the blandishments of war and terror in the pursuit of a destiny for themselves; and I fear we are now seeing that our own youth will not easily resist a cult of private sunshine, and secluded complacency which denies them a capacity or freedom for sympathy, fellowship and compassion for others. Is it any wonder that when many of these young people turn away from the elegant, prodigal world which is their inheritance they find themselves drawn into spiteful, step-on-the-gas scrambles? It is a shame, and particularly so when one hears many of these youths crying for a different, a more ordered and kindly life for themselves and for their often careless or frantic parents.

It is said so often, but still needs saying, that most youths remain faithful, directly or in a wayward, petulant fashion, to the values and ideals, or lack of them, of their parents. If we are at present appalled at a soaring, reckless criminality in our middle-class children, it is likely we are really appalled at what has happened to ourselves, because much of what horrifies us is our own assumptions and actions come to expression and perpetuation by those who know us best and are our most eager followers.

Of course, bored, self-centered and mean parents can be rejected by their children too. No one familiar with how families work can declare out of hand a series of universally applicable rules about how the human mind can acquit itself in its progressive encounters with the fateful chances and opportunities of the world. However, a society determined upon a set of ways can hardly expect them to be ignored by its young people, and the odds are heavy that most of them will take up their social legacy.

Facing this nation is the matter of real commitment to its ideals. In the thirties a near disaster forced us to take stock of one another and try to harness an economy previously expanding but in a very real sense going nowhere. Without sensible and merciful action then, Lord knows where a hungry and dazed people might have turned its eyes. Then came two decades of having to contend with countries who had indeed turned their eyes elsewhere, and in terrible directions at that. All the while our children have been growing and I suspect all the while responding to our vexing attempts to settle upon some fair goals for all citizens in this country and for this rich land in its relationship to so many poorer ones.

It has been painful, and we have made errors, just as growth involves pain and results in errors. I have been saying that much of our ambiguity of conviction and direction has now come to haunt us, picked up by our youth and, so to speak, thrown in our faces. That there is courage and idealism in our young men and women must also be said, not as an oratorical flourish to enable us to forget the very serious problems we must solve, but as a happy but urgent reminder that those men and women in the Peace Corps or working at civil rights or simply living out their youthful days in study, work and growing need every bit of reinforcement we can all manage for them.

Once and for all we must realize that the life of the child's mind lives intimately with the life of our society. If the medical and social sciences have taught us anything, it is that. The problem then is not only what we will do with this or that piece of legislation, but what continuing example in our social, political and economic life we will set for our children, hopefully knowing that our standards will establish the basis for their future deeds.

The hearts of children can die, their minds close tight, at any age, even though their bodies live out the years allotted them. A Great Society will seek after justice for all its members so that they will live rather than exist, and with them the society itself.

V. PREVENTION AND TREATMENT

EDITOR'S INTRODUCTION

The cure for delinquency cannot be separated from its causes. Psychologists and sociologists tell us this is so, and most responsible people have now come to believe it. Local, state, and Federal projects have been undertaken which seek to lessen delinquency by attacking its root causes: poverty, resentment, despair, alienation. Youth bureaus, work camps, "halfway houses," counseling systems, special programs for deprived children and their families—all these have become familiar tools in the struggle against delinquency. Juvenile courts—in which young offenders are judged separately and differently from older people committing similar crimes—have become commonplace. There is a continuing search for new ways of dealing with delinquency—a search that ranges far beyond law enforcement and that delves into the very fabric of our society: into the community, the family, and the human personality. Delinquency, we now know, is not just a matter of laws and of punishments. It is an expression of a malaise within society, and to treat delinquency means to treat the ills of society.

The first selection on various means of preventing delinquency is from a study by the Children's Bureau of the United States Department of Health, Education, and Welfare. It is followed by an article from *Parents' Magazine* by Homer Page describing one of the most experimental, and controversial, antidelinquency programs—the Mobilization for Youth project in New York. The third selection, from a Public Affairs pamphlet by Ruth and Edward Brecher, describes the police handling of juvenile offenses. Next, Judge David L. Bazelon points out some grave deficiencies in the handling of juvenile court cases—deficiencies which sometimes lead to a denial of justice to teen-agers in trouble. The following article, from the New York *Times,* describes a far-reaching Supreme Court decision designed to remedy those deficiencies by assuring to juvenile offenders the same constitutional rights that are accorded to adults on trial. The final selection, by Sydney Smith of the Menninger Foundation, argues that efforts to control delinquency by punishment evade the real problem and are doomed to failure.

PREVENTING DELINQUENCY [1]

Today in the United States, as never before, the attention of the nation is focused on its youth and its growing number of juvenile delinquents. Delinquency prevention in its broadest sense has become of prime concern to teachers, school counselors, probation workers, recreation leaders, welfare workers, physicians, and hundreds of thousands of others who work directly with children and young people. The rising proportion of youths who come into conflict with the law in America is increasingly seen as symptomatic of the lag in the adaptation of our social institutions to the accelerated pace of changes taking place in industrial American society. Our youth population is rising. Our cities are swollen by the stream of new "migrants" coming from rural and outlying areas of the United States. These developments have caused the delinquency rate to increase, and Americans have become acutely aware of the serious problem it poses to the nation. . . .

Juvenile delinquency is increasing in suburban and rural areas. But it is the "inner city" areas of the large metropolitan centers, harboring the largest concentration of economic deprivation, adult crime, school dropouts, family problems, and cultural deficiencies, that are primarily responsible for the rising rate of delinquency. "Social dynamite" is the term the American educator James B. Conant fittingly used to describe the social and economic pressures which build up in the slum areas of American cities.

In the past decade changes have also occurred in the pattern of juvenile delinquency in the United States. The average age of juveniles coming to the attention of the police has become lower with more young teen-agers being involved with the law. And a growing proportion of youthful crimes are of a violent nature.

[1] From *Juvenile Delinquency Prevention in the United States.* United States Department of Health, Education, and Welfare. Children's Bureau. Supt. of Docs. Washington, D.C. 20402. '65.

Immediately after World War II, delinquency prevention programs were undertaken primarily on a local level by privately supported, youth-serving agencies which attempted to reach out to youth on the streets of the cities to give them help and special services. Then, as the scope of the problem became more evident, city, county, and state governments began to develop new delinquency prevention measures, and a maze of public agencies—courts, police, welfare, schools, recreation departments, etc.—each of which had heretofore operated with only formal relationships to one another, began to attempt to interrelate their preventive activities more closely.

By 1960, it had become generally accepted in the United States that juvenile delinquency is a national problem, calling for national action. This view arose as it became recognized that delinquency is one of the symptoms of broad social and economic changes which cannot be dealt with at the local level alone. The population explosion and internal migration have placed unmanageable pressures on the social institutions which are expected to deal with them.

In addition, automation is changing the character of many businesses and industries. Today's labor market demands more skills and more schooling and offers fewer opportunities for the unskilled worker. Depressed areas in many parts of the country appear next to sections of high prosperity.

These economic facts have important implications for youth. Today the average unemployment rate for sixteen- to nineteen-year-olds is more than three times the unemployment rate for the civilian labor force as a whole. With an estimated 26 million new young workers entering the labor force during the 1960's, youth unemployment has become a major problem. Despite rising levels of education in the United States, it is estimated that one in every three of these new young workers are high school dropouts who are the last to be hired and the first to be fired. This situation is most acute among the children of "new migrants" to the large cities who are compelled by the pressures of poverty and discrimination to live in slum neighborhoods where economic necessity makes many parents antagonistic about older children continuing in school.

In the United States most state laws define as delinquent not only juveniles who violate state and local laws applying to adults (such as assaults, robbery, auto theft, or narcotic offenses) but also juveniles who violate special laws which apply only to youth— such as laws relating to truancy, running away from home, curfew violations, and ungovernable behavior—categories in which there is a wide range of practice in interpretation and enforcement. These special laws, which apply only to youth, account for a large proportion of the juvenile delinquency cases reported in the United States. In 1963, for example, 55 per cent of the referrals to court in the case of girls, and 20 per cent in the case of boys, were for offenses applicable to juveniles only.

Prior to World War II there was a predisposition toward thinking of delinquency as an individual malady of some kind which could be prevented if its causes could be properly diagnosed. This approach called for preventive action which would focus mainly on the individual and groups of individuals and seek to change their behavior by working with them intensively in helping them to adjust to the social institutions and settings in which they lived. In this approach to delinquency prevention, psychology, psychiatry, and intensive social casework played a primary part, although simultaneous efforts were also made to provide needed services for youth.

By the middle 1950's, however, Robert Merton's "theory of deviance" as a relationship between means and ends had led other social scientists to examine the disparity between the success goals generally held in American society and the means available to certain segments of the population for achieving these goals. This concept as it applies to juvenile delinquency was further developed by Albert K. Cohen and others. And within the past decade, particularly as a result of the work of Richard Cloward and Lloyd Ohlin, delinquency prevention theory in the United States has shifted strongly toward a sociological approach which stresses the environmental factors, the importance of changing conditions in the local community so as to provide greater opportunities for youth living in deprived areas to participate successfully in the life of the larger society.

The main target for preventive and corrective action has therefore shifted during the past decade from the individual or the group that exhibits delinquent behavior to the social setting that gives rise to delinquency. Today community facilities—schools, employment services, clinics, youth- and family-serving agencies of all kinds—are striving to reorient their programs so as to remove the barriers to opportunity (such as illiteracy, poor health, lack of job training). These barriers cut off the disadvantaged, deprived and most alienated families of our society from the mainstream of American life. . . .

By the mid-1950's the delinquency prevention effort in virtually every large city was like a huge jigsaw puzzle of services involving important government departments which had heretofore operated with relative independence. The agencies concerned with delinquency prevention included the schools, recreation departments, public housing authorities, public welfare departments giving family service and administering child welfare, private social agencies, and health departments and other medical facilities (including psychiatric hospitals and clinics). The size, shape, strength and position (role in the community) of the various pieces of the delinquency prevention picture varied greatly from one city to another. But weak or strong, large or small, each of these agencies or services invariably represented some indispensable piece which was needed to make the total structure for delinquency prevention intelligible, and it was already becoming evident that these basic services would need to be greatly strengthened and expanded if adequate progress in prevention and control was to be made.

The format for delinquency prevention services varied from city to city partly because the coordinating agency in each city was the one which happened to be the strongest—in Philadelphia it was the Public Welfare Department; in Cleveland it was the Welfare Federation; in Cincinnati it was an independent committee of prominent citizens who set up a special agency. In most large cities, coordination of activities of the major child-serving agencies was recognized as a basic requisite of effective prevention planning, even though it was an ideal which could not yet be realized. . . .

Street Club Work With Hard-to-Serve Youth

It was in the 1950's that the street club work which had begun in Los Angeles and Brooklyn the previous decade was extended to almost every large city in the United States that had delinquent gangs. The techniques which had been developed included the assignment of a "street club worker" to reach out and establish rapport with the members of a gang by creating a generally nonthreatening, useful role for himself with the gang. Once this relationship had been established, the worker was often able to shift the emphasis of the group's behavior by means of his personal ties, and in some cases even to relate the street gang to some social agency program, bringing them under the roof of an agency which was part of the institutional order of society.

Leaders of these prevention programs, however, insisted that their efforts could not be successful unless the various related agencies in the community—welfare, recreational services, police, schools, and also potential employers for the boys—accepted objectives and methods used in street club work and were willing to offer opportunities for these delinquent and predelinquent youngsters.

An unusual example of a preventive program of this kind, which was judged to be highly successful by the community, was one carried on in Cleveland during this period. Here not only was service offered to known gangs of delinquent and predelinquent youngsters, but the city's recreation department cooperated by providing "finders" on the various playgrounds of the city who identified small groups of boys (many of whom were young teen-agers) and then took them to a nearby agency or settlement house which assigned a leader who worked with the group. This particular effort at delinquency prevention in the city of Cleveland was so successful that it resulted in the late 1950's in the elimination of many "name" gangs and the end of gang warfare in that city for a period of several years. But, as in other cities, even so well organized an effort could only serve as a temporary stopgap when underlying social and economic pressures from the influx of migrant families continued to mount.

The attempts to identify problem children at the second- or third-grade level and to meet their problems preventively had been going on for a number of years, but these efforts were taken up widely as a particular approach to delinquency prevention during the late 1950's. Early detection at that time was thought of mostly in connection with the schools.

For example, in Philadelphia, as in a number of other large cities, early identification of hard-to-reach, hard-to-serve children is made possible through the school counseling system. Here the counseling division works at all age levels, identifying children who present problems to the school and to the community. A social work approach is built into the school system, with basic case work functions being offered to children and their parents. Here the counselors use all of the community agencies available to try to work out problems for the child and the family. In support of this general program a central record is kept on every child, with the school working closely with the courts, the police and all social agencies.

Another special service first offered in the late 1950's in an attempt to prevent delinquency was the providing of employment opportunities for deprived out-of-school youth. For example, in Philadelphia, the Welfare Department developed a Youth Conservation Corps, employing young teen-agers full time during the winter to work in parks and to assist in clearing park lands which were being adapted to new uses. In New York, demonstration projects in vocational guidance and employment for teen-agers in high delinquency areas began to appear. In Cincinnati, a citizens' committee organized a job training and placement program for out-of-school youths in high delinquency areas of the city. But these and similar pilot programs, forerunners of massive efforts to come, were scattered and sporadic.

With public concern about delinquency rising, all existing efforts appeared insufficient. There were many gaps in the types of services offered in any one city. And above all, the need for greater communication and coordination of effort between child-serving agencies was becoming painfully evident.

It was partly as a result of this situation that city youth commissions, most of them designed specifically to promote joint planning and coordination between related agencies in delinquency prevention, began to emerge. By 1960, approximately ten such commissions had been formed in large urban centers and about an equal number in smaller cities. Most of these commissions were supported by public funds. . . .

On May 11, 1961, President John F. Kennedy launched a new movement to curb juvenile delinquency. He established the President's Committee on Juvenile Delinquency and Youth Crime. The attorney general was named chairman of the committee, and the secretary of Labor and the secretary of Health, Education, and Welfare were its other two members. The President's action reflected the growing concern of the nation about the steady growth of youth crime, and the related problems of school failures, school dropouts and youth unemployment. It signified that the Federal Government would now accept greater responsibility in finding creative and effective solutions to juvenile delinquency in partnership with local communities. Joining the forces of three major departments of the Federal Government to coordinate their efforts in delinquency prevention and control dramatized the urgency of the problem and the necessity for agencies on every level of government (state, county and local) to close ranks in a new revitalized attack on delinquency. . . .

Outlook for the Future

The experiences of the past decade in developing approaches to delinquency prevention in the United States have sharpened our view to the nature of the problem which confronts us, and what must be done to meet this problem.

There has been increasing doubt in the United States about the validity of the term "juvenile delinquency" (as presently defined in this country) in the context of the dynamic changes in our society which have been taking place since the end of World War II. Over the past twenty years, the social structures have not been changing rapidly enough to supply the kinds and amounts of service needed by millions of "new migrants" who have streamed into our cities from outlying and rural areas. Reviewing the roster of unmet needs of disadvantaged and deprived youth today, it appears to be the social structures rather than the youth which have been "delinquent," and the volume and kinds of deviant behavior on the part of youth, particularly those found in large American cities, are understandable.

The question has been raised as to whether perhaps delinquency should be defined as those offenses which apply also to adults, and that other offenses relating only to children which come under present juvenile court laws should be considered as behavioral problems. Already in our official statistics we are classifying separately behavioral offenses applicable to juveniles only, such as running away, truancy, and curfew violations.

More important is the emergence of the new term "youth development," which sums up the approach to delinquency prevention which is most prevalent today in the United States. This term refers to the wide range of remedial and assimilative activities and programs which are going forward with hundreds of thousands of disadvantaged youth in the United States today. Hundreds of millions of dollars are being spent in these programs for remedial education, personal guidance, job training, job counseling, job development and placement, rehabilitation of health, dental care, improvement of social and communication skills, and other youth development activities. Such programs are being conducted in schools, employment services, welfare departments, recreation departments, and other youth-serving agencies in city slums, poverty-stricken rural areas, Indian reservations, and other settings. The social structures which are largely responsible for the socialization of youth (outside the home) are in the process of being remolded into patterns which fit the needs of youth who today are outside the mainstream of American life. . . .

The fragmentary, partial and intermittent approaches to delinquency prevention which marked early efforts are being rejected in favor of providing a complete gamut of services to low income families in high delinquency areas. The Mobilization for Youth program . . . has its counterpart in variations found in . . . [over sixty] cities and rural areas which are attempting to provide a comprehensive set of services to low income families. Services to children and youth are included in this constellation of programs. Not only youth but adults who have long been considered "unemployable" are being given help of all kinds—taught to read, fitted with eyeglasses, or given other needed help—and trained specifically for placement in jobs in which there are known shortages of labor. . . . Under the concept of "comprehensiveness" juvenile delinquency prevention is being broadly approached on the assumption that families, as well as children and youth, must be brought into the mainstream of American life if youthful crime is to be prevented.

MOBILIZATION FOR YOUTH PROJECT [2]

From a dismal, gray-streaked building in a lower east side slum, New York's Mobilization for Youth has been waging one of the strongest attacks on juvenile delinquency this country has seen. The battlefields are sixty-seven blocks of lower east side tenements crammed with over one hundred thousand people. Mobilization for Youth, first conceived in 1958 and in full swing since 1962, is fighting the root causes of delinquency—poverty and discrimination— in the slums where they breed. Since its beginning, Mobilization has become the pilot program for projects in nineteen cities across the country. . . .

"This is a battle we've got to win," veteran James McCarthy, Mobilization's Administrative Director, said recently. "What we do and learn is as important to the rest of the nation as it is to us."

McCarthy looked out of his office window at the teeming streets below. The melting pot for the poor of many nations and colors, this is a tough and noisy neighborhood, enlivened by pushcarts piled with used clothing, delicatessens festooned with salami, pizza parlors serving knishes, store-front churches and settlement houses.

There are the Bowery bums drifting over to rifle ash cans and sleep in doorways; the street corner baseball diamonds overrun with traffic; the cramped black asphalt playgrounds walled with hurricane wire fencing and signs reading: NO bicycle riding, NO roller skating, NO dogs allowed, NO peddling.

[2] From "We Can Beat J.D.," by Homer Page, free-lance writer. *Parents' Magazine.* 39: 56-8+. O. '64. Reprinted by permission.

And there is poverty and delinquency. McCarthy was thinking about that.

Over a million kids under eighteen [he continued] were arrested in this country last year. . . . The human cost is beyond calculation. We can only wonder about the future of a nation with millions of its teen-agers in the hands of the law before they are old enough to vote.

At Mobilization, we don't believe that pushing around tough kids is the answer to delinquency. All of us here are tired of seeing troubled kids go through the revolving doors of the social service system only to end up in reform schools, mental hospitals and detention homes.

So we attack the things that make the kids this way. We use the resources of this entire neighborhood to get at the guts of the problem. That means working with parents, schools, businessmen, unions and other social outfits to get these kids immediate and sustained help. You might say we try to help them have a chance at the American dream. If we don't succeed, they—and we—may find ourselves in an American nightmare.

Big Jim McCarthy knows what he is talking about. In the days when gangs used to fight with their fists, Big Jim's 190-pound frame was a weight to be reckoned with on the streets of New Haven. Later, after finishing at Notre Dame and Fordham, Big Jim worked for the New York Welfare Council, infiltrating two of Harlem's worst gangs. In 1957, after ten years with the Youth Board, he left to join the early studies that led to Mobilization for Youth, which is supported by the President's Committee on Juvenile Delinquency and Youth Crime, the National Institute of Mental Health, the City of New York and the Ford Foundation.

Big Jim is flanked by two other Mobilization directors, Dr. Richard Cloward, Director of Research, whose theories provided the foundation for the project, and George Brager, Director of Action Programs. Brager, a man who prefers action to words, gets to the point fast.

What's the swamp around here? Poverty. And what's the answer to poverty? Work. When we first opened the doors of our Job Center we were flooded. We figured twelve hundred kids would apply for jobs in the first year. Actually, over thirteen hundred came in the first six months. We scrambled around like the devil to keep them from going away disappointed.

That old saw about laggard youth—especially in poverty pockets like this—just hasn't proved true. What they wanted were jobs, not a lot of printed forms and fancy talk. To them, just like anyone else, a job meant social status. Soon they were crossing gang lines to come in, and looking on the program as something to protect—not wreck.

One of the boys who applied at the Job Center was Joseph Green. As a ranking member of a neighborhood gang, at first Joe took a dim view of the whole proposition, preferring to play it cool. Besides, Joe had already tried waiting in the halls of employment agencies, standing in line and filling out endless forms for jobs that didn't exist. Joe was tuned to failure, and playing it cool, he felt, was a good way to side-step the problem. Just the same, he needed a job, bad. So when word got around that the Job Center meant business, Joe moved over to survey the scene, and eased in one day. He was handed a numbered card and then sauntered into a big room with several chairs, couches and coffee tables scattered about. A few boys and girls were there, reading magazines as they waited for their numbers to be called. At the end of the room, a secretary was talking to a youngster and filling out his registration form. That sold Joe. Ever since dropping out of school, he had been privately ashamed of his poor writing and spelling. Filling out forms panicked him.

"Man," Joe said later, "that secretary was real fine. She didn't ask too many questions and she typed out that card real neat. She got me an appointment with this counselor who turned out to be a right guy. I walked out of that place feeling pretty good."

Like Joe Green (a real boy, though that isn't his real name), 90 per cent of the youngsters who come to the Job Center are school dropouts. They are gang members, parolees and just kids in need of work. Their counselors spend a minimum of time interviewing and testing them. If a youngster is capable of holding down a full-time, competitive job—and only one in ten is—he can be assigned work from the job file that the Center is busy building up. If not, he can join one of the Mobilization subsidized work projects, called the Urban Youth Service Corps, which turns out furniture and clothing, renovates stores and buildings, or finds work for the boys and girls in hospitals and offices.

For example, there are four crews which paint buildings, rebuild interiors or improve playgrounds. On each crew, the kids get practical experience under a skilled foreman. Not a social worker. The foreman is interested in putting out a good piece of work on time, not in coddling kids. And he has authority. He can dock any kid who shows up late, and he can reward good work on a pay scale ranging from $1.00 to $1.25 an hour.

The kids soon realize that this is no hand-out; it's a job. They like the idea that Mobilization will help them if they help themselves. In fact, it was the boys, themselves, who made the rule docking late arrivals on the job.

Some of the most successful work projects are the brain-children of Dr. Mel Herman, who runs the Work Program. Herman doesn't seem to care much for regular social agency rules.

When I first came up with the idea of buying and running a luncheonette [he recalls] some of the staff gently suggested I'd been working too hard lately. They wanted to know if I expected the kids to handle the cash and work all day next to open shelves stacked with candy and cigarettes. "Precisely," I said. They were ready to take me quietly away until they found that it worked.

The luncheonette now hums merrily along with 2,500 weekly customers. It pays for itself and four experienced personnel, while Mobilization, as on other projects, pays the wages of the nine youngsters working there. Recently, a congresswoman took a grass-roots sampling at the luncheonette. She asked a boy behind the counter how he liked the work and if he had learned anything. "Yes, ma'm," he answered on both counts. "Next week I start as an assistant cook at the Americana." That happens to be one of New York's luxury hotels.

As the result of another Herman brain-child, Mobilization leases and runs a twenty-four-hour gas station on Houston Street. Elmer Williams, crack mechanic and foreman of the ten-boy crew, says with a hint of pride that, so far, accounts have balanced.

I expect these kids to toe the line [he says]. At the same time, I got to remember they're just kids. For instance, we're missing one screwdriver. But I must admit, if I was a kid, I might have thought about securing it. It was a new jazzy type with a reversible shaft. Just the same, when I find out who took it, he gets his pay docked. Maybe double.

Funny what a job does for a kid. Take that big, blond guy washing the car. He left automotive high school to bail out the family when his father died. He wasn't here a month before he found out how little he really knew about car mechanics. We got him back into school at night and kept him on the job at the same time. One day, he'll be a good mechanic working on his own.

Since an apprentice mechanic soon finds he has to know how to read a manual to get ahead, or a young waitress learns she must add swiftly and accurately to hold a job, Mobilization backs them up with help in subjects they may need. When ready, they move out of the fully-subsidized work program to job training where Mobilization splits the cost of wages with the new employer for a few months until the youngster can pull his own weight. Then he is hired like the next man. When the Work Program is in full stride, it will have about 220 youngsters on subsidized work, about 300 on job training, and a turnover of about 2,000 a year.

The unions, well aware of the danger of having 700,000 youngsters in this country out of school and out of work, are sympathetic to Mobilization's job program. The UAW, the Teamsters and the Clerical Union have given their support to the program. Five locals of the ILGWU have contributed $4,000 to purchase machines for a sewing center, and their membership is represented on the center's Advisory Committee. The Lavenburg-Corner House Foundation has put up $20,000 for training at public trade schools.

Mobilization's work program is backed up by an education and neighborhood program. Each attack is directed toward a different aspect of delinquency, but all apply the same principles. All are ready to improvise, should some aspect of this plan prove ineffective. They strive to follow through on each case without becoming simply do-good handholders.

Especially important in the development of Mobilization's program was a theoretical basis for action as presented by Dr. Richard Cloward and Dr. Lloyd Ohlin in their book *Delinquency and Opportunity*. The authors point out that the kinds of opportunities available to youngsters largely determine whether or not they are forced into delinquent behavior. They see racial discrimination and poverty as the basic causes of restricted opportunity. These ideas have already set the pace for community action proposals in the President's poverty bill.

Rehabilitation programs for youngsters [Dr. Cloward explained] have had a tendency to concentrate on the casualties, such as school dropouts. At Mobilization, we want to draw attention to some of the underlying facts of delinquency. You cannot solve the delinquency problem unless you do something about total unemployment. Nor can you solve the delinquency problem unless you do something about the homes, neighborhoods and schools in areas like this. If you want people to behave differently, you must provide them with the opportunities.

Mobilization's Education Program has worked to knit the homes and lives of the children more closely to the classroom, as well as to educate teachers to the particular problems of the poor. Teachers have visited the homes of all the children in their classes. Though at first many of them were apprehensive about walking into the tenements, for mostly they were middle-class women who had never seen slum apartments, they soon learned that the poor can be quite as gracious and hospitable as anyone else.

In school, as Dr. Abe Tannenbaum, Coordinator of the Education Program, explained:

Ungraded primary classes were formed (grouping the first three grades together), to give slow starters a chance to get on their feet before entering fourth grade, instead of holding them back and conditioning them to failure. Also problems and stories have been designed for these youngsters —material which has something to do with their lives, instead of the Dick-and-Jane-have-a-large-house-and-a-nice-dog approach.

Homework helpers are another way of giving more attention to children who need it. The homework helpers are chosen from the upper third of high-school students, and are paid to tutor younger children after school. This scheme, like others, works two ways. It helps and encourages the children and it gives prestige to the tutors. Conceivably the tutor could replace the gang leader as someone to admire and emulate.

Job and education programs are still not enough. Slum families need day-to-day help. Not long ago, a teacher phoned Dom Sala-mack, a Mobilization caseworker, to tell him that three children from a single family had not attended school in weeks.

I went to the apartment immediately [Dom recounts]. There, I found the mother, Mrs. Sanders, badly shaken by the recent death of her husband. She had delusions that he was talking to her. Her apartment was in good order and the children were neatly dressed. She was keeping them safely at home because, she said, her husband had told her to do so.

I called in our psychiatrist who felt that Mrs. Sanders could be treated at home. That way, we could hold the family together. Then, I made arrangements to take the kids to and from school and for a homemaker—one of the capable neighborhood women we hire—to come and help out.

But Dom arrived too late the following day to prevent a grim scene from unfolding. A policeman had already taken Mrs. Sanders to Magistrate's Court because of her truant children. The magistrate talked to the woman, discovered her delusions, and committed her to the psychiatric ward at Bellevue Hospital for observation. The children were sent to a center run by the city.

Dom's psychiatrist conferred with the Bellevue doctor and, at the final hearing, Dom and his doctor succeeded in getting the commitment, originally recommended for six months, reduced to six weeks.

"But we could have saved that family from being broken up and institutionalized at all," Dom says, "if only we could have gotten everybody together in time."

This case is representative of those handled every day by social workers at the four Mobilization Neighborhood Service Centers. These Centers are located directly on the street in storefronts scattered throughout the neighborhood. Their doors are always open to anyone who wants to walk in and visit or talk about a problem. And problems range from the outpouring of a child about to run away from home to a discussion of rat control. Workers can recount any number of rat stories. One of the pleasanter of these involves a mother who, unable to cope with the rats infesting her apartment, began to feed them so they would not bite her baby. The caseworker's quick and practical first step was to send a cat over right away.

Margaret Shea, who directs the Service Centers, says:

Thirty years ago, when I started social work, we went out and helped the poor. Then the profession became more specialized and more remote. Now we have come full circle back to the poor. We think the best social worker is a very good neighbor who believes people are entitled to respect and brings skill and compassion to their problems. We try not to do anything for these people. We try to do it with them.

Social workers at the Centers concentrate on solving families' immediate practical problems, realizing that this will lighten their emotional burdens, as well. When they assign a homemaker to the job of helping a housewife organize her chores, budget her scarce dollars and join a mothers' baby-sitting club, they perform tangible services and also ease emotional strains. When tenants are helped to deal with authorities about an exorbitant rent increase, they take a step away from the helplessness that keeps the lower fringes of the poor in a state of social starvation. . . .

Helping the poor presents Mobilization with some sticky problems.

Some slumlords [Big Jim McCarthy says] are not going to jump for joy when they find their tenants—who were easy to intimidate before—are now informed of their rights. Neither are other local powers likely to be happy to find Mobilization encouraging more poor people to exercise their voting franchise. However, since the residents are going to have to solve their problems eventually, the more they know, the better. We hope to see them discussing election issues that bear on their lives, and encourage them to register; we don't care which party.

New York City's Mobilization for Youth has been the first of the truly forceful attempts to meet the urgent needs of urban slum dwellers. Now, nationwide, the United States Department of Labor has planned a national network of Youth Opportunity Centers in one hundred and five cities to provide education, job training, guidance—and work—for disadvantaged young people. And recently the White House has announced a $1.5 million grant to Mobilization, in recognition of its effectiveness "in several major areas in attacking the roots of juvenile delinquency."

THE DELINQUENT AND THE LAW [3]

Despite all the forces making for peace and lawkeeping in a well-organized community, some youngsters will break loose and commit acts which bring them to the attention of the police. Such an act may be relatively minor: Boy Scouts waking the neighborhood on their way home from a troop meeting. Or it may be far more serious: a gang of young hoodlums attacking a man in a park, stealing his wallet, and beating him up or even killing him. In between lies a vast range of other acts which make a child or teen-

[3] From Public Affairs Pamphlet no 337, by Ruth and Edward Brecher, free-lance writers. Public Affairs Committee. 381 Park Ave. S. New York 10016. '62. Copyright © 1962 by the Public Affairs Committee, Inc. Reprinted by permission.

ager an object of police concern. The police become involved in one of two ways:

(1) Someone phones in a complaint and a police officer is sent to investigate.

(2) A policeman actually observes the act and intervenes.

In either case, there follows a scene of crucial significance: a face-to-face confrontation between the policeman, representing the forces of law and order, and youngsters who have transgressed or are thought to have transgressed. . . . In the course of each contact with a child, the policeman must decide what action to take. Four main courses of action are open:

First, he may "adjust" a minor matter himself by talking it over with the children or young people concerned, then writing a brief report on the incident, and bearing it in mind in case the same problem or the same individuals come to his attention again.

Second, he may call the problem to the attention of some other agency. . . .

Third, he may call the matter to the attention of the child's family. In some cases, he may also suggest to the parents that they seek help from some other agency.

Fourth, he may bring the matter to the attention of the juvenile court.

In the past, and in a very few backward jurisdictions today, the police make use of a fifth alternative: they "lock the little hoodlums up" in the precinct station or even in the county jail.

Both authorities on child behavior and thoughtful police officials universally condemn this *lock-'em-up* approach to juvenile delinquency for a wide variety of reasons.

In the first place, it is illegal and in most cases unconstitutional. Under American law, an accused person is deemed innocent until proven guilty. Detention and punishment are *judicial* rather than police functions; the police force which takes punishment into its own hands is usurping the role of the judge. The law protects adults from illegal detention in a variety of ways: the right of habeas corpus, the right to counsel, the right to bail, the right to recover from the police for false arrest. A police force alert to the rights of juveniles, and a community alert to the importance of sound police procedures are the child's best protection against unwarranted or unlawful detention by the police.

In the second place, authorities are agreed that the use of police detention as a form of punishment for juvenile delinquency doesn't work. The central goal in the treatment of delinquents is to help them grow into useful, law-abiding adult citizens. Many methods aimed at this goal have been developed and are discussed below. Far from contributing toward the healthful maturing of a young person, the slapdash use of detention as a punishment cure-all actually defeats the helpful effect of other measures. The police, and the forces of law and order generally, become identified as "the enemy" in the child's mind. Once released, moreover, the detained child takes on a new prestige as a leader in neighborhood delinquency. "I'll bet you told those blankety-blank coppers where to get off," his companions comment admiringly while he struts.

The misuse of detention as a form of punishment by the police is likely to be particularly harmful where the place of detention is a jail or police lockup. There contacts between children and hard-ened adult offenders are quite likely to occur. "Come see me at Joe's when we get out and I'll give you the real lowdown," is an invita-tion likely to be heard again and again. But even if under-age offenders are segregated in jails from adults, another set of evils follows. Detained children are then at the mercy of the tougher, older, juvenile delinquents who may abuse them mentally, phys-ically, or even sexually—without even the presence of adult pris-oners to intervene in their behalf. Suicides and murders are not unknown under such circumstances. Finally, locking a child up all alone—in solitary confinement—is a cruel and inhuman punish-ment which cannot be too roundly condemned.

Police detention, moreover, is almost certain to be capricious. The police officer can know very little about the inner roots of a child's misbehavior when he picks him up on the street and locks him up; and there simply is not room in the jails, police lockups, and detention centers for all the children who come to the attention of the police each day. Hence, while some unfortunates are detained, countless others—some of whom may be in need of much more intensive treatment—are given a tongue-lashing, a lecture, and a little table-pounding, and then turned loose. This procedure may help a poorly trained police officer to let off steam; but it doesn't really reform the child's behavior or affect the community's underlying delinquency problem. Well-trained police officers are aware of this and do not place undue reliance on either "locking 'em up" or "bawling 'em out." They know that more effective procedures are available.

Some children, it is true, do need to be detained in secure quarters immediately, on an emergency basis—for their own protection or that of society. But with children as with adults the law specifies and common sense dictates that this must be a *judicial* rather than a police decision. Indeed, decisions with respect to the detention constitute one of the primary functions of the juvenile court. To see just how this works in a well-organized community, let's examine the court's role in the handling of delinquency.

Juvenile Courts

Throughout the United States, legislatures have established specialized juvenile courts for the handling of juvenile delinquency and other matters affecting the welfare of children. These courts, though they vary widely from jurisdiction to jurisdiction and from judge to judge, have one common goal: to help every child, and especially delinquent, neglected, and dependent children, grow into a competent, self-reliant, law-abiding adult citizen.

The philosophy of the juvenile court—and an increasing number of adult courts as well—is not centered on the concept of *punishment* for criminal acts, but rather on *treatment*—the kind of treatment most likely to assist the processes of healthy growth toward law-abiding maturity.

The juvenile court seeks to accomplish this goal in many ways. In the first place, it maintains close contact with other community agencies—the schools, social agencies, youth groups, churches, recreation programs. It can and often does call on these agencies for assistance. Where a child's delinquent behavior appears to have grown out of the family conditions in his home, for example, the problems may be referred by the court to a family service agency.

Where a gang of youngsters is repeatedly getting into trouble in a neighborhood lacking recreation facilities or adult leadership, the juvenile court may move through its contacts with appropriate agencies to fill the lack.

A well-organized juvenile court, moreover, has its own staff, made up of men and women skilled in the problems of children and young people; these men and women are usually called *probation officers*, and have several basic functions.

They are the eyes and ears of the court, assigned the task of investigating fully the background of each child brought to the court's attention. Their "social investigation" is not concerned primarily with questions of guilt or innocence, or with the precise legal nature of the child's act; such matters are generally the subject of the police officer's investigation and report. The probation officer's investigation is instead concerned with the child's essential character, his needs, his attitudes, and the circumstances in his family and environment that caused him to deviate from the community pattern.

At a later stage, the probation officer is the effective arm of the court in carrying out the treatment decided upon. This often involves the supervision for a period of many months or even several years of the child who has been "placed on probation" by the court. Skilled probation officers play many roles in their work with delinquent children; they may be counselors, or authority figures, or helping "big brothers," or ideals upon whom the child tends to model himself—all depending upon the needs and circumstances of the particular child in question.

The judge, of course, is the central figure in the court. It is he who decides what form of treatment shall be administered. Before deciding, he hears the story from the child himself, his parents, and others familiar with the child's behavior. He also studies the police report and the probation officer's investigation report. He may arrange, in appropriate cases, for a psychological or psychiatric examination of the child. The juvenile court judge is also the policy-deciding head of the investigation-detention-probation system.

Just as the great majority of illnesses can be treated without hospitalization of the sick person, so the great majority of children brought to the attention of the juvenile court can be and in many places are handled without detaining the child or committing him to an institution. But just as some illnesses require emergency hospitalization and others require long-term treatment in an institution, so some delinquent children need to be taken out of the home-school-neighborhood environment where their delinquency developed and given intensive short-term or long-term treatment in an institution established for the purpose—a state training school, for example.

This is a decision for the judge to make; in part because he is by law the official empowered to reach such decisions, and in part because as a practical matter he alone is in a position to bring together the information available from so many sources.

In this picture of the juvenile court, the policeman has two important functions.

First, he is in the great majority of cases the official who first brings the child to the attention of the court.

Second, his report supplies the court with all the relevant information he has obtained concerning the child and his behavior.

In many cities and counties, let us confess at once, the juvenile court does not live up to the picture we have painted. Often it is seriously understaffed, lacking the probation officers, social workers, and psychiatric consultants needed for effective operation. Sometimes the judge is a part-time appointee, uninterested in juvenile problems and unsuited to his role. Many courts lack essential facilities—a well-designed, well-staffed detention center for the emergency care of delinquents who must be detained, for example, or various clinic services to which the child can be referred.

In such cases, the court stumbles along without really solving children's problems. The police, as a result, may experience frustration, and feel that their efforts to enforce the law are thwarted. You can hardly blame them. They see the juvenile court as a mere paper institution, and complain that "if I take that brat to court, he'll be back on my beat before I am," or that "that old judge doesn't know what he's doing; when I pick up a young punk all he does is take away his library card."

The moral of such remarks points directly to the principle with which we began: a police force by itself cannot curb juvenile delinquency. A sound school system, sound social agencies, and above all a sound juvenile court are also needed. Sometimes the greatest single step a community can take in improving police services to juveniles lies not in reforming the police force at all, but in improving its juvenile court or other agencies so that the police can resume their proper, important, but limited, role in the total delinquency program.

If you are evaluating the work of your own community's police force in handling juvenile problems, remember that it does not function in isolation. The police officer is one member of a team which centers around the juvenile court and involves the entire community. Delinquency crises may not be the fault of the police; a weak spot anywhere can destroy the whole team's effectiveness.

JUSTICE FOR JUVENILES [4]

The legal profession has been engaged in more than one revolution during the past decade. And a new one is beginning now. The spark was Morris Kent, a seriously disturbed Negro boy of sixteen, who in 1961 was picked up for housebreaking, robbery and rape. He was brought before the then only juvenile court judge in Washington, D.C., who, according to the statutes and cases in my jurisdiction, was supposed to give Morris "care," "concern" and "adequate and suitable treatment." But these fine principles sound false in the real world of the nation's capital. The juvenile court judge was in an impossible situation. Here was a lad "seriously disturbed," desperately in need of professional care and treatment, and yet, as Judge Lawson who was appointed to our Juvenile Court after the *Kent* case was later to say, we simply "don't have a place in the community for this type of child." Well, this was the problem for the juvenile court judge in the *Kent* case. And he chose a rather ingenious solution. He washed his hands of the whole sorry mess and "waived" his jurisdiction to the adult criminal courts.

[4] From article by David L. Bazelon, Chief Judge of the United States Court of Appeals for the District of Columbia Circuit. *New Republic.* 156:14-16. Ap. 22, '67. Reprinted by permission of *The New Republic,* copyright 1967, Harrison-Blaine of New Jersey, Inc.

Morris stood trial as an adult criminal and the jury found him guilty of the housebreaking and robbery charges, although it acquitted him by reason of insanity on the rape charges. The criminal court judge sent him to a mental institution until he recovered his sanity, after which he was to serve a sentence of thirty to ninety years.

My own Court of Appeals affirmed the conviction and sentence even though, as one of my colleagues frankly put it, "it [was] a fair inference from the record before us that one of the reasons why the Juvenile Court waived jurisdiction was because [Morris] was seriously disturbed and the Juvenile Court lacked facilities adequately to treat him." To me, it was "shocking that a child was subjected to prosecution and punishment as a criminal because he was thought to suffer from a serious mental or emotional disturbance."

At first, Morris' lawyer asked my Court of Appeals to rehear the case, but then he decided to seek immediate review by the Supreme Court. At the time, observers thought his chances were rather slim. Since Illinois established the nation's first juvenile court at the turn of the century, the Supreme Court had never reviewed a case coming from any children's court. But the Supreme Court agreed to hear Kent's case. For the first time in more than sixty years of juvenile courts, the Supreme Court of the United States decided to look into the record of a juvenile proceeding. The Justices opened the door cautiously, and, judging from their opinion, they recoiled from what they saw within:

While there can be no doubt of the original laudable purpose of the juvenile courts, studies and critiques in recent years raise serious questions as to whether actual performance measures well enough against theoretical purpose to make tolerable the immunity of the process from the reach of constitutional guarantees applicable to adults. . . . There is evidence, in fact, that there may be grounds for concern that the child receives the worst of both worlds; that he gets neither the protections accorded to adults nor the solicitous care and regenerative treatment postulated for children.

What are the legal justifications for our juvenile court system?

All of us know those two Latin words *parens patriae*. But what does that phrase really mean? *Black's Law Dictionary* tells us that *parens patriae* refers to "the sovereign power of guardianship [of the state] over persons under disability such as minors, and insane and incompetent persons." Unfortunately, for sixty years courts have been using that phrase as if it were the answer. The judge closes his eyes, waves his magic gavel, intones the magic phrase, and the problems go away. Well, they don't.

A chief difficulty with discussing the justification for juvenile courts is that they deal with so many different kinds of children: children who have committed antisocial offenses; children who are neglected or abandoned; children who are disturbed or "beyond parental control," and the like. There are nine different categories in the District of Columbia. Some jurisdictions provide different labels for these categories. New York, for example, classifies children as "neglected," "delinquent" or "in need of supervision." The law of the District of Columbia makes no distinction whatever although, in practice, the juvenile court classifies children as "dependent" or "delinquent." It is understandable, then, that judges and scholars have suggested different justifications for society's right to deal with the child at all.

First, there are those who think that the function of a juvenile court is to punish. According to these people, a child, like an adult, who commits an antisocial act, should be held responsible for it unless he can show that he has some kind of mental condition which excuses him from responsibility. This is the position taken by Justice Oliphant of the New Jersey Supreme Court. He says, in one of his opinions:

> A peaceful citizen has the right to be protected by his government, and to have a spade called a spade, and if young hoodlums are mentally incapable of a criminal intent they should be put to the burden of establishing that proposition in a court of law under established rules and are only entitled as a matter of right to the constitutional guarantees afforded to other citizens.

I do not say that a juvenile court cannot or should not ever undertake to "punish" children, although I think that is an extremely narrow view of the problem. And, of course, it completely ignores the neglected child or the child who is "beyond parental control"—children who may be deeply disturbed but who surely are not "young hoodlums." But regardless of whether juvenile courts should sometimes punish children, it is evident that punishment is not the central justification for the juvenile courts as they exist today. If it were the central concern, we wouldn't need juvenile courts at all. We would need only a few more criminal court judges and some extra cells in the adult jails.

There are others who suggest that our juvenile courts exist to protect society. In the large view, I cannot quarrel with this concept. If we succeed in helping the child, we will have made our society safer also. Unfortunately, too much talk about protection ignores the element of treatment and rehabilitation. Then protection means nothing more than getting the child out of the way, getting him off the streets. If we are going to follow Justice Oliphant's advice and call a spade a spade, I'd like to call this particular spade preventive detention. Without discussing the constitutional or moral objections to preventive detention, I think I can assert with some confidence that it is not, nor does anyone claim it is, the only or even the primary purpose of our juvenile courts. Here, again, if removal from the streets were the goal, the criminal courts could provide the solution just as quickly and perhaps more effectively than a juvenile court, which is restricted to essentially nonpunitive processes and whose jurisdiction is limited by the happenstance of the child's birthdate.

It is only when we turn to the treatment and rehabilitation of the child that we approach a satisfactory justification for our juvenile courts, at least as they exist today. I do not mean that punishment and safety are not factors to be considered, but I do claim that standing alone they do not and cannot provide suitable underpinning for our present system. The central justification for assuming jurisdiction over a child in an informal, nonadversary proceeding is the promise to treat him according to his needs.

We look around us and see that promise broken at every turn. It is full of cant and hypocrisy. And yet, it is made to do double duty. It is used to justify the informal nonadversary procedures of the juvenile court; used again to justify the child's confinement.

The Denial of Due Process

The Supreme Court now has a case dealing with a boy from Arizona, Gerald Gault. Gerald and a friend were supposed to have made a lewd telephone call to a neighbor. While his mother was at work, a probation officer took him into custody and questioned him. His mother returned home that evening, and neighbors told her that her son was "detained." She went to the detention home where the officer told her that a hearing would be held the following day. The hearing was held in the judge's chambers and no record of the proceedings was made. There was no lawyer. The neighbor did not testify, although, seemingly, Gerald admitted placing the call. When asked what section of the law Gerald had violated, the officer stated, "We set no specific charge in it, other than delinquency." There is considerable doubt about the judge's ultimate determination. At one point, he thought Gerald's calls amounted to a breach of the peace, elsewhere he said Gerald was "habitually involved in immoral matters"—a phrase used in Arizona's juvenile court statute—and again he stated there was "probably another ground, too."

Probably not a single justice of the peace in this country would permit an adult to be convicted in such a proceeding. According to the briefs and allegations in the Supreme Court, almost every ingredient of the civilized procedures and safeguards which we refer to as due process of law was missing: Gerald did not have notice of the charges, he did not have an opportunity to confront and cross-examine the witnesses against him, he did not have counsel, he was not warned of any privilege against self-incrimination, no appellate review was provided, and the lack of a transcript made subsequent review of what actually happened virtually impossible. I understand that juvenile proceedings are not criminal proceedings and that these procedures and safeguards are not necessarily applicable. It is important to notice, though, that the Arizona Supreme Court sought to justify these shortcuts because of the promise to treat the child. This is from the Arizona court:

We are aware of the tide of criticism inundating juvenile proceedings. The major complaint deals with the informal, nonadversary procedure for determining delinquency rather than the treatment rendered after a finding of delinquency. On the other hand, juvenile courts do not exist to punish children for their transgressions against society. The juvenile court stands in the position of a protecting parent rather than a prosecutor. It is an effort to substitute protection and guidance for punishment, to withdraw the child from criminal jurisdiction and use social sciences regarding the study of human behavior which permit flexibilities within the procedures. The aim of the court is to provide individualized justice for children. Whatever the formulation, the purpose is to provide authoritative treatment for those who are no longer responding to the normal restraints the child should receive at the hands of his parents.

[The Supreme Court decision in the *Gault* case is reported in the next selection.—Ed.]

I do not find it objectionable to deprive the child of some procedural safeguards if the individualized treatment he is supposed to get requires the sacrifice and if the new procedures are reasonably fair. We should not blind ourselves, though, to what individualized treatment in our juvenile courts really is.

Blindness and Insensitivity

In the District of Columbia, for example, the juvenile court is overloaded with work. We have too few judges, too few supporting personnel, too few public institutions, and too few dollars. Last year, 10,000 delinquent children had their cases heard by a juvenile court judge in Washington. We have only three of these judges, so each judge had about 3,500 cases, about 14 a day. You can readily understand why 85 per cent of the children "waived counsel" and "acknowledged" their involvement. With a caseload of 14 per day, the juvenile judge simply cannot take the time to hold trials.

If our blindness extended only to these formal procedural matters, our juvenile court system would probably be in decent shape. But, in fact, blindness and insensitivity pervade the whole system. A short while ago, a Negro girl named Betty Jean from the slums of Washington was brought before the juvenile court. Her attorney asked for a psychiatric examination. He submitted the following facts: His client had commenced sexual relations at the age of ten; she was the mother of an illegitimate child; she was raped by a neighborhood boy at the age of sixteen; she had nightmares and saw people staring at her when the lights were out. A physician who had treated her from time to time added the opinion that Betty Jean was "known . . . to have been a disturbed child since early childhood" and that she needed "nothing short of a complete psychiatric study." The juvenile judge recognized that, under the law, he had discretion to provide for such an examination and that the community had hospitals available for this purpose. But he did not. Here is why:

> Such experiences are far from being uncommon among children in her socioeconomic situation with the result that the traumatic effect may be expected to be far less than it would be in the case of a child raised by parents and relatives with different habits and customs.

So, sexual activity at the age of ten—rape at sixteen—are "far from being uncommon" in the slums, and Betty Jean's experiences would not touch her as deeply as they would others, and so the judge can deny her access to a psychiatrist.

Different people *may* be affected differently by the same experiences. But the insensitivity of the judge's statement and similar statements amaze me. And the statement contains an internal contradiction which wrenches the whole system. . . .

For the purpose of denying her a psychiatrist, the judge saw that Betty Jean was a Negro from the slums; but for the purpose of putting her away, he did not, or would not, see the same thing. For that purpose Betty Jean might as well have been a white middle-class child from the suburbs, for it was white middle-class suburban values to which the judge was asking her to respond. Suburban children do not appear regularly before our juvenile courts. It is not that there is no delinquency in the suburbs, or that these children have no problems. But they have families and communities which are interested. And effective or not, at least they care and make the attempt. Betty Jean is the kind of girl we must deal with in the courts. And if we recognize that she is what she is for some purposes, how can we ignore that fact for other purposes?

I do not know how to make that promise to treat a child according to her needs a reality, and perhaps nobody does. But I do know that the first step is to awaken our consciousness to the fact that there is a promise. The people who are on the inside, running our receiving homes, and training schools, and prisons and hospitals, know that things are radically wrong, but they will not speak out. And the people on the outside do not want to see the truth, so they go through elaborate rituals in order to blind themselves. . . .

Learning What the Facts Are

We judges are a resourceful lot, and there are numerous legal doctrines we can use, and do use, every day to avoid seeing what is before us. Not many months ago, a Federal judge in California received a hand-written complaint from a prisoner in a state institution. Such complaints are common and often without foundation in fact. And courts have adopted a shorthand method of ridding themselves of such matters. In the ordinary judicial opinion one reads that such complaints touch matters of "internal discipline" and that the courts cannot deal with these problems. Something in this particular pleading struck the judge and he ordered an evidentiary hearing. This is what he found: The prisoner was confined in a windowless cubicle, deprived of the basic rudiments of civilized existence including functioning toilet facilities so that the concrete box was lined with the stench of human excrement. The judge quickly forgot about "internal discipline" and ruled that the prisoner was being subjected to "cruel and unusual punishment" and directed the prison officials to remedy the situation immediately or else release the inmate.

I hope that there would be the same shock if judges would allow themselves to know what was happening to juveniles. But we don't. The other day, a severely disturbed seventeen-year-old sought a judicial hearing on his claim that he was being illegally held in our District of Columbia Receiving Home for Children without receiving any psychiatric assistance. He had been at the home for eight months awaiting disposition of a pending charge in the juvenile court. The judge did not hold a hearing to learn what the facts were—because, in his opinion, whether or not the child was receiving psychiatric assistance "was not germane to the lawfulness of [the juvenile's] confinement." I can scarcely imagine anything more "germane" to the "lawfulness" of the child's confinement than a claim—a claim which incidentally the attorney for the superintendent of the institution candidly conceded was true—that he was receiving no treatment at all, although he was desperately in need of it, and although the promise of treatment was the justification for holding the boy.

The fact that we are judges makes this deliberate blindness even more serious. A child comes before us and claims that he is being held illegally. The society asks us to say whether or not he is correct. There are some judges who think that they need only approve the way in which the juvenile home got custody of the child; that is, were the proceedings proper, was the order of confinement signed by the right person, and so forth. Even if this were the extent of our duty, and I do not think it is, society perceives that we are doing much more—namely deciding, in effect, that everything about the child's confinement is legal, the proceedings, the place of confinement, the conditions of confinement. The appearance becomes the reality, and in effect we are putting our stamp of approval on his confinement and on the whole system under which he is held. When we refuse to discover the facts we are participating in society's fraud—worse, we are the high priests in black robes who soothe society into thinking there is no fraud. . . .

In May of 1966 the Juvenile Court for the District of Columbia adopted a new policy memorandum outlining the factors which must be considered before a juvenile is waived to the adult court. It is now the juvenile court's stated policy that if treatment is not available the child should be waived. The question raised is clear: Are we to punish someone because the community has not provided the means and facilities for his treatment and, perhaps, cure?

If the juvenile court judges did require treatment for these youngsters, the judges would have to face the possibility that treatment itself is a ruse, at least when we are talking about mental and emotional disorders particularly associated with the slums. Perhaps we can never be satisfied with treating the individual unless we also treat his society.

JUVENILES GIVEN BILL OF RIGHTS PROTECTION [5]

The Supreme Court ruled . . . [on May 15, 1967] that juvenile courts must grant children many of the procedural protections required in adult trials by the Bill of Rights.

[5] From "High Court Rules Adult Code Holds in Juvenile Trials," by Fred P. Graham, member, New York *Times* Washington Bureau. New York *Times*. p. 1+. My. 16, '67. © 1967 by The New York Times Company. Reprinted by permission.

The landmark decision is expected to require that radical changes be made immediately in most of the nation's three thousand juvenile courts.

In New York, judges said that the Supreme Court ruling would not affect juvenile cases, since "it already is the law" that minors have the same rights as adults. The change became effective in September, 1962 with the adoption of a new Family Court Act by the state legislature.

In a detailed opinion by Justice Abe Fortas, the Supreme Court held that in delinquency hearings before juvenile court judges children must be accorded the following safeguards of the Bill of Rights:

Timely notice of the charges against them.

The right to have a lawyer, appointed by the court if necessary, in any case in which the charge might result in the incarceration of a child.

The right to confront and cross-examine complainants and other witnesses.

Adequate warning of the privilege against self-incrimination and the right to remain silent.

Rights Applied to All

"Neither the Fourteenth Amendment nor the Bill of Rights is for adults only," Justice Fortas declared.

"Under our Constitution, the condition of being a boy does not justify a kangaroo court."

The decision was supported at least in part by eight of the justices, with only Justice Potter Stewart dissenting outright. He said the decision was "a long step backwards into the nineteenth century," because, he contended, it would abolish the flexibility and informality of juvenile courts, and would cause children once more to be treated as adults in courts. . . .

Justice Hugo L. Black wrote a separate concurring opinion, in which he disclosed that he had opposed reviewing the matter in the first instance because the case "strikes a well-nigh fatal blow to much that is unique about the juvenile courts in the nation."

But Justice Black agreed with the outcome because of his belief that all of the guarantees of the Bill of Rights are applicable to all state criminal trials, including juvenile ones, by the Fourteenth Amendment.

Justice Fortas took pains to state that the decision applied only to juvenile trials, and did not affect the handling of juvenile cases before or after trial. This means that the decision does not automatically apply the Supreme Court's limitations on police interrogation to the investigation of juvenile suspects.

However, the Court's opinion mentioned several instances of improper questioning of young suspects, and Justice Fortas noted that "it would indeed be surprising if the privilege against self-incrimination were available to hardened criminals but not to children." . . .

The case before the Supreme Court was brought by Paul L. and Marjorie Gault, parents of Gerald Gault of Globe, Arizona, with the assistance of attorneys furnished by the American Civil Liberties Union. Gerald was adjudged to be a juvenile delinquent in June 1964, when he was fifteen years old, after a juvenile court judge found he had made lewd telephone calls to a female neighbor. [See preceding selection.—Ed.]

Young Gault served six months in the state industrial school. His parents challenged the constitutionality of the Arizona juvenile court law in a habeas corpus petition for his release.

They asserted, among other things, that they had been given inadequate notice of the charges, that the woman had not testified, that they had not been offered the assistance of counsel, that Gerald had not been warned that his testimony could be used against him, that no transcript had been made of the trial and that Arizona law does not permit an appeal of juvenile court decisions.

Old Doctrine Rejected

Justice Fortas' opinion rejected a basic premise on which juvenile courts have operated since the first one was established in Chicago in 1899—that juvenile court trials are essentially civil in nature and that the children's rights are adequately protected by the judges, acting as *parens patriae*, or substitute parents.

He cited studies to show that about half of the nation's juvenile court judges have no undergraduate degree, a fifth have no college education and a fifth are not members of the bar.

He also cited data from the national crime commission showing that persons under eighteen accounted for about one fifth of all arrests for serious crimes and over one half of all the arrests for serious property offenses, in 1965. About one out of nine children will eventually face charges of juvenile delinquency, the Justice further said. . . .

Lack of Protection Found

Justice Fortas noted that this was the first Supreme Court case involving the constitutional rights of children in juvenile court. He concluded that the *parens patriae* concept had not protected them, and held that they must be accorded the protection of the Bill of Rights.

The most far-reaching aspect of today's decision is expected to be the new requirement that counsel be provided in juvenile court.

According to the opinion, only New York, California, Minnesota and the District of Columbia now provide free counsel, and some of them do so only when the charge would be a felony in adult court. Today's decision requires counsel whenever the child might be incarcerated. . . .

In declaring that the Fifth Amendment's privilege against compulsory self-incrimination applied in juvenile cases, Justice Fortas acknowledged that in practice it might not operate as rigidly as in adult cases, since children are encouraged to talk things out informally with the judge.

But he said that the privilege had been violated in this case because young Gault had not first been told of his right to remain silent. . . .

The dissent by Justice Stewart conceded that the record of juvenile courts did not measure up to their ideals, but he said that the solution "does not lie in the Court's opinion in this case, which serves to convert a juvenile proceeding into a criminal prosecution."

To illustrate the possible abuses of this, he related the case of a twelve-year-old New Jersey boy named James Guild, who was hanged for murder in the nineteenth century.

"It was all very constitutional," he said.

IS PUNISHMENT THE ANSWER? [6]

Almost everyone today is impressed with the fact that juvenile delinquency is a serious social problem. The number of children throughout the nation referred to the juvenile courts for delinquency has almost doubled in the last twenty years, and the statisticians tell us that this jump in the juvenile crime rate is out of proportion to the increase in juvenile population. The President's Committee on Juvenile Delinquency has declared that juvenile crime has reached epidemic proportions, and the statistical reports on crime circulated by the Federal Bureau of Investigation continue to paint a bleak picture. To what extent this "increase" in delinquency can be accounted for largely by the remarkable improvements in detection and apprehension of offenders is still a basis for argument, but it is important to note that the increase is in police referrals to juvenile courts.

Whatever the nature of the increase, it has provided justification for a reassessment of our methods and procedures in handling juvenile offenders, and not too surprisingly the juvenile code itself has come in for a critical reappraisal. It is the so-called "protective philosophy" of most state juvenile laws that has received the sharpest criticism. However legitimate and well-based another look at our management of juvenile problems might be, the scene is largely dominated by the anguished cries of citizens and law-enforcement personnel demanding a new "get tough" attitude toward juvenile offenders. The emphasis should be on punishment rather than protection, they say, and we must bring to a quick end the sixty-five years of mollycoddling that "soft" juvenile laws have been encouraging. One of the indignant voices in the front lines of this movement is that of Judge Robert Gardner of Santa Ana, California, who

[6] Article entitled "Delinquency and the Panacea of Punishment," by Sydney Smith, staff psychologist, Division of Law and Psychiatry, the Menninger Foundation. *Federal Probation.* 29:18-23. S. '65. Reprinted by permission.

. . . [in 1964] published an article in the *FBI Law Enforcement Bulletin* entitled "The Error of 1899?" He advises taking a more punitive approach toward children who transgress the law, and suggests that the guardianship of the court over delinquent children, first established in Chicago in 1899, has been abused, and that the answer to our juvenile problem lies instead in the quick application of deserved punishment.

In various communities citizen-action groups have begun similar crusades, calling for a revision of the laws, and in some cases even demanding that the philosophy of the juvenile court be abandoned in favor of pushing juvenile offenders into adult courts where they can suffer the same penalties as adult criminals. During the past year, as an example, in one sizable southwestern city a group of community leaders, forearming themselves with the imposing title of "Citizens Task Force," succeeded through various pressure tactics in stampeding a superior court judge out of his juvenile court assignment, despite his long record of dedication to individualized service and a close adherence to the provisions of the law. Elsewhere in the country incensed citizens and juvenile court judges have suggested that juvenile offenders should suffer the "shame" of a complete public exposure of their behavior, and in some quarters enforcement officials have urged a return to the use of the public whipping post.

Punishment a Simplistic Philosophy

These efforts at control grow out of an urgency to "do something" about the problems of delinquency. However, the phrase "problems of delinquency" is a deceptively simple and misleading one. Simple questions invite simple answers, and few can resist the temptation of succumbing to the seemingly straightforward analysis of the juvenile crime issue as "just a bunch of ornery kids who haven't spent enough time in the woodshed." Put in these terms, the problem suggests an equally simple answer: Punishment. But no problem that involves the complexities of human personalities interacting with an equally complex culture can be considered simple.

The return-to-the-woodshed philosophy has great appeal. It permits us to ignore the fact that delinquency is not a single entity but a term that covers a manifold variety of behavior—everything from traffic violations to homicide. It also permits us to ignore the fact that a significant percentage of the children who come to juvenile court have misbehaved in the very face of punishment, often harsh punishment, and that with many delinquent children their behavior is irrational, beyond self-control, or self-understanding, possessing a quality of compulsion that cannot be contained by punishment even when the child himself genuinely wants to behave differently. Oversimplification makes it easy for us to bury our heads in the sand and refuse to recognize that there are some children who are actually delinquent out of a need for punishment and for whom punishment only exacerbates the underlying pathology.

The framers of the original juvenile court philosophy seem to have had some understanding that there are numerous causative influences at work in the life of the delinquent that demand close investigation. The juvenile court procedure opens the door for individualized treatment, for a meeting of a child's problems before they have hardened into a way of life; indeed, in extreme cases, for stepping into the role of parent and safeguarding the child from a malevolent, often destructive home environment. The philosophy, in a word, is that if we can treat the child today, we won't have to incarcerate the prisoner tomorrow.

The contrasts between points of view on how to deal with the youthful offender are clearly drawn:

There is first of all the simplistic view that delinquency is a monosymptomatic behavioral expression caused, as Judge Gardner states, by the overindulgent parent who through his weakness has been unable to punish the child for his badness.

In reaction to the explicit punitiveness of this position, there has arisen, secondly, a tradition of humanitarianism which correctly has tried to understand delinquency in its multifarious forms and to see the criminal as a product and often a victim of his circumstances. Not uncommonly the humanitarian view succumbs to a sentimentality that looks suspiciously (especially to those who espouse punishment as "the answer") like a maudlin effort to establish alibis for delinquent behavior. There is, however, a third alternative, a scientific point of view which permits deviant behavior to be viewed objectively and dispassionately, taking not a judgmental nor an excusing attitude, but an inquiring approach that seeks for realistic, empirically testable solutions to critical social problems.

What Motivates the Punishment Philosophy?

Those most vociferous in their demands for a return to the philosophy of punishment seem to be fearful of the old adage, *Tout comprendre c'est tout pardonner* [To understand everything is to forgive everything], as a dictum implying a good many dangers for society which abandons the concept of culpability. Perhaps at bottom—if this is not investing the argument for punishment with more depth than it deserves—the issue is imbedded in the age-old polemic of free will versus determinism. Punishment is, of course, based on the premise that the delinquent child quite consciously and deliberately decides to transgress the rules regardless of the consequences, and that he could if he wanted to put an end to all his willful misbehavior. If one abandons this concept in favor of dealing with the "illusory" factors that could have contributed to the child's delinquency, one tacitly condones and encourages the misbehavior. There is the fear that if one becomes concerned with the child himself and the context in which the delinquency occurs, one is likely to be seduced into permissiveness or overindulgence. Since "going easy" with the offender is not in the best interests of society, and since too much psychological or sociological information merely delays or softens the blow delivered by the arm of the law, it is best not to engage in the unconstructive luxury of too much professional attention by psychiatrists or psychologists.

At a recent public conference on delinquency a juvenile court judge indicated that we should stop looking for the causes of delinquency because when we find them they merely serve as justifications to the child for his delinquent behavior. This statement is another form of the plea to keep things simple, even if it means flying in the face of reality. Could you imagine how much confidence you would have in a physician who indicated he was not interested in discovering the cause of your fever because it would merely provide you with an excuse for having it?

The current wave of hostility in the delinquency field against professionally trained people seems in part based on the apprehensive conviction that their interest is merely to save the child from the firmness and punishment that would "do him good." There is also a certain amount of anxiety aroused by the psychiatrist's interpretations of delinquent behavior because they make apparent the fact that the rest of us—parents, educators, even policemen— must share the blame for the child's misbehavior.

One should consider in the motives of people bent on punishing other people the role that retribution plays in their own personality dynamics. Dr. Karl Menninger long ago pointed out (see his article reprinted in *A Psychiatrist's World*, entitled "What Is Wrong With Our Prisons") that the populace needs to see criminals punished in order to reinforce the control of its own antisocial impulses. Every person has aggressive wishes which he may not act upon, at least not in a way that arouses the interest of the law, but which he may feel guilty about. The punishment of others may assuage his own guilt and help him keep his own antisocial impulses in check. Perhaps this concept helps explain the fact that for centuries harshly punitive procedures have been employed against those convicted of crime, despite a mountain of evidence that the severity of punishment has had no deterrent effect at all. Everyone knows the story of the pickpockets diligently plying their trade among a crowd of people gathered to witness the hanging of another less fortunate pickpocket.

In regard to complex social problems, when people offer solutions that emerge, as the solution of punishment so often does, out of their anger and indignation, one can justifiably raise the question of the extent to which such emotionally tinged solutions can be trusted. In general, the more vehemently a person subscribes to the idea of punishment and the more vindictive he wishes that punishment to be, the less one can rely on his point of view, for the more likely it is to be a reflection largely of his own emotional problems or, almost as bad, his ignorance. But there is another element, too, in that the simplicity of the punishment philosophy often represents a general harkening back to the formulations of the past, an almost nostalgic groping for a world uncomplicated by rapid cultural changes, unscarred by the revolution of a new industrial technology, and uninfluenced by the insecurities and the uncertainties of nuclear science. The wish is for a return to an age free from disturbing psychological insights when problems could be etched in black and white without concern for the mysterious intricacies of the human personality.

But this kind of argument is only a dangerous form of wishful thinking. When a society lags in its constructive efforts to deal early and effectively with its disruptive byproducts—and delinquency is one of the byproducts of society—then the vacuum this lag creates begins to be filled with essentially destructive efforts. It is this state of affairs that now prevails in many parts of the country. Too many of our states have followed a short-sighted policy of neglecting the mentally ill, of refusing to provide adequate facilities for disturbed children, of flaunting a sanctimonious pride in keeping morally crippled people off the welfare rolls in the interests of some shibboleth about budgets and taxes, and they are now reaping a harvest in broken lives, in teen-age violence, and in a hundred different forms of trouble that makes some of us question the wisdom if not the sanity of society itself.

Flaws in the Argument for Punishment

In the juvenile court setting it has become less easy to hold the line against those who would supplant treatment efforts and the social work approach with programs built largely around punitive measures. In many departments there is mounting pressure on the probation officer to forget his formal training in preference for the role of the moralistic disciplinarian and the purveyor of punishment. The impossible caseloads with which the officer may be burdened is an implicit expression of a lack of respect for his skills and a destructive way of making any fulfillment of his capacities completely unrealizable. One citizen group recently suggested to county officials that juveniles coming before the court be organized into chain gangs for weekend work-shifts over which the probation officers, most of whom had graduate degrees, could serve as guards.

Somehow those who have a concern for society and some knowledge of a child's behavior problems must stem the tide against these primitive concepts of child care. If one listens closely to the arguments of those most determined in their advocacy of punishment, one begins to understand that the concept of delinquency is allied in their minds to the popular notion of sin, and it is then only a short step to archaic explanations of motivation in terms of "bad seeds," devils, evil spirits, and at this point reality issues are no longer in focus.

Some Fallacious Assumptions

Perhaps it would be helpful to engage in a closer examination of the punishment argument and point up its more glaringly fallacious assumptions.

1. *All children are alike and can be treated the same.*—In the first place, there is the assumption that all children are alike, and thus all can be treated in the same manner. This point of view effectively wipes out whatever gains the science of human behavior has made in the recognition of individual differences. It holds that since children are so much like each other, there is no room either for concepts of differential pathology or differential prognosis. The important point the doctrine of punishment has to make is that delinquency emerges out of willful meanness, not out of helplessness or distress or sickness. The number of research studies indicating the seriousness of the emotional disturbance characteristic of a great percentage of delinquents is entirely discounted, and the experiences of many psychiatric practitioners working in juvenile court settings who have dealt at first hand with character disorders not only in the child but in the whole family are discarded as if they were personal idiosyncrasies of the psychiatrist. The truth of the matter is that while some children who are not psychiatrically ill unquestionably come to the attention of law-enforcement agencies, there is a significant percentage of delinquent youngsters suffering from diagnosable psychiatric disorders. No amount of figure-juggling will alter this fact, and until it is freely admitted and expertly dealt with, disturbed delinquents, whether they are punished or not, will continue to engage in troublesome behavior.

2. *Delinquents escape punishment.*—There is also the assumption that children who get into trouble somehow have miraculously been spared from previous experience of punishment, particularly at home. Granted there are instances in which children have been reared in an atmosphere of inconsistency where value training of any kind was entirely missing; but even in these cases it is the lack of loving guidance and structure rather than the lack of punitive retribution that has triggered the behavioral manifestations of delinquency. In a high percentage of court cases, there is evidence that the child has met with punishment that has not only been frequent but in many cases excessive. In fact, one of the sources of the child's own inadequate development is the model of open violence provided by the parent who has resorted repeatedly to corporal punishment, usually because of his own limited imagination. This indoctrination into a world where only might makes right and where all strength is invested in the authority of the mother or of the father not only makes it easy for the child to develop aggressive patterns of behavior but makes him emotionally distant and distrustful.

3. *The delinquent act is an isolated phenomenon.*—Those who support the doctrine of punishment usually have no perception beyond the fact that the delinquent act is in violation of the law. What is necessary is an appreciation of the fact that behavior does not occur in a vacuum; behavior is motivated. The delinquent act is a form of communication; in some cases, as we know, it is a cry for help, a reaching out for understanding and support, albeit in an aggressive and often self-destructive way. The choice of the form of communication may emerge out of the child's anger about what he feels is happening to him, or it may be that his cultural background has provided him only with limited models of interaction. What form the communication takes is not as important as whether or not the message is understood. The offense itself may mask the true picture of the child's motives, and without bringing this picture into focus, no efforts at help will be effective, least of all punishment. One can think analogically of what might be called for the sake of comparison "neurotic misbehavior" where an individual may suffer from a body or facial tic, or manifest an hysterical

paralysis of the arm, or engage in persistent sleepwalking. Because these disorders do not involve the destruction of property or an aggressive assault on others, it is easier to accept them as merely surface symptoms of underlying psychological problems. In this respect the case is not different for the delinquent; his behavior too is symptomatic, and in his case as much as in those with neurotic symptoms, efforts at help must get beyond the superficial manifestations of the problem. How vital, then, becomes a revealing psychological and sociological investigation of the delinquency and, in the face of such knowledge, how impotent and futile becomes the limited prescription of punishment!

4. *The protective philosophy of the juvenile court has been tested and failed.*—There is also the accusation that the protective, i.e., educational or treatment, approach has been amply tried for over half a century but has utterly failed to accomplish its mission. Society is thereby left without proper safeguards. This argument, too, has great appeal for those who cherish simple solutions.

For sixty-four years we have tried the guardianship and protective philosophy in handling antisocial young people [says Judge Gardner]. The results would hardly qualify as a howling success. Sixty-four years seem to me to be a long enough time to try an experiment. Why not go back to the philosophy of deterrence for sixty-four years. . . . By the year 2000 we should have the answer. One system or the other would certainly have been proven more effective.

But is it true that we have given the philosophy of the juvenile court a fair trial? Have we in truth insisted on adequate, let alone the best, care and treatment that the probation officer and the professional consultant know how to give? Haven't we allowed knowledge to run foolishly ahead of application in the way that we do not take advantage of all we know about doing a better job? And haven't we, in addition, crippled the probation officer with caseloads so heavy he cannot even become acquainted with the children in his own district, and further demoralized him through inadequate salary, lack of recognition, and incredible demands on his personal tolerance for frustration? Haven't we been too smugly satisfied with a delimited diagnostic function, attaching outmoded and unserviceable labels to the child's behavior problems instead of demanding facilities where treatment and research on delinquency could result in some positive movement in solving our social ills? When is society really protected against the destructiveness of the delinquent: When, for the sake of punishment, he is isolated in a custodial institution for a few months only to return to the same neighborhood more embittered than before, or when a program of rehabilitation, education, or treatment brings about lasting changes in the self-concept and self-controls of the troubled youngster?

It goes without saying that where an educational or treatment program is successful, society is the winner from every conceivable standpoint. Where we can appeal to research results, we find that those communities willing to experiment with providing the probation staff with the time and the money to do the best possible job they know how to do—invoking drastically lowered caseloads and engaging in one-to-one casework experience with delinquents and their families—the results have been startlingly successful. As one example, the Saginaw Probation Demonstration Project of the Michigan Council on Crime and Delinquency showed that less than 20 per cent of previously confined probationers were returned to the institution. There was also "a reduction in violation rates and there were substantial savings in welfare costs as a result of a greater use of probation."

5. *Treatment is merely condoning delinquency.*—Another simplistic assumption in the argument for punishment is that the only alternative to punishment is a mollycoddling attitude that nurses the delinquent child along in his misbehavior, never permitting him to discover that his maladaptations are not socially acceptable. The fear is that if the child is not punished for his misdeeds, he will "have it free and easy," sidestepping the debt he has incurred to society. Running through the arguments in favor of a punitive approach to delinquency is the implication that treatment is itself a giving-in to weakness in managing problem behavior. The notion is abroad that if a child enters psychotherapy or if he is placed in a psychiatric hospital or a school, he has successfully "weaseled-out" of being punished, and is thus escaping just retribution. The corollary assumption is that the therapists or teachers themselves are rather fuzzy-headed do-gooders who become an easy prey to the clever manipulations of the wily delinquent.

The truth of the matter is that it is the therapist who is the hardheaded realist in the matter of handling delinquency. He knows that four or five or six months in a custodial institution is of no value either to the child or to the community such institutions serve. In fact, a good case could be made to demonstrate that custodial institutions themselves make a large contribution to the juvenile delinquency problem. The therapist is aware that real changes in the delinquent child, real progress in the treatment of aggressive personalities, may take years, not months, and that individualized treatment must be combined with casework with the whole family. And he knows that the self-confrontation and the struggle toward personal growth are painful, arduous processes, involving skill and toughness on the part of the therapist and corresponding hard work and suffering on the part of the patient. He knows that the child must be constantly confronted with the unacceptability of his behavior, and that his responsibilities toward the child must be carried out with a firmness that does not exclude kindness. Therapy is never an easy road. It is expensive and lengthy by some standards of comparison, but it is cheap when one considers it is human life at stake, and it is short when one considers that it may make unnecessary an entire life spent behind bars.

6. *Treatment costs too much.*—The issue of the expense of individualized treatment has frequently been exploited as another reason to abandon the treatment philosophy. The state cannot afford high-priced professional help for delinquent children, the argument runs, and punishment is not only effective, it is economical. But is it? Many states have poured hundreds of thousands of dollars into custodial institutions which often serve no other purpose than a training ground for the state prison. Conservative estimates indicate anywhere from one half to two thirds of the children now sentenced to such institutions could, with short-term, family-oriented treatment, be kept out of confinement altogether. Recidivism rates in custodial institutions are notoriously high, and the cost of continued crime both in human life and in property is enormous. How much more economical it would be to shift to an investment in human beings rather than in elaborate, security-oriented buildings intended simply for the punitive containment of misguided

children. In effect, it would cost less in actual tax dollars to do the right thing for our delinquents than to perpetuate the wrong thing.

7. *Punishment cures delinquency.*—Finally, it should be pointed out that the idea that simple punishment will eliminate delinquent behavior is the biggest assumption of all. There is no evidence, experimental or otherwise, to indicate that mere punishment can do that job. Indeed, if punishment were the answer, we should have rid ourselves of crime and delinquency centuries ago. What is needed is a revolution in the whole manner of perceiving and handling criminals of any kind, child or adult.

The history of the treatment of mental illness in this country is illuminative. Fifty years ago there was no solution for those who became "insane" except to indicate that they must be "beset by the devil," a notion readily seized upon as a justification for beating the devil out of them. It was not so long ago that mental patients were chained to stone walls or whipped for their misdeeds. But a half century of patient study by dedicated scientific practitioners who were willing to replace inaccurate moral judgments and vindictive treatment with meaningful research and intelligent insight has worked a miracle of change, a change so dramatic that patients who would in years past have no future but to languish hopelessly in some back ward, can now be returned to productive life in record time. Some hospitals have closed down whole wings no longer required because of new and more effective procedures.

There is a lesson to be learned in this chapter of history. What is to prevent us from bringing about the same revolution in the treatment of the delinquent? Only our own lack of resourcefulness and our lazy willingness to allow reaction-dominated citizens' task forces, wherever they may be, to tempt us by their simple thinking into the errors of the past. The self-appointed experts make us recall with Goethe that "there is nothing more frightening than ignorance in action."

BIBLIOGRAPHY

An asterisk (*) preceding a reference indicates that the article or a part of it has been reprinted in this book.

Books, Pamphlets, and Documents

Aichhorn, August. Delinquency and child guidance. International Universities Press. New York. '65.

Aichhorn, August. Wayward youth; foreword by Sigmund Freud. Viking. New York. '65.
Originally published in 1935.

Amos, W. E. and others. Action programs for delinquency prevention. C. C. Thomas. Springfield, Ill. '65.

Bernstein, Saul. Youth on the streets. Association Press. New York. '64.

Blaine, G. B. Youth and the hazards of affluence; the high school and college years. Harper. New York. '66.

*Brecher, Ruth and Brecher, Edward. Delinquent and the law. (Public Affairs Pamphlet no 337) Public Affairs Committee. 381 Park Ave. S. New York 10016. '62.

Bromberg, Walter and Bellamy, F. R. How to keep out of jail. Watts. New York. '66.

Burchill, G. W. Work-study programs for alienated youth. Science Research Associates. Chicago. '62.

Cavan, R. S. Juvenile delinquency; development, treatment, control. Lippincott. Philadelphia. '62.

Cavan, R. S. Readings in juvenile delinquency. Lippincott. Philadelphia. '64.

Chein, Isidor and others. Road to H; narcotics, delinquency, and social policy. Basic Books. New York. '64.

Cloward, R. A. and Ohlin, L. E. Delinquency and opportunity—a theory of delinquent gangs. Free Press. New York. '60.

Coleman, J. S. Adolescent society. Free Press. New York. '61.

Conant, J. B. Slums and suburbs. McGraw. New York. '61.

Conger, J. J. and Miller, W. C. Personality, social class, and delinquency. Wiley. New York. '66.

Council of State Governments. Juvenile delinquency; a report on state action and responsibilities. The Council. 1313 E. 60th St. Chicago 60637. '65.

Erikson, E. H. ed. Childhood and society. Norton. New York. '64.

Erikson, E. H. ed. Youth: change and challenge. Basic Books. New York. '63.

    Same with title: Challenge of youth. Doubleday (Anchor Books). Garden City, N.Y. '65.

Fleisher, B. M. Economics of delinquency. Quadrangle Books. Chicago. '66.

Ford Foundation. Society of the streets. The Foundation. Office of Reports. 477 Madison Ave. New York 10022. '62.

Friedenberg, E. Z. Coming of age in America. Random. New York. '65.

Friedenberg, E. Z. Vanishing adolescent. Beacon. Boston. '59.

Fyvel, T. R. Troublemakers: rebellious youth in an affluent society. Schocken. New York. '62.

Glueck, Sheldon, ed. Problem of delinquency. Houghton. Boston. '59.

Glueck, Sheldon and Glueck, E. T. Predicting delinquency and crime. Harvard University Press. Cambridge, Mass. '59.

Glueck, Sheldon and Glueck, E. T. Unraveling juvenile delinquency. Harvard University Press (for the Commonwealth Fund). Cambridge, Mass. '50.

Glueck, Sheldon and Glueck, E. T. Ventures in criminology. Harvard University Press. Cambridge, Mass. '64.

Goodman, Paul. Growing up absurd. Random. New York. '60.

HARYOU [Harlem Youth Opportunities Unlimited]. Youth in the ghetto—a study of the consequences of powerlessness and a blueprint for change. HARYOU. 2092 Seventh Ave. New York 10027. '64.

Hanson, Kitty. Rebels in the streets: the story of New York's girl gangs. Prentice-Hall. Englewood Cliffs, N.J. '64.

Jones, Howard. Reluctant rebels. Association Press. New York. '60.

Keniston, Kenneth. The uncommitted: alienated youth in American society. Harcourt. New York. '65.

Kvaraceus, W. C. Anxious youth; dynamics of delinquency. Merrill. Columbus, Ohio. '66.

*Kvaraceus, W. C. Juvenile delinquency: a problem for the modern world. Unesco. Paris. '64; New York. '65.

    Reprinted in this book: Federal Probation. 28:12-18. S. '64. [Excerpts from the book in condensed form.]

Martin, J. M. and Fitzpatrick, J. P. Delinquent behavior. Random. New York. '65.

Michael, D. N. Next generation. Random. New York. '65.

Myers, C. K. Light the dark streets. Doubleday. Garden City, N.Y. '61.

National Federation of Settlements and Neighborhood Centers. Young people and the world of work. The Federation. 232 Madison Ave. New York 10016. '65.

Neumeyer, M. H. Juvenile delinquency in modern society. Van Nostrand. Princeton, N. J. '61.

New York City. Youth Board. Manual of procedures for application of the Glueck prediction table, by Maude M. Craig and Selma J. Glick. The Board. 79 Madison Ave. New York 10016. '64.

New York City. Youth Board. Ten-year trends in juvenile delinquency in New York City. The Board. 79 Madison Ave. New York 10016. '64.

O'Connor, G. W. and Watson, N. A. Juvenile delinquency and youth crime: the police role. International Association of Chiefs of Police. 1319 18th St. N.W. Washington, D.C. 20036. '64.

Remmers, H. H. and Radler, D. H. American teenager. Bobbs. Indianapolis. '57.

Riccio, Vincent and Slocum, Bill. All the way down [the violent underworld of street gangs]. Simon and Schuster. New York. '61.

Rosenheim, M. K. Justice for the child: the juvenile courts in transition. Free Press. New York. '62.

Rubenfeld, Seymour. Family of outcasts; a new theory of delinquency. Free Press. New York. '65.

Rubin, Sol. Crime and juvenile delinquency. Oceana. Dobbs Ferry, N.Y. '61.

Salisbury, H. E. Shook-up generation. Harper. New York. '58.

Scudder, K. J. and Beam, K. S. Twenty billion dollar challenge: a national program for delinquency prevention. Putnam. New York. '61.

Shoham, Shlomo. Crime and social deviation. Regnery. Chicago. '66.

Shulman, H. M. Juvenile delinquency in American society. Harper. New York. '61.

Smith, B. K. Chance for a life. Hogg Foundation for Mental Health. University of Texas. Austin. '66.

Spergel, I. A. Racketville, Slumtown, Haulburg; an exploratory study of delinquent subcultures. University of Chicago Press. Chicago. '64.

Stinchcombe, A. L. Rebellion in a high school. Quadrangle Books. Chicago. '65.

Thrasher, F. M. The gang; rev. and abr. ed. by James F. Short, Jr. University of Chicago Press. Chicago. '63.

Time, Inc. Young Americans. Time. New York. '66.

Tunley, Roul. Kids, crime and chaos. Harper. New York. '62.

United States. Congress. Senate. Committee on the Judiciary. Juvenile delinquency; hearings before the subcommittee to investigate juvenile delinquency; part 16, July 30, 1964: Effects on young people of violence and crime portrayed on television. 88th Congress, 2d session. Supt. of Docs. Washington, D.C. 20402. '65.

*United States. Congress. Senate. Committee on the Judiciary. Juvenile delinquency; report by subcommittee to investigate juvenile delinquency, pursuant to S. Res. 52. (S. Rep. no 1664) 89th Congress, 1st session. Supt. of Docs. Washington, D.C. 20402. '66.

United States. Department of Health, Education, and Welfare. Children's Bureau. Control and treatment of juvenile delinquency in the United States. Supt. of Docs. Washington, D.C. 20402. '65.

United States. Department of Health, Education, and Welfare. Children's Bureau. Delinquent children in penal institutions, by William H. Sheridan and others. Supt. of Docs. Washington, D.C. 20402. '64.

*United States. Department of Health, Education, and Welfare. Children's Bureau. Juvenile delinquency prevention in the United States. Supt. of Docs. Washington, D.C. 20402. '65.

United States. Department of Health, Education, and Welfare. Children's Bureau. Police work with children, perspectives and principles, by Richard A. Myren and Lynn D. Swanson. Supt. of Docs. Washington, D.C. 20402. '62.

United States. Department of Health, Education, and Welfare. Children's Bureau. Report to the Congress on juvenile delinquency. Supt. of Docs. Washington, D.C. 20402. '60.

United States. Department of Health, Education, and Welfare. National Institute of Mental Health. National Clearinghouse for Mental Health Information. Current projects in the prevention, control, and treatment of crime and delinquency. Supt. of Docs. Washington, D.C. 20402.
Semiannual.

United States. Department of Health, Education, and Welfare. National Institute of Mental Health. National Clearinghouse for Mental Health Information. International bibliography on crime and delinquency. Supt. of Docs. Washington, D.C. 20402.
Bimonthly.

*United States. Department of Health, Education, and Welfare. Office of Juvenile Delinquency and Youth Development. Culture of youth, by M. E. Wolfgang. Supt. of Docs. Washington, D.C. 20402. '67.

United States. Department of Health, Education, and Welfare. Office of Juvenile Delinquency and Youth Development. New approaches: prevention and control of juvenile delinquency. The Office. Washington, D.C. 20201. '65.

*United States. President's Committee on Juvenile Delinquency and Youth Crime. Juvenile gangs, by Gilbert Geis. Supt. of Docs. Washington, D.C. 20402. '65.

United States. President's Committee on Juvenile Delinquency and Youth Crime. Report to the President. Supt. of Docs. Washington, D.C. 20402. '62.

Vermes, H. G. and Vermes, J. C. P. Helping youth avoid four great dangers: smoking, drinking, VD [and] narcotics addiction. Association Press. New York. '65.

Wakefield, Dan, ed. The addict. Fawcett. New York. '63.

Whyte, W. F. Street-corner society. University of Chicago Press. Chicago. '55.

Wills, W. D. Common sense about young offenders. Macmillan. New York. '62.

Wolfgang, M. E. and others, eds. Sociology of crime and delinquency. Wiley. New York. '62.

PERIODICALS

ALA Bulletin. 59:516-22. Je. '65. Can reading affect delinquency? address, January 1965. W. C. Kvaraceus.

America. 108:795. Je. 1, '63. Jobs for youth.

America. 115:271. S. 17, '66. Today's rebellious generation.
   Discussion: 115:684-7. N. 26; 828-30. D. 24, '66.

American Bar Association Journal. 47:804+. Ag. '61. Shall we punish the parents? J. A. Kenny and J. V. Kenny.

American Bar Association Journal. 49:44+. Ja. '63. Juvenile delinquency —also a federal problem. Richard Mills.

American Catholic Sociological Review. 24:3-53. Spring '63. Juvenile delinquency.

American Education. 2:1-4. D. '65. Children and the badge; Atlanta board of education's school detective department. Richard Hardwick.

Annals of the American Academy of Political and Social Science. 338:1-143. N. '61. Teen-age culture. Jessie Bernard, ed.

Annals of the American Academy of Political and Social Science. 339:11-23. Ja. '62. Crime and delinquency in the United States. Thorsten Sellin.

Annals of the American Academy of Political and Social Science. 339:157-70. Ja. '62. Juvenile delinquents and their treatment. P. W. Tappan and Ivan Nicolle.

Annals of the American Academy of Political and Social Science. 347:20-9. My. '63. Juvenile gang; a cultural reflex. H. A. Bloch.

Annals of the American Academy of Political and Social Science. 355:90-7. S. '64. Helping the child who comes into conflict with the law. R. G. Farrow.

Annals of the American Academy of Political and Social Science. 355:98-104. S. '64. Residential treatment center. J. G. Milner

Annals of the American Academy of Political and Social Science. 364:96-112. Mr. '66. Violent crimes in city gangs. W. B. Miller.

Atlas. 8:79-82. S. '64. Britain's new super-gangs.
   Reprinted from New Society.

California State Bar Journal. 39:773+. S.-O. '64. Youngest delinquents. Ernest Lenn.

Children. 8:170-4. S.-O. '61. Youth workers and the police. M. E. Blake.

Children. 11:21-6. Ja.-F. '64. Adolescent delinquent girls. Gisela Konopka.

Christian Century. 79:1475-8. D. 5, '62. Delinquent youth in a normless time. Robert Lee.

Christian Century. 83:879-80. Jl. 13, '66. Tucson's dangerous alliance: school-police liaison.

Commonweal. 82:285-9. My. 21, '65. Mobilizing the poor. Frank Riessman.

Crime and Delinquency. 7:201-12. Jl. '61. Schools and the problems of juvenile delinquency. B. M. Moore.

Crime and Delinquency. 9:29+. Ja. '63. Problem drinking among juvenile delinquents. J. R. Mackay.

Crime and Delinquency. 10:1-7. Ja. '64. Halfway houses pay off. R. F. Kennedy.

Crime and Delinquency. 12:165+. Ap. '66. Lawyer and his juvenile court client. J. L. Allison.

Ebony. 20:43-4+. Jl. '65. Cool world: controversial movie changes lives of New York delinquents.

Ebony. 21:110-12+. My. '66. Godfather to delinquent boys.

Esquire. 64:30-9+. Jl. '65. Special issue; teen-agers in America; symposium.

Farm Journal. 87:82. Ag. '63. Why young people get into trouble.

Federal Probation. 26:49+. Mr. '62. Gangs need not be delinquent. G. E. Jereczek.

Federal Probation. 27:3+. D. '63. Delinquency and socially and economically deprived youth. A. W. Silver.

Federal Probation. 28:20-5. Je. '64. Why can't we understand juvenile delinquency? D. J. Tyrell.

Federal Probation. 28:25-30. Je. '64. Alienation as a factor in delinquency. Jacob Chwast.

Federal Probation. 28:50+. Je. '64. Chronic "mess-up" and his changing character. William Crain.

Federal Probation. 29:50-3. Mr. '65. The place of religion in the lives of juvenile offenders. M. E. Miller.

Federal Probation. 29:12-16. Je. '65. How delinquent children think and feel. E. P. Sharp and E. S. Grayson.

*Federal Probation. 29:18-23. S. '65. Delinquency and the panacea of punishment. Sydney Smith.

*Harper's Magazine. 225:50-2+. N. '62. Bored and the violent. Arthur Miller.

Harper's Magazine. 232:16+. Ja. '66. Substitutes for violence. John Fischer.

Same abridged with title: What young men need: a substitute for violence. Reader's Digest. 88:82-5. Mr. '66.

Journal of Marriage and the Family. 27:139-47. My. '65. American teen-agers of the 1960's—our despair or hope? B. R. M. Porter.

Kentucky Law Journal. 53:781-9. Summer '65. The juvenile offender, some problems and possible solutions. Scotty Baesler.

Ladies' Home Journal. 78:34+. Mr. '61. Treatment of delinquency. Benjamin Spock.

Ladies' Home Journal. 78:36+. Ap.; 27-8. My. '61. Can we prevent delinquency? Benjamin Spock.

Ladies' Home Journal. 79:72-3+. Jl. '62. Why did they steal? Glenn White.

Ladies' Home Journal. 80:26+. S. '63. New open door policy for wayward girls. Hannah Lees.

Life. 54:4. Ap. 5, '63. Two new ways to curb juvenile delinquency.

*Look. 27:17-23. Ag. 27, '63. Tense generation. Samuel Grafton.
    Same abridged: Reader's Digest. 83:61-6. N. '63.

Look. 30:27-9. My. 17, '66. Discarded third; unstable family life. D. P. Moynihan.

Look. 30:30-5. My. 17, '66. Life without father; Holman family of Harlem. E. Dunbar.

Look. 30:40-3. S. 20, '66. Fifteen years of trouble; Gail White at Livingston school for girls.

NEA Journal. 51:22-4. S. '62. Delinquency international: ambivalent obsession. W. C. Kvaraceus.

NEA Journal. 54:26-28. Ap. '65. Saving the trouble-prone. N. E. Hall, Jr.

NEA Journal. 54:10-13. D. '65. Student violence and rebellion. David Iwamoto.

*NEA Journal. 55:8-12. My. '66. Teen-age drinking and drug addiction. J. H. Pollack.

Nation. 193:31-2+. Jl. 15, '61. Rebellion or delinquency? Joseph Margolis.

Nation. 196:439-43. My. 25, '63. Surplus youth; a future without jobs. J. S. Coleman.

*Nation. 199:137-40. S. 21, '64. Why youth riots: the adolescent ghetto. Frank Musgrove.

Nation. 200:522-6. My. 17, '65. Motorcycle gangs: losers and outsiders. H. S. Thompson.

Nation. 200:662-66. Je. 21, '65. Anatomy of violence. J. P. Scott.

New Republic. 148:11-13. F. 23, '63. Tryout in Harlem. Murray Kempton.

*New Republic. 151:59-64. N. 7, '64. Youth: opportunity to be what? Robert Coles.

New Republic. 154:10-12. Ja. 1, '66. Watch out, Whitey. Lewis Yablonsky.

New Republic. 154:28-9+. Ja. 29, '66. Causes and cures of delinquency. Robert Coles.

*New Republic. 156:13-16. Ap. 22, '67. Justice for juveniles. D. L. Bazelon.

*New York Times. p 1+. Ja. 4, '65. Narcotics a growing problem of affluent youth. Martin Arnold.

*New York Times. p 1+. My. 16, '67. High court rules adult code holds in juvenile trials. F. P. Graham.

New York Times Magazine. p 41+. F. 12, '61. Open doors for young prisoners. Gertrude Samuels.

New York Times Magazine. p 14+. Jl. 23, '61. Rescue for the wayward girls. Gertrude Samuels.

New York Times Magazine. p 14+. F. 18, '62. Making of a boy killer. I. H. Freeman.

New York Times Magazine. p 9+. Jl. 8, '62. Summer walk with Carlos. Samuel Kaplan.

New York Times Magazine. p 82-3. My. 10, '64. Evening at Club 169.

New York Times Magazine. p 13+. My. 24, '64. New lost generation: jobless youth. Michael Harrington.

New York Times Magazine. p 47+. Jl. 19, '64. When teenagers start to drink. B. Lang.

*New York Times Magazine. p 13+. O. 4, '64. Paradoxical case of the affluent delinquent. Joseph Lelyveld.

*New York Times Magazine. p 12-13+. Ja. 31, '65. Arithmetic of delinquency. Julius Horwitz.

New York Times Magazine. p 40+. Mr. 7, '65. They no longer bop, they jap. Gertrude Samuels.

New York Times Magazine. p 12-13+. Je. 13, '65. Teen-agers are an American invention. B. M. Berger.

New York Times Magazine. p 60+. N. 28, '65. Absent father haunts the Negro family. C. E. Lincoln.

New York Times Magazine. p 56-7+. N. 27, '66. We can't appease the younger generation. Spencer Brown.

Newsweek. 64:94+. N. 16, '64. What triggers violence?

PTA Magazine. 59:8-10. Je. '65. Does get tough work? G. B. Hunt.

Parents' Magazine. 36:80-1+. O. '61. Teen-age drinking can spell disaster. Garrett Oppenheim.

Parents' Magazine. 38:47+. Ag. '63. Jacksonville's jury of juvenile peers. Frederic Sondern, Jr.
    Same abridged: Reader's Digest. 83:82-5. Ag. '63.

*Parents' Magazine. 39:56-8+. O. '64. We can beat J.D. Homer Page.

Parents' Magazine. 39:42-5+. D. '64. Young rebels with a cause. Homer Page.

Parents' Magazine. 41:50-1+. F. '66. Keeping kids out of trouble; program in New Castle, Pa. W. F. Burmester.

Parents' Magazine. 41:64-7+. D. '66. Employment lab for teenagers in trouble: youth and work project, New York. S. L. Horwitz.

Phi Delta Kappan. 42:283-91. Ap. '61. National policy for alienated youth. R. J. Havighurst and L. J. Stiles.

Reader's Digest. 82:31-2+. Mr. '63. It's tough to be a teen-ager; ed. by R. L. Smith. J. F. Phelan, Jr.

Reader's Digest. 85:79-81. Ag. '64. Let's stop kicking the kids around: excerpts from address. Whit Hobbs.

Reader's Digest. 86:125-30. My. '65. It's a dead-end road for the dropout. J. N. Miller.

Reader's Digest. 86:92-5. Je. '65. Hijinks that can haunt your life. J. M. Lasky.

Reader's Digest. 88:66-70. Je. '66. Pills, glue and kids: an American tragedy. Earl Selby and Anne Selby.

*Redbook. 127:73+. My. '66. Why young people are seeking new values. Richard Schickel.

Redbook. 127:20+. Jl. '66. Kinds of rebellion in adolescence. Benjamin Spock.

*Reporter. 34:41-3. F. 24, '66. Youth, crime, and the Great Society. J. W. Symington.

Saturday Evening Post. 236:74-6. Ap. 6, '63. Death of a youth worker. Gertrude Samuels.

Saturday Evening Post. 236:10+. Je. 22, '63. Speaking out—too many kids are loafing. Robert Gardner.

Saturday Evening Post. 237:19-25. Ap. 4, '64. Dope invades the suburbs. R. P. Goldman.

Saturday Evening Post. 238:10+. S. 11, '65. Teen-agers are the greatest people. Philip Wylie.

Saturday Evening Post. 238:32-9. N. 20, '65. Hell's Angels. William Murray.

Saturday Evening Post. 238:23-7. D. 4, '65. Thrill-pill menace. Bill Davidson.

Saturday Evening Post. 239:12+. N. 19, '66. Speaking out: you force kids to rebel. Steven Kelman.

School and Society. 93:388+. O. 30, '65. Early identification of delinquency.

Science Digest. 55:76. F. '64. How to spot a pre-delinquent.

Science News. 89:260. Ap. 16, '66. Delinquents find values; rehabilitation at Essexfields.

Science News. 90:122-3+. Ag. 20, '66. Children in conflict. B. Culliton.

Senior Scholastic. 86:sup 14. My. 6, '65. Can delinquency be predicted? James Olsen.

Senior Scholastic. 88:6-9. F. 4, '66. Today's teen-agers: youth in ferment or youth playing it safe?

*Time. 86:16-17. D. 24, '65. On not losing one's cool about the young; Time essay.

Time. 87:114. My. 20, '66. Reformers in crisis.

Today's Health. 44:40-3+. S. '66. Malady of our times: alienation. A. A. Messer.

U.S. News & World Report. 54:83-5. F. 18, '63. Growing worry for U.S.: young people out of work.

U.S. News & World Report. 54:62-7. Ap. 1, '63. Why young people face a shortage of jobs; interview. W. W. Wirtz.

*U.S. News & World Report. 58:56-60+. Ap. 26, '65. Why young people "go bad"; interview. Sheldon Glueck and E. T. Glueck.

Vital Speeches of the Day. 30:734-6. S. 15, '64. Unemployed youth in our affluent society; address, September 3, 1964. R. F. Male.

Vital Speeches of the Day. 33:162-5. Ja. 1, '67. Policy for youth; address, November 16, 1966. W. W. Wirtz.

*Washington Post. My 3-8, 10-15, '65. Children and society: partners in crime? [12 articles]. J. J. Carmody and others.
    Reprinted in this book: VI. 20% of slum children find status in thievery. My. 8, '65. J. J. Carmody; IX. How experts explain making of a criminal. My. 12, '65. J. J. Carmody.